NEWHAVEN COURT

NEWHAVEN COURT

LOVE, TRAGEDY, HEROISM AND INTRIGUE

HELEN MURRAY

First published 2022

The History Press
97 St George's Place, Cheltenham,
Gloucestershire, GL50 3QB
www.thehistorypress.co.uk

British Library Cataloguing in Publication Data.
A catalogue record for this book is available from the British Library.

ISBN 978 1 8039 9107 8

Typesetting and origination by The History Press
Printed and bound in Great Britain by TJ Books Limited, Padstow, Cornwall.

Trees for Lyfe

Contents

When at Newhaven
Court we meet you,
This is the welcome
that shall greet you.

A.D.

12·iv·97

Kate Greenaway Newhaven illustration with poem by Austin Dobson. (Family collection, KG courtesy of Michael Dad

Acknowledgements

Enormous thanks and love are due to my husband, Anthony, and my three dear children, Tristan, Austin and Alexandra. Grateful thanks also go to my extended family around the globe, those who have so kindly furnished me with memories, anecdotes, photographs and documents: Ellie Sturrock, Diana Patoir, Julian Delmar-Morgan, Janie and Peter Fowler, Conway Ellison, Miranda Delmar-Morgan, Rachel Connor, Clare Herring, Jonathan Locker-Lampson, Anthony Locker-Lampson, Maranda Locker-Lampson and Patricia Walker.

My sister, Miriam Jamieson, not only provided an original piece of artwork but along with my cousin, Ellie, provided unfailing support and encouragement. I couldn't have done it without you both. I have been lucky that the family left a considerable paper trail behind them, including biographies and letters and, as prominent members of society, they were frequently mentioned in newspaper columns of which I have made good use.

Significant contribution to this work has been made by family members who are no longer with us. Locker Madden, Jane Madden, Rosa Mornard and New Zealand historian and author Stephen Locker-Lampson, I have much to thank you for.

Along the way, I have been fortunate enough to meet several Cromer residents who have been immensely helpful. Author Brenda Stibbons helped me gain access to family letters and Robbie Nash, as well as helping with research and maps, kindly shared his uncle Philip Colman's recorded memories of working for Oliver Locker-Lampson. George Baker, whose father and uncles served in Russia with Oliver Locker-Lampson, gave me considerable time to explore his memories, books and treasured photo collection.

The more recent occupants of Newhaven Court were instrumental in filling in the later years of the house. Grateful acknowledgement goes to Anna Jansz, Phillip Shaw, Brian Welham and the brothers, Ian and Roy Boyd-Stevenson. Their spare time, memories and photos were of immeasurable help. Jenny Scally also shared her happy memories of Newhaven Court. Special thanks must go to Anna's mother, the late Josephine Towle, who preserved many priceless family letters from being lost forever.

Grateful thanks also go to the Locker-Lampson family of New Zealand, Kim Woodrow of AG Brown, Jane Hunt, Steve Snelling, Mike Rogers, Philip Colman, Christopher Dreyfus, Val Edmondson, Alexandra Shackleton, Caroline Jarrold, Michael Dadd, Pam Griffiths, David Pope, Terry Mace, Philip Griffin, Jacqueline Regis, Stephen Scott-Fawcett, Trevor Barton, Phyllida Scrivens, Jurg Linggi, Tony Spurgeon, Norwich Writers Circle, Stuart McLaren, David Clay, Paul Brighton, Paul Browne, Norfolk Record Office, Norfolk Museums Service, Leeds University Archive, Wayne Kett of Cromer Museum, Chris Bennett of Hertfordshire Archives and Local Studies, Keith Giles of Heritage Collections, Auckland Library and Yasmin Ramadan of the Beinecke Rare Book and Manuscript Library.

Credit must also go to my siblings, who have supported me all these years, and my nieces and nephews whose company bring me so much joy. My love goes to my dad, who would have encouraged me to write this. I hope I have done you proud. Lastly, my amazing mum whose endless determination, drive and ambition to do more, learn more and see more has given me the courage to try.

Preface

This is the house by Cromer town,
Its bricks are red, though they look so brown.
It faces the sea on a windswept hill –
In winter it's empty, in summer it's chill:
Indeed, it is one of Earth's windiest spots
As we know from the smashing of chimney pots.
In August I ask for an extra quilt –
This is the house that Jane built!

Newhaven Court. (Courtesy of Miriam Jamieson)

With characteristic touches of humour, this is the poem written by Frederick Locker-Lampson to describe his newly built summer property, Newhaven Court, an imposing red-brick house that once stood exposed and proud on a windy hill overlooking the north Norfolk sea-side resort of Cromer. Designed and built in 1884, under the instruction of Frederick's wife, Hannah Jane, with the help of her charismatic American father, the elegant Victorian mansion with its ornate chimneys, turret and jumbled architecture, stood braced against the North Sea under the wide-open Norfolk skies for almost eighty years before its dramatic destruction by fire in 1963.

For almost four decades, Newhaven Court was the grand summer home of the Locker-Lampson family, Frederick and Hannah Jane (known to all as Janie), with their children, Godfrey, Dorothy and the twins, Oliver and Maud, who decamped to Cromer every year to spend the warmer months by the sea. The wealth of the family's social, cultural, literary and political connections meant their many and varied family and friends followed, invited to stay under their roof where they laughed, argued, danced and dined within its walls. It was a happy and welcoming home where people spent their leisure time but also where they fell in love, sought refuge, had affairs, conducted business, found comfort during illness and prepared to go to war.

Frederick and Janie's younger son Oliver, whose electric personality burns bright throughout this history, inherited Newhaven Court on the death of his mother in 1915. Following the Great War, Oliver converted the building into an exclusive guest house. Thousands of pounds were spent updating the property and adding an impressive ballroom and two enormous indoor glass-roofed tennis courts. With the help of his fashionable young wife, Bianca, whom he married in 1923, the couple entertained some of the most prominent figures of 1920s society.

In his son Jonathan's words, Oliver was a man who managed 'to ingratiate himself with royalty wherever he went'. A grand statement but not one over-stating the facts. While serving during the Great War with his armoured car squadron in Russia, Oliver engineered a meeting with Tsar Nicholas II and later, when he and his men were in Romania, he personally introduced himself to Queen Marie. Oliver's association and friendship with the Romanian royals led to the exiled King and Queen of Greece staying at Newhaven and to a lengthy visit from Marie's daughter, the young and glamorous Princess Ileana. Oliver was also friendly with Princess Marie-Louise, a granddaughter of Queen Victoria, along with King Albert of Belgium. It was through his association with the latter that Professor Albert Einstein, on the run from the Nazis, came to be Oliver's guest in 1933.

Once financial considerations and family tragedy forced Oliver to sell Newhaven, the house experienced several custodians moving through its rooms, each in turn leaving their mark on the grand house through years challenged by a further conflict and the seismic changes inevitably faced by a post-war society.

It was on one of those long summer days of endless blue skies and warm sunshine, seemingly only found in the distant vista of childhood, that I first became dimly aware of Newhaven Court. My mother's mother, Jane Madden, had taken my sister and I for a day out to Cromer. We drove there from nearby Norwich, bumping along the country lanes in her outlandishly bright orange Volkswagen Beetle, sucking on travel sweets all the way. A picnic lunch was eaten on the golden sands and in a lull after the food, as waves gently lapped at our toes, we listened as she told us of a big house on the hill above the town, once owned by her charismatic Uncle Oliver. She quickly became lost in her memories of days on the beach with her cousins, eating ice creams and splashing in the cooling surf.

We must have shown a reasonable interest as, later in the day, we were taken to Cromer Museum. I have a clear recollection of being shown a large black and white photograph of a family enjoying a picnic on the beach. My Grandma showed me her mother, Dorothy, who sat immortalised in the picture, looking back at me with her beautiful large, dark eyes.

Grandma was fond of talking about her childhood, from where her memories remained clear and strong. Anecdotes and rec-ollections, oft repeated, became familiar to us

Jane Madden on a visit to Cromer, 1939. (Family collection)

all. We heard about gentle Aunt Maud reading Tennyson poems to her by the warmth of a fire, a beautiful carnival princess, kings and queens, her notorious practical joker godfather, and an intriguing story of her meeting Albert Einstein. Many of the stories revolved around the house in Cromer and her time there both as a child and a young woman.

As we lived in nearby Norwich, we occasionally drove to Cromer for some fresh sea air. After a day spent walking on the beach and drawing letters in the sand, we headed for home. Driving up and out of Cromer, we passed two roads on our right, named Newhaven Close and Court Drive. With Grandma's tales in our thoughts, the car came to a stop so that we could walk up these roads looking for a trace of the mysterious house that we had heard so much about. But we were disappointed to find nothing and soon drove on.

Twenty-five years later, in the brief summer respite from the covid pandemic in 2020, I paid a visit to a cousin, the keeper of many of the family records. Out came a heavy square volume of blue leather, inlaid with big, bold, gold lettering spelling out the name 'NEWHAVEN'. It was the visitors' book that I had been shown so many times as a child. Written in black spidery handwriting, names like Shackleton, Churchill and Tennyson jumped out at me. Other names, so familiar from anecdotes, felt like they had been waiting patiently for me to find them and tell their stories. I was immediately fascinated, and so began my epic journey of discovery culminating in this volume.

With the project set in my mind, I again made the 25-mile trip north to Cromer. On a scorching August day and armed with a map, I walked up towards where Newhaven would have been. On the top of the hill, with the sun beating down, I stood admiring the clear view down onto the picturesque blue sea below. On the opposite side of the road, a lady was enjoying the sunshine from a deckchair in her garden. On enquiring whether she knew anything of Newhaven Court, she told me that her house had probably been built where the tennis courts had been and that it was not unusual to still find little burned pieces of Newhaven glass from the fire of 1963.

Having spent the morning exploring the boundary and grounds of the old estate, I sat down to rest on a concrete kerb on the very spot where the grand entrance hall would have been. Closing my eyes against the warm sunshine, I imagined the large Queen Anne-style house rising from the ashes behind me. There was Alfred, Lord Tennyson in his long, black cloak and hat taking a solo stroll around the grounds, occasionally stooping to pick a strawberry or admire the pretty rose garden. And then Janie, my great-great-grandmother, walking purposely through the grounds to check on the explorer Shackleton, lined and worn from his recent Antarctic expedition, then occupying one of the little huts in the grounds to write a book about his adventures.

Walking down the sweeping drive over 100 years before, I may have encountered the author M.R. James ambling along thinking up a new ghost story to scare the guests with after supper, or possibly the children's illustrator Kate Greenaway returning from a walk on the beach with the children, their intention to join Janie busily conducting a game of croquet on the lawn.

I imagine a carriage conveying the troubled Oscar Wilde whistling past, and then one of Oliver's men thundering by in a noisy armoured car. Then there is the familiar figure of Winston Churchill, puffing on his cigars, deep in conversation with Oliver.

Moving forward just a few years, I spot the stunt pilot Winifred Crossley standing at a window, waiting for her call-up papers to arrive. Then, in the late 1950s, I might have even been knocked aside by a young American couple walking carefree arm in arm to dance the night away on Newhaven's sprung-floor ballroom where the latest rock 'n' roll music played from the stage.

As well as the story of Newhaven Court, this is a story of those who dwelt within, so bound up in the history and fortunes of the house.

A NOTE ON THE TEXT

The spellings 'Newhaven', 'New Haven' and 'NewHaven' were used inter-changeably. For clarity, I have used the spelling Newhaven throughout.

1

The Beginning of the End

TUESDAY, 22 JANUARY 1963

As dawn broke on the grey and bitterly cold Tuesday morning of 22 January 1963, the residents of Cromer reluctantly began to rise for work and school. Freezing temperatures meant that, for the majority without central heating, it was a struggle to emerge from their warm beds. While the adults quickly dressed to get downstairs to put the kettle on, their children marvelled at the swirled ice patterns that had formed on their windows before racing each other to the front room to grab the best spot in front of the coal fire. Those who could on that wintry day stayed at home, others, who had to go out, by late afternoon rushed home along the dark, frozen streets, looking forward to a hot dinner.

On the windswept incline above Cromer town sat the Newhaven Court Hotel. On that chilly afternoon, enjoying their tea in the lounge were the hotel owners, Donald and Violet Boyd-Stevenson, and their three boys, 15-year-old Ian, 11-year-old Christopher, and Roy who, just days earlier, had celebrated his 10th birthday.

Though partially sheltered from the easterly winds by the neighbouring lighthouse hill and the wooded areas that surrounded the hotel, the family still shivered in the frigid breeze blowing in over the North Sea as it whistled down the towering chimney stacks, finding its way in through the edges of the old window frames. All winter it had been a battle to keep warm and despite having central heating and a fire burning constantly, the old house with its numerous roomy spaces, corridors, projections and turret struggled to retain any semblance of warmth.

The peaceful family meal that afternoon was suddenly interrupted by a man who burst into the room. 'The hotel is on fire!' he shouted breathlessly.[1] It was a tremendous shock. All were unaware that as they had sat eating, the top floor of Newhaven Court was already a mass of smoke and flames.

As the Boyd-Stevenson family hurried out of the hotel, Cromer residents watched with alarm as smoke poured from the roof of the old Newhaven Court. Most of those who had spotted the fire assumed that someone else had already called the emergency services. When the engines failed to arrive, Arthur Mayes, who lived with his family on nearby Arbor Hill, called to ask where the fire engines were, only to be told his was the first call they had received.

The call handler asked him where the fire was. Not realising the line had connected to a central number and not the Cromer station, Arthur told them 'Newhaven Court!'

The handler replied, 'Where is Newhaven Court?'

Incredulously, Arthur replied, 'In Cromer, of course!'[2]

NOTES

1   Interview with Ian Boyd-Stevenson, 2021.
2   David Pope, Facebook 'Cromer' Group, 2021. Mr Mayes was the manager of Travis & Arnold Builder's Merchants.

2

The Lockers Meet the Lampsons

To tell the story of Newhaven Court, we must travel back to the year 1806, to the small community of New Haven Mills in the American state of Vermont. It was here that 44-year-old mill owner and sheep farmer William Lampson lived with his wife Rachel and their nine children. The Lampsons were well established and prosperous residents of the close-knit community and had lived in the pleasant small town since at least 1790. First chartered in 1767, the town by 1806 boasted a population of over 1,300, who ran a blacksmith, tannery, general store, wagon shop, creamery and cheese factory as well as a small village school.

The settlement was next to a river, and we can be sure the substantial Lampson homestead, in common with the other houses in town, enjoyed a scenic backdrop of rolling hills, fields, forests and the beautiful Green Mountains in the distance. Every September, the trees would explode with colour, cloaking the landscape in the fiery red and orange foliage that signalled the onset of autumn.

It was on the 21st of that month, and most probably at home, that Rachel gave birth to her tenth child, a robust, healthy boy. Rachel, who was nearly 39, must have been relieved to survive another pregnancy and birth. The little boy was quickly welcomed into the noisy household by his three older brothers and six sisters. He was named Curtis Miranda Lampson, his unusual middle name a tribute to the once-celebrated South American emancipator, Francisco de Miranda, a figure admired by Curtis's parents.

Curtis was enrolled at the local school, where he received a rudimentary education and showed early signs of his later entrepreneurial aptitude. The boy was given the job of stoking the school fire and was paid in the form of the wood ashes, from which he made soap to sell to the townsfolk. Alongside school, he helped his father run the mill and farm. Any spare time was spent roaming the forests hunting deer and fishing in the tumbling clear waters of New Haven River, both pursuits that would become lifelong passions.

This carefree early childhood was rocked in the spring of 1813 when an epidemic affecting Vermont known then as 'spotted fever' carried off his 3-year-old little sister, Laura Anne, followed by his mother, a month later. The illness, which modern-day doctors would probably identify as cerebral spinal meningitis, was terrifying. In 1814, Dr Hale wrote that his patients would commence with 'severe pain in the head and back … pain increased until in a short time it produced a delirium'.[1] In fatal cases, the afflicted would develop dark blotches or spots, nausea and vomiting, then become comatose and die within hours, sometimes before doctors could reach them.[2] Curtis was just 6 years old when he stood in the New Haven evergreen cemetery and watched as his mother and sister were laid to rest together.

William supported the family with a combination of sheep farming and working in the clover mill. The children picked up work when and where they could, including Curtis, who at 13 was working in the general store. William was an opportunist, a trait also seen in his youngest son. In 1820, at the age of almost 60, his diary reveals that he began working in the fur trade for his older son, William. He writes, rather excitedly, that he had bought in preparation 'thick shoes and a beaver hat'.[3]

Curtis grew into a tall, broad-shouldered young man with a strong, handsome face and head of wavy, fair hair, combed into a side parting. He was energetic, kind, optimistic and full of adventurous spirit. His future son-in-law, Frederick Locker, writing in his own reminiscences, wrote of Curtis, 'I am told that as a youth, he was wise beyond his years and intelligent in advance of his experience; that he was confided in for counsel by people old enough to be his father.'[4]

By the age of 17, Curtis had outgrown the small township and left to join his father and older brother, who were already working with the Hudson Bay Trading Company in Canada. Bright, ambitious and driven and not afraid to start with the most menial of jobs, it was not long before Curtis began making a name for himself. He showed a natural flair for business, and before long he was regularly sent to New York and London on behalf of fur dealers, including the financier, John Jacob Astor, who was well on the road to amassing a personal fortune.[5]

It was during a spell in New York that Curtis met Jane Walter Sibley of Sutton, Massachusetts, one of a pair of 'very beautiful' daughters of Gibbs Sibley and his wife Hannah.[6] Jane was just 17 and Curtis 21 when they married in 1827. A portrait survives of Jane in her wedding dress, revealing her curved figure and attractive heart-shaped face, framed by curling, chestnut brown hair. She and Curtis made a handsome young couple.

Three years after their marriage, Curtis took his wife to London where, at the age of just 24, he set up a successful business, trading in furs under the name C.M. Lampson. London, with its busy streets, squares, grand buildings and wealth of culture, must have suited Curtis, who quickly made England his home. He would never live in his birth country again. The fur venture was a success and Curtis and Jane quickly became very wealthy.

With great success came invitations and introductions, often from other extremely wealthy individuals. One of these was the influential American philanthropist George Peabody. George, all but forgotten today, was a millionaire who rendered assistance to charity. Brought up in deprived circumstances himself, Peabody gave very generously to public schemes both in America and the UK, predominantly involving housing for the poor.

Although not as active as Peabody, Curtis collaborated with his friend on several occasions. In 1851, the two men donated £40,000 to fund American participation in the Crystal Palace Great Exhibition and the following year, £5,000 was spent to fit out SS *Advance*, which was sent far north to look for the missing John Franklin expedition.[7]

Six years after their marriage, Jane gave birth to her first child, a boy named George Curtis. Two years later, a brother for George arrived, little Henry. In 1846, after a gap of over ten years, Jane gave birth to Hannah Jane, the builder of Newhaven Court, followed by a further son, Norman George, in 1849.

'Rowfant' was the name of the enormous Sussex Tudor mansion purchased by Curtis for under £50,000 in the year after the birth of his daughter.[8] This enchanting manor house, 'with the pointed old-world gables, the Horsham tiling mortared with moss and grey stone walls' was to become the Lampsons' country home.[9] The family divided their time between Rowfant and their city address at 80 Eaton Square in London. Curtis also leased a hunting forest and lodge at Inchbae in Scotland. Having firmly established himself in England, 43-year-old Curtis became a naturalised British citizen in May 1850.[10]

All four of Curtis and Jane's children were energetic and lively but their only daughter, Hannah Jane, known to her family as Janie, was singled out by her affectionate father from the start. He doted on his daughter and the two became solid companions. Janie's son, Oliver, later wrote, 'The Americans are far more affectionate than the English and the bond between my mother and her father was American in its touchingly tender strength. They adored each other.'[11] Perhaps Curtis saw much of himself in the wide-eyed, dark-haired and cheerful little girl, or maybe her vulnerability from childhood brushes with death, once from rheumatic fever and later diphtheria, made him particularly protective of her.

Rowfant House c. 1890. (Family collection)

The family lived a life of luxury, employing a large staff of servants, maids, footmen, stable hands, nannies and chefs. Having only received rudimentary schooling himself, Curtis placed value on a good education. George, Henry and Norman were all sent to a prestigious private London school before further education at Trinity College Cambridge. As a girl, Janie was educated at home by a governess.

Janie was taught the basics of reading, writing and arithmetic, in addition to receiving tuition in French, German and Italian. As befitting a lady of her class, she was introduced to the key accomplishments of deportment, conversation, dancing, drawing, needlework, horse riding and music; all skills to ensure that she would stand out in the competitive marriage market.

Janie was, as her father before her, easily pleased but naturally bright. She became a proficient pianist and a skilled choral singer as well as a talented dancer. She loved reading and a favourite pursuit of father and daughter was reading Tennyson poems aloud to each other.

A good governess was expected to press on her pupil Bible study and a strict adherence to the moral code. Janie's governess would not have been disappointed in this regard, as she showed early signs of her lifelong religious zeal. Occasionally, she would be the only member of her family to attend church on a Sunday, once remarking in her diary that she had been left alone in the pew sitting 'like an owl in an ivy bush'.[12]

However, Janie was not solely academic and serious minded. Her diary for 1864, the year she turned 18, shows the lighter, fun side of her personality. Using rushed sweeping paragraphs, she describes attending parties with her brothers where she danced the quadrille and the waltz as well as taking part in after-dinner games such as Blindman's Buff, Forfeits and Twenty-One Questions. She wrote about eligible young men, games of croquet, shopping trips with her mother, theatre shows with her father and taking regular, long walks with her friends and American cousins. It was also the year when she was presented at Court before Queen Victoria, and the outfit she wore, reported in *The Evening Standard*, gives us an idea of her young, fashionable style, 'Miss Lampson wore a train and corsage of rich mauve satin, ornamented by tulle over a petticoat of rich white satin, trimmed with tulle and bows of satin ribbon. Head dress of plume, lappets; parlure of diamonds.'[13]

By this time, George Curtis, Janie's elder brother, was already causing his parents distress with activities for which he would later become renowned and which would also later lead to his sister inheriting what, by birthright,

Sir Curtis Miranda Lampson. (Family collection)

should have been his.[14] Rumours of shady, underhand financial dealings and other disreputable behaviour were rife, leading Lord Battersea to allegedly proclaim that George and his brother Henry were, 'the biggest bounders he ever met'.[15]

Curtis was rumoured to have been offered a partnership with merchant bankers, the Baring Bros, only to have had the offer withdrawn when the directors met his wayward sons. Perhaps the more disappointment Curtis felt in relation to his older sons, the more he revelled in the company of his daughter. Curtis was fond of taking Janie to view his projects, one of which became his most celebrated achievement.

In 1856, the Atlantic Telegraph Company was formed to lay the first deep-sea transatlantic telegraph cable, with the ambitious aim of connecting the 2,000 miles between England and America. Curtis was appointed as a director and later promoted to vice chairman. The project was beset by delays and repeated failures and as the company struggled to achieve success, several of the directors became despondent. Ever the optimist, Curtis persevered, expending his own time, money and considerable effort. He was eventually rewarded when, on 27 July 1866, the project came to completion and a transatlantic telegram was sent and received. Queen Victoria was said to have been greatly pleased and it was at a formal dinner in Liverpool in October that year that Lord Derby, then prime minister, announced that Curtis would receive a baronetcy.

Although already well respected, newly titled Sir Curtis and Lady Lampson were now invited to mix in the most influential of social circles. It was on one of these occasions, a New Year party in January 1873, that their daughter Janie first met 51-year-old Frederick Locker, the man who would later become her husband.

❋   ❋   ❋

Frederick was born in 1821 to Edward Hawke Locker and his wife Eleanor, the second son and third child of six in an upper-middle-class family of considerable interest. Edward Hawke Locker was the youngest son of Nelson's friend and mentor, Captain William Locker, later Lieutenant Governor of Greenwich Hospital.[16]

As a young man of 17, Edward entered the navy as a clerk before becoming a civil secretary. His naval duties took him to Europe during the Peninsular War and in 1814 he met ex-Emperor Napoleon Bonaparte during his incarceration on Elba.[17] Later in his career, he became Resident Civil Commissioner of Greenwich Hospital and with the appointment came beautifully appointed, fine, large living quarters for him and his family that faced the River Thames. A talented watercolour artist and author himself, Edward fulfilled his father's ambition of a painted hall at Greenwich, in addition to filling his own bright, roomy apartments with carefully chosen paintings and interesting books.

It was an idyllic home for the young Locker family. Frederick and his closest two siblings, Edward and Ellen, took brisk walks with their father in the scenic park behind the hospital or stopped to chat to the resident 'old salts' – Greenwich naval pensioners – who entertained them with high tales of adventures at sea. On rainy days they took dancing lessons, played the piano or fed the stray cats in the cellars. Occasionally, they stood at the water's edge to watch the boats on the river or sat at the large Georgian windows where in the street below Dutch women in their high, white caps and stout petticoats sang as they sold brooms to passers-by. On bright days, they played outside with bows and arrows or took Strawberry the pony for a ride around the courtyard.

Frederick's mother, Eleanor, was the daughter of the intelligent conservative scholar, Reverend Jonathan Boucher, who as a young man had taken off to Virginia and found himself tutor to the stepson of the future president, George Washington. Boucher and Washington had been firm friends until they found themselves on opposing sides during the American War of Independence.

Loyalist Boucher was an eloquent preacher, and his outspoken proclamations of 'God save the King!' made him extremely unpopular. Fearing physical harm, he spent his last few months in America preaching with two loaded pistols on his pulpit. He eventually fled back to England in 1775 for his own protection, where he later settled with his second wife and large brood of children in Epsom, Surrey.

Edward had fallen for the considerably younger Eleanor on first sight. She was charming, with 'a fine figure, beautiful face, sprightly, with gentle feminine manners'.[18] The courtship was short, and the couple married within weeks of meeting.

Although short in stature, Edward commanded respect, and though imbued with many good qualities, he was also prone to an irritable temper made worse by a series of chest complaints that frequently made him weak and tired. Family legend has it that Eleanor, when she first married her older husband, was 'scared of him'.

Despite being loving and warm towards her children, Eleanor was vulnerable to influence, and during Frederick's earlier childhood fell in with the morally questionable and frightening Mrs Shore, who terrified the children with stories of eternal damnation, insisting 'the road to everlasting punishment was extremely broad and very crowded'.[19] This was all terrifying to a little boy who already, from his own admission, was a nervous child.

Frederick went through a succession of unhappy school placements, made worse by his sensitive nature and slow learning. It led to his father, a man of immense energy, intelligence and drive, to write in frustration, 'Fred cannot read even tolerably, though almost eight!' After schooling, and out of options, his parents placed him in unsatisfactory monotonous clerking positions before finding him a place in the Admiralty.[20]

However, it was his early life at Greenwich Hospital that had the greatest effect on his life. His father's rich circle of literary and political connections meant there were always interesting people invited to dine at Greenwich and the children were allowed to come down and join the guests for dessert. Sir Walter Scott, the Poet Laureate, Robert Southey, and astronomers working in Greenwich all came to dine with the Lockers.

At the end of the evening, after the guests had left, the children sat with their mother in the bedroom along with their black Newfoundland dog, Argus. After a short time, Edward, dressed for bed in his white cap and grey gown, would join them and encourage them to converse and ask questions. He would also regale them with tales of his own experiences, such as in 1820 when he listened to Quaker Elizabeth Fry lecture the Newgate prisoners or when he ascended to the skies in squally conditions in the summer of 1802 with celebrated Parisian balloonist André-Jacques Garnerin.

Edward also enriched them with experience, taking the children to the Continent to view the site of the Battle of Waterloo or to see the first omnibus, as well as making frequent trips into the centre of London where watermen would row them from their Greenwich apartments to Westminster Bridge.[21] Frederick and his siblings grew up with a talent for socialising and a passion for literature, art, book collecting, paintings and beautiful *objets d'art* that was to colour and determine the course of their lives.

Along with a nervous disposition inherited from his mother, Frederick also suffered from a gastric complaint which he called 'the hag, dyspepsia … who waits upon grief and anxiety, and had always more or less tormented me'.[22] In 1849, aged 28, the symptoms were debilitating enough for him to obtain a lengthy leave of duty from his naval position. It is impossible to determine an exact diagnosis, but the symptoms described, such as vomiting and, at times, weight loss, could suggest a chronic serious bowel disease or could easily be due to physical manifestations of severe anxiety, for, in 1844, his father had suffered a breakdown which put enormous stress on the entire family. Though his mother, fearful of losing her home and income, initially tried to hide her husband away, his mental health and memory were failing. Edward was forced to retire his position and apartment in Greenwich and died in 1849. Soon after, Frederick fled to the Continent with a small inheritance and a pocket full of introductions.

In his late twenties, Frederick was a good-looking and fashionably dressed young man, 5ft 9in tall, slim with dark eyes and a mop of curly chestnut-brown hair and well-trimmed sideburns. With his interesting personality, talent for conversation and love of the arts, he was a captivating man to be around.

Lady Charlotte Bruce, daughter of Lord Elgin and four years his senior, was one of many rich and attractive young women Frederick met on his travels. He was immediately smitten, calling her his 'beneficent angel'. They fell quickly in love. Frederick proposed, and Charlotte accepted. The happy couple married in Paris in July 1850.

Frederick Locker as a young man. (Family collection)

His marriage to Charlotte was a fortunate move and changed Frederick's life, instantly solving the problems of both money and status. He was now the son-in-law of Lord Elgin and relatively well off.[23]

In an age where money and connections meant everything, his wife opened doors. Charlotte's sister, Lady Augusta Stanley, was one of Queen Victoria's favourite ladies-in-waiting and the queen also had a warm regard for Charlotte. Frederick found himself invited to formal meals at Buckingham Palace and introduced to other eminent figures, including the great Victorian Poet Laureate, Alfred, Lord Tennyson.

A daughter was born in 1854, named Eleanor Bertha. Eleanor grew up 'a solitary child in an atmosphere of books and bindings',[24] who 'shared her father's enthusiasm in art and poetry, won with her piquant and ingenious charm the affection of his friends, was petted by Queen Victoria and played with the young princesses'.[25] The little family of three went about creating a network of literary friends, including George Elliot, William Makepeace Thackeray, Henry James and Charles Dickens. Bright little Eleanor accompanied her parents to dinner parties and collected a library of her own, full of signed copies of the books of her parents' friends.

His happy marriage allowed Frederick to spread his wings and indulge in his hobby of collecting and his creative talent for poetry. A small volume of popular rhymes called *London Lyrics*, published in 1857, became a hit and made Frederick a minor celebrity.

Through their mutual occupations and interests, Alfred Tennyson and his wife, Emily, became close friends of the Lockers and the families holidayed and spent much time together. Eleanor was of a similar age to Tennyson's sons, Hallam and Lionel, and spent so much time with them that she was considered one of the family. Emily, particularly, saw Eleanor as the daughter she had never had. Unfortunately, Charlotte's health, always precarious, began to fail and she died suddenly in April 1872, while only in her mid-fifties.

Frederick and 17-year-old Eleanor were heartbroken. On hearing the news, Alfred and Emily Tennyson, who were staying at Farringford, on the Isle of Wight, wrote to Frederick to offer their support, 'When you are able to come to us, and it will be good for you to come, you must come. We will do all the little we can for you, you know, with all true love.'[26] It was not an empty gesture. When they arrived back in London, the couple saw how ill and sad Frederick and Eleanor had become and took the Lockers under their wing, joining them most evenings for dinner.

Within a year, desperately lonely Frederick consciously made the decision to seek a new wife. Remembering the meeting he had had with Sir Curtis Lampson and his attraction to his striking tall, elegant and unmarried daughter, Frederick made moves to renew the acquaintance. Janie was 27, twenty-five years younger than Frederick and the opposite in personality in every way. He had only a wavering faith, whereas she was zealous and orthodox; he suffered from ill health and she was robust and energetic.

Frederick courted her gently, sending her letters touched with humour and light flirting. Referring to a bookplate he had sent her featuring two lovebirds, he asked, 'Do you like the little bird who is singing to his mate?'[27] By December 1873, he had received an invitation to stay at Rowfant, where it is likely he proposed.

Hannah-Jane 'Janie' Lampson around the time of her marriage. (Family collection)

Friends were astounded by the apparent incompatibility of the couple. Some more cynical folks, observing Janie's fabulous wealth, accused Frederick of being a fortune hunter. Despite the two later becoming firm friends, hardworking man of business Sir Curtis was initially suspicious of Frederick's lack of occupation and Lady Lampson actively disliked him. However, opposites attract, and Frederick found Janie's energy, drive, 'never flailing animal spirits'[28] and optimism a tonic to his naturally melancholy disposition and she found that his eccentricity, kindliness, connections and love of learning made him interesting and attractive.

Emily Tennyson, although morally disapproving of second marriages, had to admit that Frederick was a changed man and was pleased for her friend. It was, therefore, after a short engagement that Frederick made a second fortunate marriage. On 6 July 1874, they wed in Janie's local church at Worth in the presence of Tennyson, among others. The wedding caused considerable interest, with *The Graphic* describing the day:

> From the lych gate to the church door the path was lined with children, who not only strewn flowers before the happy pair on the return journey but

literally pelted them with roses and lilies as a token of their affectionate regard, the bride being an especial favourite with all classes. Nine bridesmaids looked charming in their muslin skirts, peacock blue jackets and dainty caps. After the ceremony, the wedding party drove under triumphal arches … horses were taken out of the bridal carriage which was part drawn home by labourers to Sir Curtis's beautiful seat at Rowfant.[29]

Nineteen-year-old Eleanor, Frederick's daughter, had grown into a strikingly attractive, highly intelligent and witty young woman with a slim figure, turned-up nose and wavy thick, dark hair. Although her new stepmother was kind, Eleanor found her overbearing, especially when it came to religion. Due to his earlier experiences with Mrs Shore, Frederick was not a man of strong religious beliefs, and it is reasonable that Eleanor held similar views. In contrast, Janie was evangelical. She banned games on Sundays and busied herself writing religious children's stories, studying scripture, conducting Bible classes and writing pamphlets for the Christian Association.

Increasingly alienated, Eleanor began spending more time with the Tennysons and, particularly, Lionel, their thoughtful youngest son. Soon after, their relationship developed into something more and when Lionel proposed to Eleanor on a holiday in Italy, she accepted. They married in a beautiful ceremony at Westminster Abbey in February 1878, witnessed by George Eliot and William Gladstone, among others. Three children quickly followed in the proceeding years, Alfred (Ally),[30] Charles (Charlie) and Michael.

Frederick and Janie enjoyed a long honeymoon touring the cathedrals and art galleries of Belgium, Holland and France and after an extended stay in Sir Curtis's Scottish hunting lodge, Janie found herself pregnant. The couple were delighted when on 25 September 1875, Janie gave birth to a son, who they named Godfrey Tennyson.

In 1878, the dark, curly haired little boy gained a sister, Dorothy Jane Charlotte, known as Dolly, and then, in 1880 they were joined by twins, Oliver Stillingfleet and Maud Hannah. Oliver later recounted their birth:

It was behind the burnished brass knocker of our green door at 25 Chesham Street, London, that I was born … My Father, Frederick Locker, the poet was waiting in the room adjoining that in which my mother was confined when the nurse burst through with a baby boy. 'Another coming' she announced and disappeared. She returned shortly, and my sister joined me on his sagging lap. 'A girl this time-twins!'[31]

Eleanor, who had grown up as an only child, now found herself in the peculiar position of having children the same age as her own half-siblings. The growing Locker household was a noisy, happy and boisterous one. Janie was a caring, loving mother and Frederick, although older, was an approachable and interested father.

However, like most other parents in their social class, the everyday childcare was left to others. One of several servants working for the family was the children's nanny, Harriet Lucas, who was 48 when the twins were born. She was a tiny but fierce woman and much loved by the four little children.

Below left: *Eleanor Locker. (Auckland Libraries Heritage Collection, 1342-Album-244-23-5)*

Below right: *Lionel, the youngest son of Poet Laureate Alfred, Lord Tennyson. (Auckland Libraries Heritage Collections, 1342-Album-244-23-6)*

Little Nanny Lucas came with a good reference from the Colman family of Norwich mustard fame, from whose employ she had come. Nanny, garbed in black and barely 4ft 6in tall, was a force to be reckoned with when it came to the children, whom she adored. Oliver later wrote of her:

> She was like an old child, with veined hands and knuckly joints which distressed us because we felt like they had grown like that in our service. Her face, as large as a tennis racquet, was surmounted by a pad of false hair, which flapped as she darted about.[32]

Almost a second mother to the children, she was especially close to Oliver, whose insistence that she could never possibly leave him saved her from being fired on more than one occasion. Godfrey also remembered her fondly, 'She loved only us children, with a fierce maternal love. Her little flame of life, that tiny lamp, fed by the oil of love, burnt for us and us alone.'[33]

The relationship lasted into adulthood. When Oliver, then aged 35 and serving in France during the Great War, received a letter from Dorothy telling him that Nanny had suffered a stroke, he paid the doctor's bill without question. He then sent Nanny the most touching letter in which he reminded her that he loved her 'better than anyone' and to 'let my love cure you until I can return myself and make you well'.[34]

Sir Curtis warmed to Frederick and stayed exceptionally close to his daughter and her growing family. He loved his grandchildren dearly and took visits to see his daughter and the children whenever occasion allowed. He was particularly close to Godfrey and took the little boy out fishing or for long walks and carriage rides. When apart, warm letters and generous gifts would fly between them, 'We miss our grandchildren more than we do you!' he jokingly wrote to Janie, then heavily pregnant with the twins.[35] Curtis always signed off his numerous letters with 'your affectionate Dad, CML'.[36]

Now in his late seventies, Curtis had never truly retired. He was remarkably energetic for a man of his age and his letters to Janie are full of accounts of his frequent hunting and fishing trips in Scotland. Janie's mother, though sociable, tired easily and often stayed with her daughter instead of accompanying her husband on long trips north.

During the early stages of her pregnancy with the twins, presumably feeling exhausted and nauseous, Janie took the children and the nannies and left

Above left: *Nanny Lucas, 'garbed in black and barely four feet and a half tall'. (Taken from Godfrey Locker-Lampson,* Life in the Country *[1948])*

Above right: *Sir Curtis with his grandson, Godfrey Locker. 'We miss our grandchildren more than we do you!' he wrote to his daughter, Janie. (Family collection)*

for the Isle of Wight. She took lodgings at Beach House in Freshwater, on the invitation of the Tennysons, and stayed for the summer, enjoying allowing Godfrey and Dorothy to splash and play in the cool refreshing waters. Janie wrote to her father with news of their stay. 'I am glad to hear you are still enjoying your seaside trip,' he replied.[37]

The successful Freshwater summer break was a revelation. Janie clearly revelled in being close to the sea. In the year after her twins turned 1, Janie decided on another summer by the coast. On the invitation of the owner, Francis Hoare, a family friend, Janie took lodgings at Weylands, a property on the Cromer coast with stunning sea views.

Where Janie went, her parents followed. After returning home after an idyllic July fortnight spent with his daughter and his grandchildren in the Norfolk sunshine, Sir Curtis found his wife keen to return. 'We enjoyed our visit to Cromer greatly,' Curtis wrote to Janie, 'Mother is in love with the place.'[38]

NOTES

1   'Dr Webber's Essay on Cerebral Spinal Meningitis', *New England Journal of Medicine* (6/9/1866).
2   Woodstock History Center website, 'Spotted Fever Epidemic' (accessed 1/2/2019).
3   William Lampson's diary, 'Journal of My Life', 11 April 1820. Source: Pat Walker, MyHeritage.com.
4   Frederick Locker-Lampson, *My Confidences*, p.385.
5   Father of John Jacob Astor II, who sadly met his end on SS *Titanic* in 1912.
6   William Addison Benedict and Rev. Hiram Tracy, *History of the Town of Sutton, Massachusetts 1704–1876*, p.272.
7   Source: Pat Walker, MyHeritage.com. Captain John Franklin had gone missing in an attempt to traverse the Northwest Passage in 1845. Neither SS *Advance* nor other rescue missions were successful in finding the missing men or boats.
8   Around £6 million. Source: Bank of England Inflation Calculator.
9   Stephen Locker-Lampson, *Nothing to Offer but Blood*, p.20.
10 Naturalisation Papers: Lampson, Curtis Miranda, from New York. Certificate 1118, issued 14 May 1850. The National Archives, ref: HO 1/33/1118.
11 Stephen Locker-Lampson, *Nothing to Offer but Blood*, p.44.
12 Hannah Jane Lampson diary of 1864. Referenced in Madison C. Bates, 'Sir Curtis Lampson: Vermont Baronet', *Vermont History*, Vol. XXVII (Vermont Historical Society, January 1960) p.11.
13 *Evening Standard*, 4 May 1864.
14 In 1862, George married Eliza Anne Kaye, under an abbreviated name to conceal the union from his disapproving parents. A long-lasting affair with Dutch-born Sophia Van Gelderen produced several children. George was later involved in a messy affair, leading Eliza to petition him for a divorce for desertion and misconduct.
15 Stephen Locker-Lampson, *Nothing to Offer but Blood*, p.42.
16 Captain William Locker (1731–1800). Admiral Lord Horatio Nelson served as a lieutenant under Locker's command on HMS *Lowestoffe*. The men remained lifelong friends and correspondents.
17 Edward's account of this meeting can be found in *My Confidences*, by his son, Frederick Locker-Lampson.
18 Ellen Dobie, unpublished recollections (family collection).
19 Frederick Locker-Lampson, *My Confidences*, p.51.
20 *Ibid.*, p.99.
21 Ellen Dobie, unpublished recollections (family collection).
22 Frederick Locker-Lampson, *My Confidences*, p.150.
23 Thomas Bruce, Lord Elgin of 'Elgin Marbles' fame.
24 Augustine Birrell, *Frederick Locker-Lampson: A Character Sketch*, p.67.
25 Charles Tennyson, *Stars and Markets*, p.44.
26 Alfred and Emily Tennyson to Frederick Locker, 28 April 1872. Quoted in Hallam Tennyson, *Alfred, Lord Tennyson: A Memoir. Volume II*, p.113.

27 Letter from Frederick Locker to Hannah Jane Lampson, 1873 (family collection).
28 Frederick Locker-Lampson, *My Confidences*, p.202.
29 *The Graphic*, Saturday, 11 July 1874.
30 The 'golden-hair'd Ally' of Tennyson's poem, 'To Alfred Tennyson, my Grandson'.
31 Stephen Locker-Lampson, *Nothing to Offer but Blood*, p.2.
32 *Ibid*., OLL, p.5.
33 Godfrey Locker-Lampson, *Life in the Country*, p.123.
34 Letter from Oliver Locker-Lampson to Nanny Lucas, 1915 (family collection).
35 Sir Curtis Lampson to Hannah Jane Locker, 9 September 1880 (Beinecke Rare Books and Manuscript Library).
36 Madison C. Bates, 'Sir Curtis Lampson'.
37 Sir Curtis Lampson to Hannah Jane Locker, 13 April 1880 (Beinecke Rare Books and Manuscript Library).
38 *Ibid*., 20 July 1882.

3

Arise – Newhaven!

You should have gone to Cromer, my dear, if you went anywhere.
Perry was a week at Cromer once, and he holds it to be the best
of all sea bathing places. A fine open sea, he says, and very pure air.

Mr Woodhouse advises on sea bathing in Jane Austen's *Emma*, 1816.

Before its transformation into an exclusive seaside resort, Cromer was a small but prosperous coastal village inhabited predominantly by fishermen and their families. Change began during the late eighteenth century as the wealthy flocked to the pretty little town eager to 'take the waters' or to soak up the beautiful scenery. Artists and writers followed, inspired by the dramatic clifftops, yellow gorse and heath.

Those who came to Cromer for their health did so in the belief that the purifying air and seawater was a remedy for a host of maladies such as consumption, digestive problems and fevers. Some took long constitutional walks under the wind-beaten clouds. Others came to drink the salty seawater, believing it to have medicinal effects. Visitors who wanted to take a dip in the chilly waters made use of beachside bathing machines, wooden-walled carts on wheels pulled by horses or men into the sea. Bathers undressed in private inside the dark sandy-floored hut before descending the steps into the frigid North Sea, the shock of which was supposed to aid the constitution.

Railways came late to Cromer, and it was not connected until 1877 when a station was built on an elevated plot on the north side of Norwich Road to serve as the terminus of the Great Eastern Railway line from London.

Cromer beach c. 1870. (Author's collection)

Initially, the railways brought a moderate number of extra summer visitors, but it was generally more of a convenience for the existing inhabitants and the town remained fairly remote and sedate.

Nearby seaside resorts like Great Yarmouth, whose railway links had come earlier, attracted a different clientele to Cromer. Comparing the summer scene in Yarmouth to Cromer in 1883, *Daily Telegraph* travel writer Clement Scott wrote:

> At Yarmouth, the babies swarm between one jetty and another. Holes and hollows are dug in the sand and down in it the miserable infant is plunged with a feeding bottle in mouth whilst the nursemaid turns aside and coquets the photographer's assistant.

Cromer, he said, had a distinctly different air and the only children one would tend to see would be public school boys home for the holidays. In comparison to Punch and Judy shows, dancing and raucous drinking at Yarmouth, visitors to Cromer would more likely be found on little pony traps that drove up in the afternoons to the Roman encampment on Beacon Hill. There were 'no brass bands, no fashionable promenade, no evening dances'. When the sun set over Yarmouth, the air was still alive with music and noise, the smells of food and babies crying, whereas Cromer's 'fields and cliffs look chilly and deserted' and 'when the clock struck ten, the best part of Cromer is asleep'.[1]

Janie loved the atmosphere at Cromer and after the successful summer season of 1882 spent in the town, she became convinced that her young family needed a permanent home of their own in the area. It seemed a perfect destination. Cromer was far away from the unhealthy congestion and pollution of London and a place where her four young children, Godfrey, Dorothy, Oliver and Maud, now 7, 4 and 2, could grow and thrive in the healthy air. Cromer had an air of wealthy exclusivity that appealed to Janie and the local prominent interrelated Quaker families. The Birkbecks at The Grove, the Barclays at The Warren, the Buxtons at Upton House, the Gurneys at Beach House and Sir Samuel Hoare MP at Cliff House all shared her penchant for socialising, religious sentiments and high moral values. 'I do not think I could stay so long in so quiet a village,' wrote Sir Curtis to Janie in 1882, 'but I can understand your liking it for all the neighbours are so kind to you and it is no doubt a most desirable place for your children.'[2]

Having set her mind on Cromer, Janie was determined to find land on which to build her summer home. By September 1882, she had found what she considered to be an ideal plot on an elevated position above the town with an excellent view straight down to the church tower and blue sea below. It was an easy ten-minute walk down the hill to the town centre, church and beach, but it was also far away enough from the town to avoid feeling crowded. The Eastern boundary was marked by the main thoroughfare into Cromer, the Norwich Road, which made it convenient for easy carriage access to the railway station, which was just a little further up the hill. The newly rebuilt white lighthouse to the east across the valley was a striking landmark, lighting up the land once a minute and the grand Cromer Hall estate, to the west through a small dense wooded area that broke up the sparse plot, made a genteel neighbour.

The plot was a field of several acres that had once been ancient heathland before being divided and cultivated into arable land. Various tenants throughout the eighteenth and nineteenth centuries had occupied the site, including the Bennet family, George Bull, Henry Sandford and Joseph Pull, but the land comprised part of the vast Cromer Hall estate. Once owned by the powerful Wyndham family, the estate, which covered much of the land around Cromer, was bought in 1852 by wealthy barrister and MP Benjamin Bond Cabbell for £65,000. Cabbell died in 1875, leaving the estate to his nephew, John, who in turn left it on his death in 1878 to his son, Benjamin

Bond Cabbell II. Just prior to John's death, plans had been drawn up for a mass sale of land, but he had died before the sale took place.

Janie excitedly wrote to her father, asking for his advice and financial backing. 'The financial part of the business can be arranged but I see no reason for hurrying the matter,' he replied. Sir Curtis was not immediately taken with the plot Janie had found and considered the high price of £500 per acre 'about equal to that demanded for land in the out-laying parts of London'. A man of business, Sir Curtis had the foresight to predict that Cromer was on the verge of a building boom and feared the house would soon be surrounded by new buildings. 'I do not like the position,' he wrote, 'too near and not isolated.'[3]

Despite her father's concerns, Janie had her way. Initially, she purchased just 6 of the 10 available acres of land, those on the higher ground overlooking the town and the sea. By the spring of 1883, with advice and help from her father, Janie had consulted and employed an architect. Sir Curtis was no stranger to funding and arranging a build, having given money as a gift in 1868 to build a school in his American hometown of New Haven Mills.[4]

Janie was a young woman and naturally wanted her new house designed in the most on-trend style in England in 1883 – Queen Anne Revival. The style had become popular following sketches by British architect Norman Shaw, after his pen and ink drawings began to appear in trade journals in the 1870s. It was quickly adopted by the Americans before becoming popular in the UK. Janie was a woman with strong convictions and Frederick was happy to allow his young, energetic wife free rein to indulge her ideas.

The architect employed by Sir Curtis and Janie was probably John Bond Pearce.[5] Born in 1843 in Norwich, Pearce was an architect in demand having designed and completed several large-scale builds to excellent standards. In 1882, he designed the Agricultural Hall in Norwich, considered to be a decided success, and in June of the same year, he designed the impressive new town hall on the quayside at Great Yarmouth.[6] The town hall was grand enough to warrant an opening ceremony attended by HRH The Prince of Wales. As the architect, Pearce had the important job of presenting the prince with a silver key with which to unlock the building.

Sir Curtis and the Lockers probably consulted Pearce at his premises in Surrey Street in Norwich, where plans were drawn up and finalised. There was much to think about beyond the layout. The 1878 Building Act set down details that would have to be considered, such as thickness of walls, damp-proof courses, underfloor ventilation and ceiling heights. By the end of July 1883, Sir Curtis had the architect's papers sent to builders for inspection and an estimate for the cost for the build.

By August 1883, labourers were digging down into the sandy earth, ready to lay foundations. Janie was active in making suggestions that she felt would improve the build and was eager for progress. Occasionally, Sir Curtis had to slow her down, 'The pavement outside the house can next be determined and arranged after the roof is on and I would say nothing more about it now.'[7]

Father and daughter made an exceptional team. Janie supervised as red brick, stone and slate were brought in and Sir Curtis approved alterations and gave sensible advice about building, boundaries, contracts and solicitors. Though younger in years than his father-in-law, Frederick was decidedly more delicate and often ill with his gastric complaint and appears to have had little input into the build.

Over the winter of 1883–84, the building took shape. On a sunny and cloudless day in early July 1884, Sir Curtis boarded the train to Cromer to meet his daughter at her completed summer home. Frederick stayed in London. The two traversed the site and examined the finished build. Previously referred to in letters simply as 'Cromer Lodge', it was probably at this point that the pair decided the house should be named Newhaven Court, in honour of Sir Curtis's birthplace.

The final result was striking. Pearce had designed the three-storey mansion with every defining exterior characteristic of the Queen Anne Revival style. It had an asymmetrical and picturesque frontage with a single large, turreted corner tower, large stone-mullioned windows, warm red-brick facade, jumbled, steep-gabled rooves, balconies and a slated roof topped with dramatic chimneys.

The central shadowed-porch entrance with artistic stone portico led to double doors opening into the tessellated-floor hallway. Through the doors, on the immediate left, was a strongroom, followed by the foot of the staircase that led to the first floor. The staircase was bathed in light from the magnificent feature window, which spanned the height between the two floors. Past the stairs and across the hall was a door opening into a lofty lounge area that led through to the drawing room and library.

The rooms were well proportioned with large fireplaces. French casement windows in the drawing room opened onto a south-facing gravel area and a planned rose garden. To the right of the front door, opposite the stairs, was a dining room with a fireplace, oak-panelled walls and dado. In the corner was the turret annexe with a bay window that allowed natural light into the dark room.

An oak door from the dining room led to the kitchen and pantry, and in the furthest corner were steps to the wine cellar and storage rooms. Also on the ground floor was a school room, housekeeper's lounge, servants' hall and a toilet.

On the first floor, leading off a large landing, were three spacious bedrooms named 'Jessamine', 'Crocus' and 'Myrtle' after the flowered paper that covered the walls. Two dressing rooms were on the same floor, in addition to various smaller bedrooms, all with fireplaces. The principal and prettiest room was the large turret bedroom, which looked across the valley to the lighthouse. Although each bedroom had a convenient washstand, there were also two bathrooms on the first floor, fitted with the most modern conveniences of flushing toilets, foot bath and a sink and another separate toilet. A night and day nursery were on the same floor. Another small staircase led to a further set of ten small bedrooms on the floor above, some with a balcony and one with a pleasant little terrace. A back landing and passage led down to the servants' hall beneath.[8]

Every window framed a picturesque view – and what a view it would have been! A photograph from 1885, taken shortly before the massive housing boom that shortly followed, shows Newhaven in an expanse of empty fields.[9] With no surrounding houses, it stood dominant on the landscape and would have had a clear vista down to the sea below.

With the house now constructed, and being keen on an aesthetically pleasing look, father and daughter next set to work on the large, bare plot and gardens. The architect had placed an advertisement in a local paper in July 1884 for an experienced gardener in Cromer, who, he stated, 'must be thoroughly up to his work'.[10] Presumably, the gardener was employed to help lay out the grounds around the newly erected house.

The front of the house faced the Norwich Road and beyond to the lighthouse, while one side of the house faced the church and beyond, the sparkling blue sea. Newhaven backed onto a small established, square, wooded plot that had once been rented from the Cromer Hall estate by wealthy banker Henry Baring, and led through to a hedge running parallel to a sunken lane that was said to have once served smugglers from the coast. Sir Curtis suggested building a brick wall on the northern boundary, 'ten foot high and fourteen inches thick, so there is no fear of the wind blowing down the wall'. It was erected at the considerable cost of £3 per yard and later solidly marked with a datestone, still standing today, with their initials and the date, 1885.[11]

View of Cromer from the High Station in 1885. The newly built Newhaven Court can be seen on the left of the photo. (Courtesy of Cromer Museum/Norfolk Museums Service, CRRMU: 1980.80.69)

On the sunny, sheltered, southern side of the house was a large area ready to be laid out for gardens. Janie had initially been offered the whole field of just over 10 acres but had bought 6. With the house finished, Janie looked over to the neighbouring 4 acres and considered she had been unwise not to have purchased all 10. Frederick agreed, and the couple approached the land-owning Cabbells. Though it was a poorer plot of land, the price was inflated by over £300 (about £35,000 today). Unsure of what to do, Janie wrote to her father. 'It is evident you have to deal with sharp persons,' came the reply. 'Had you taken the whole field at first, ten ½ acres, they would have been very glad. Now that you have put up a good house on the best part of the land, they charge you an extra price for the poorest part of the field.'[12] Sir Curtis advised them to approach Mr Bond-Cabbell directly and ask him to split the difference and accept £2,125. If not acceptable, then he advised them to accept the cost, but whatever they agreed should be settled at once. Negotiations were successful and by the end of August 1884, the land was theirs.

Within the bare plot, Frederick and Janie were now free to instruct the gardeners to lay out a varied, pretty garden full of flowerbeds, potted shrubs and cone-shaped yew hedges, surrounded by an expanse of lawn. On the southern side, the grounds were naturally graduated. Gardeners worked to create a large, flat, rectangular area for a tennis court.

Nearer to the house was a pretty rose garden. A section of the grounds behind the kitchen was laid out to grow herbs, fruit and vegetables, and strawberries grew so well in the sandy soil that a bumper crop grown in 1885 made the local papers.[13] Pine and ilex trees were planted around the boundaries to shield the house from the busy main Norwich Road thoroughfare. Frederick fancied himself as a gardener and was particularly keen on getting his knees and hands dirty by 'lopping off boughs' and 'digging up dock-weeds'.[14]

On the northern side of the house was a large, sweeping, circular carriage driveway and on the eastern side, the main entrance opened onto a terrace edged by a stone balcony with wide central steps. At the bottom of the steps, a generous path cut through the sloping green gardens to the road beyond. While creating the main driveway that connected the Norwich Road to the house in 1885, the children were fascinated by the skeleton of an ancient man that was dug up by workmen, later becoming the source of many a chilling ghost story.[15] In the back corner of the grounds, behind the house was a large stable and carriage shed that housed fine horses for the family, all being keen and competent horse riders.

Despite the impressive build, the house was not without its faults and not everyone appreciated the eclectic style. Without a mature garden, some thought the house looked stark, jutting out of the surrounding picturesque landscape. One early visitor, Kate Greenaway, initially did not like the exposed position and thought it very bare but felt 'the trees will grow up in time and inside it is a very nice house'.

Charles 'Charlie' Tennyson, the son of Eleanor Locker and Lionel, stayed in the house frequently as a child, where he and his brother Alfred 'Ally' got up to 'antics and exuberances in the gardens and corridors'. He was not impressed by the house ,which, in his view, had little architectural charm. He called the site 'bleak, sandy and apparently capable of producing little but an unending host of earwigs'.[16] The house had spring-hung doors that guests found would suddenly open on touch, leading to 'large draughty rooms and cold hallways'.[17] A large log fire was almost perpetually burning to counter the cold, damp and the wind that whistled down the great chimney stacks. Frederick himself, in his usual humour, penned a poem about the windy house on the hill where in August he would 'ask for an extra quilt'.[18]

To soften the bare brick exterior, gardeners planted ivy on the northern and eastern sides of the house. Easy to grow, the shade-tolerant evergreen helped keep the house cool in the summer but also helped to lessen the damp during the colder months. It was not long until the glossy green leaves gave the house a pleasant look.

A home is made by the people inside it, and Frederick's talent for collecting soon turned the house from a house that was 'new and raw without' to a 'pavilion of charm'.[19] As much as Janie oversaw the project and the exterior design of the house, Frederick indulged his passion for interior design. The fashions of the time were busy rooms, heavy curtains, large intricately designed rugs and heavy wallpaper. Though for everyday leisure and tasks, oil lamps and candles were used, the new building was fitted with modern gas lighting contained within beautifully designed glass shades.

To decorate the large rooms, Frederick scattered *objets d'art* that 'might not be costly, or even always rare but they were an expression of a taste, flawless within its modest range'.[20] He had an innate sense of style as to where to place furniture and where pictures should hang, always with the eye to enhancing their beauty. Furniture, including an old Elizabethan chair, was brought up from Rowfant, while other attractive pieces such as chiming clocks and a large barometer were bought locally or from nearby Norwich.

Carefully chosen paintings and pencil etchings by Holbein, sketches by William Blake and inked Van Dyck heads covered every available wall space. Ever the clever poet, Frederick was fond of taking a piece of artwork from the wall to examine through his eyeglass before penning an inspired stanza or two. It would then be replaced with the neatly written poem hanging on a chain from beneath the picture.

With a thought to his expected guests, Frederick bought display cabinets with glass lids, which he filled with interesting treasures: coins, fossilised amber, birds' nests, jewellery boxes, snuff pouches and valuable antique pocket watches, all designed to be conversation starters. In the master bedroom hung quotations from Chaucer and miniature portraits of the children.

Frederick enjoyed scouring antique shops, where he would pick up an unusual piece and place it in an unexpected spot to delight and surprise his guests. He was often successful, but from time to time, Frederick's good nature saw him swindled. On one occasion, he bought a china owl for a costly £4 from a shop in Norwich. The dealer had given him a long story of the owl's lineage and pointed out its various time-ravaged chips and faults. Frederick believed he had a rare antique and placed the owl proudly dominating the dining room. On a visit to Norwich, eight months later, he stopped at the same shop only to find an identical bird in the window. In shame, the owl was swiftly taken from his perch and deposited 'in the dust of the Dutch cabinet with the highly populated pieces of amber'.[21]

Though Janie clearly allowed Frederick to express his own tastes when decorating the interior, she did add touches that reflected her own personality and interests. Mottos and religious texts hung on her dressing room walls, and downstairs, *Sunday at Home* magazines lay strewn about the drawing room.[22]

Once it had been completed, the youngest Lockers, Godfrey, Dorothy, Oliver and Maud, were excited to stay in their new summer home. They were, by several accounts, 'four extremely lively and noisy children', who Charlie Tennyson recounted, 'had inherited all their mother's energy and none of their father's sensibility'.[23]

Down they came on the train from London to Cromer, with 'a welter of trunks, luncheon baskets, pails and nurses'.[24] The journey from Liverpool Street, with the stop in Norwich, took over three hours and was a hot and noisy affair. Although the household had their own carriage with plush, but-toned, comfortable seating, the number of bodies and luggage in the small space was stifling and the air was thick with the pungent odour of burnt coal and steam. There was a lack of distraction for the four overexcited children, who bounced up and down and squabbled among themselves. Nanny Lucas was in control, occasionally barking at the children in her cockney accent to pipe down. As they neared Cromer, Frederick would place each child at a window with the promise of a sixpence for whichever child spotted Cromer lighthouse first.

On arrival, the excitement reached a crescendo as the children tumbled out into the bustling station. Seagulls circled overhead and the inviting blue sea could be seen on the horizon. Porters, eager for a good tip, helped the household staff to swiftly unload the contents of the carriage to the wait-ing cabs, which were standing ready to convey the group the short journey down the Norwich Road to Newhaven Court. Though the children were used to grand houses and fine objects, the house was new and exciting, and being so close to the seaside there was the promise of fine days to come.

Although all sharing a lively spirit, the Locker children differed in their individual personalities. Godfrey, the eldest, at 9 in 1884, was a dark-haired, serious-minded little boy. He thrived in nature, often heading out to the lighthouse to capture wasps and butterflies in a net or to examine the rock-pools at the foot of the cliffs for crabs and long-spined sea scorpions. He went out looking for birds in the hope of spotting an unusual golden oriole or crossbill or hunted for bird's nests, where he sat quietly and watched, resisting the temptation to steal an egg for his collection.

He had inherited a love of poetry from his father and would often send home lines from Eton boarding school to be critiqued. Other letters home from boarding school show that he was sensitive and frequently bullied, once prompting a kindly and pragmatic reply from Frederick, 'I am very sorry the boys tease you – bear it as well as you can and if you are amiable and kindly, and obliging and show a bold front, they will soon leave off.' Later in the same letter, he finished with the excellent advice, 'If you ask boys to tea to meet us, ask those who are not pleasant to you.'[25] Unfortunately, boarding school was not the ideal place for a boy with a sensitive nature and the bullying continued.

Frederick and Janie with their children. (L–R) Godfrey, Dorothy, Maud and Oliver, c. 1887. (Family collection)

Godfrey was also prone to sulkiness and was frequently out of sorts with his mother and father, on one occasion running away from home only to have to be retrieved by a kindly retainer. Although not musically talented, music could move him to tears.

Dorothy, who was closest to Godfrey in age, was petite, hardy and fair haired. She loved to go hunting for birds' nests with Godfrey and showed an element of his sensitive nature, which she channelled into her early talent for drawing and her love of art. Dorothy was excited to visit the stables to sit on a horse, something she did regularly over the years, becoming quite an equestrian. Like Godfrey, Dorothy enjoyed poetry and particularly the funny limericks of Edward Lear. She loved telling stories, often sparked with clever wit, and was the first to seek her father and listen to his literature readings, looking up at him enraptured with her striking dark eyes.

Maud was just 4. Along with her twin, Oliver, she was the baby of the family. Maud was loved by all, especially as she seemed to suffer from more childhood illnesses than her siblings. Thankfully, she bore her frequent isolations and coughs and colds with her naturally cheerful disposition and was kind, caring and thoughtful. She also showed signs of a religious piety, like her mother. Maud had long, wavy hair which framed her dark eyes. She squinted due to short sight and this, combined with her frequent illnesses, made her the most cosseted of the four children. A piano was placed in the large lounge and Maud, who was musically inclined, tinkered her small fingers on the piano keys while singing along.

Oliver, Maud's twin, was loud, boisterous and confident, with an adventurous and at times mischievous spirit not unlike his Grandfather Curtis. It was not unusual to find the little boy with a peashooter or noisily banging a toy drum. In looks, he was strikingly like his mother, with dark hair and a penetrating gaze. He also inherited her boundless energy, social skills and outgoing personality. Referring to his tenacity, Frederick affectionately named him 'little dog'.

Occasionally he could come across as arrogant. In later life, Dorothy would often recount a story about the first time the poet Tennyson, 'with his great shock of hair, had appeared for dinner'. Oliver, 'in a loud voice had demanded of his father if this was the new tutor'.[26] Oliver, who was just 4, was particularly taken with Cromer, and for him it was the start of a lifelong association with town.

The year 1884 soon gave way to 1885 and all the children, along with Sir Curtis, Jane, Frederick and Janie, were excited about the coming summer season, which would see Newhaven full of visitors for the first time. However, a dark cloud was on the horizon.

Sir Curtis, who had always enjoyed robust health, was nearing his 80th year. He still pursued his hobbies and interests with vigour and as late as the autumn of 1884, he sent Janie a letter describing his day salmon fishing on his Scottish estate. Characteristically enclosed with the letter were seeds he had gathered for her of wild lupine.

It was around this time that Sir Curtis had begun to suffer from intermittent pains attributed to angina. Over the winter, he stayed in his London home in a chair by the fireplace, increasingly exhausted by the pain that prevented him from sleeping. Gradually, he grew gaunter and Godfrey, who was taken to see him, was shocked at his appearance. 'His coat hung baggily upon him,' he later wrote. 'Great veins stood out on his wasted hands and his eyes were closed.' As Godfrey was led away, he heard Curtis say, 'Goodbye darling'.[27] Janie, who was there by her father's bedside, was distressed by his struggle to hide the pain from her.

Curtis suffered heart failure and on 12 March 1885, with his family gathered around him and with 'the look of love in his eyes', he died.[28] Janie was nothing short of devastated and, according to Oliver, she never got over the loss. He had finished Newhaven for his daughter, but he did not live to see the home full and happy with the laughter of the family that he loved so dearly.

Letters of condolence flooded in from all over the country, from friends and colleagues in every rank of English society, aristocracy, his neighbours at Rowfant, Inchbae, Newhaven Court and London, clergy, men of letters and old friends in England and America. Tennyson wrote to Frederick, 'I am very grieved by your sad news. You know I have always admired and loved Sir Curtis. Please tell Janie how much I sympathise with her.'[29] The condolences were sincere and deep.

Curtis's long and detailed will was read after his death. His personal estate amounted to over £400,000, a huge sum for the time.[30] Lady Jane, Curtis's wife, was given £20,000 and his personal effects, furniture, carriages and horses. She was also given the use of Rowfant for life, after which it would pass to Janie. It would have been natural for Sir Curtis to have left his properties of Rowfant and Newhaven Court to his eldest son but, bucking tradition, he left them to Janie in the knowledge she would be a worthy custodian. He also left his daughter £100,000 in trust and a third of his estate. Janie's eldest brother, George, inherited the baronetcy, a third of the estate and

£175,000, and her younger brother, Norman, received £40,000 with a further £100,000 in trust for life, along with the remaining third of the estate. Henry, Janie's other brother, had died in 1876. Sir Curtis bequeathed smaller amounts to family and friends, including £5,000 to Frederick, £1,000 to his wife's companion, Emily Clarke, and gifts of £1,000 to Lampson siblings, nieces and nephews. Curtis also left money to recognise loyalty, £250 for each clerk employed in his firm and £50 to each servant.[31]

The properties of Rowfant and Newhaven Court were left to Janie on the understanding that the name Lampson be added to her own and the family known thereafter as Locker-Lampson.

NOTES

1 Clement Scott, *Daily Telegraph*, 17 August 1883. The beautifully vivid descriptions of the poppy-strewn landscape of north Norfolk, written by Clement Scott and published in the summer of 1883, coined the enduring phrase 'Poppyland'. These articles, and later his poetry, romanticised and popularised the area, initiating a building and visitor boom.
2 Sir Curtis Lampson to Hannah Jane Locker, 20 July 1882 (Beinecke Rare Books and Manuscript Library).
3 Sir Curtis Lampson to Hannah Jane Locker, 11 September 1882 (Beinecke Rare Books and Manuscript Library).
4 Lampson School still stands today, although it is now converted to residential use.
5 A.D. Boyce, *Harmonious Houses in Exquisite Surroundings* (Cromer Preservation Society, 2008).
6 *Norwich Mercury*, 11 November 1882.
7 Sir Curtis Lampson to Hannah Jane Locker, 10 September 1883 (Beinecke Rare Books and Manuscript Library).
8 Cromer Electricity Company Invoice, 1919 (Norfolk Record Office).
9 View from Cromer High Station, 1885 (Norfolk Museums Service).
10 *Norfolk News*, 26 July 1884.
11 Equivalent to £380 per yard. Sir Curtis later disliked the wall, thinking it too high and expensive, but it still stands 140 years later. A stone with the date 1890 is further down the wall, laid presumably after the driveway was completed.
12 Sir Curtis Lampson to Hannah Jane Locker, 28 July 1884 (Beinecke Rare Books and Manuscript Library).
13 *Eastern Daily Press*, 1 December 1886.
14 Stephen Locker-Lampson, *Nothing to Offer but Blood*, p.14.
15 Alfred Savin, *History of Cromer*.
16 Charles Tennyson, *Stars and Markets*, p.46.

17 Rodney Englen, *Kate Greenaway*, p.173.
18 Quote from the poem 'This is the House that Jane Built' by Frederick Locker-Lampson. Charles Tennyson, *Stars and Markets*, p.46.
19 Stephen Locker-Lampson, *Nothing to Offer but Blood*, p.11.
20 *Ibid.*, OLL.
21 *Ibid.*, p.13.
22 Oliver Locker-Lampson, 'Recollections of Frederick Locker-Lampson', *Cornhill Magazine* (1921).
23 Charles Tennyson, *Stars and Markets*, p.47.
24 Stephen Locker-Lampson, *Nothing to Offer but Blood*, p.15.
25 Augustine Birrell, *Frederick Locker-Lampson: A Character Sketch*, p.151.
26 James L. Clifford, *From Puzzles to Portraits: Problems of a Literary Biographer* (1970).
27 Godfrey Locker-Lampson, *Life in the Country*, p.13.
28 Stephen Locker-Lampson, *Nothing to Offer but Blood*, p.45.
29 Madison C. Bates, 'Sir Curtis Lampson: Vermont Baronet', *Vermont History*, Vermont Historical Society, p.15.
30 Worth approximately £36 million in 2021 (source: Bank of England Inflation Calculator).
31 The will of Sir Curtis Lampson, 1885 (Principal Probate Registry).

4

Frederick and Janie

My wife submits, and I obey –
She always lets me have her way.

Frederick Locker-Lampson

O n the eve of his funeral, Sir Curtis was brought from his London residence and gently placed in the library at Rowfant. The house was quiet, save for the crunch of footsteps on the gravel drive as numerous friends, family and employees came to pay their last respects. On the following cool morning of 18 March, Curtis was conveyed to nearby Worth Churchyard on an open-topped hearse. As the procession worked slowly down the daffodil-lined lanes, workmen and tenants from the estate followed behind. Behind the men was a funeral cortege of a further nine carriages containing his sons, George and Norman, son-in-law Frederick, friends and local gentry. After a service in the crowded little church, the mourners gathered around as the large, polished oak coffin, covered in beautiful wreaths and adorned with brass work and an inscription, was laid to rest in the same plot alongside his second son, Henry, who had died in 1876.[1]

To busy and distract herself from her grief, Janie began the move to Newhaven Court for the summer season, which was expected to run from June to October. It would be the first summer that guests could be entertained and accommodated on a grander scale and Janie, with her customary pragmatism and energy, sent out numerous letters to friends and family inviting them to stay. The family had originally planned to leave for Cromer around Whitsun week, but they had delayed their leave due to Curtis's death and the reading of the will.

By July, affairs seemed in order and a date was set to leave. As the day drew closer, excitement among the children mounted. Bags and trunks were packed, buckets and spades brought down from the attic and summer clothes purchased. Final instructions were given to the Rowfant staff before the family, nannies and maids boarded a carriage that took them to the railway station.

The troupe arrived at London, Liverpool Street to find the station a cacophony of noise and heaving with every class of society. Wealthy ladies rushed past, dragging their tired maids behind them, businessmen hurried to catch their trains and children crowded around the ticket booths, much to the consternation of the railway staff. Porters, eager for a tip, were more than happy to help load the train carriage that had been set aside for the party. Among swirls of steam, the excited group took their seats. They all heard a whistle blown before feeling the gleaming black engine start to move. Out of the station it puffed, to rattle and bump its way east.

One of the first guests to join the family in Cromer was Annie Ritchie, who had been invited by Frederick's older daughter, Eleanor Tennyson. Annie was the daughter of *Vanity Fair* author William Makepeace Thackeray, and a talented author in her own right. William Thackeray had been a friend of both Frederick and Tennyson, and when he died in 1863, Annie and her sister Minny spent large amounts of time with both families at the Tennyson property on the Isle of Wight, where she mixed with both Lionel and Eleanor.

Annie surprised her family and social circle when, at the age of 39 in 1877, she married her quiet, dark-haired first cousin Richmond Ritchie, seventeen years her junior. The unusual match caused less sensation than might be expected, with many in society feeling that young Richmond had done well for himself. 'Her charm depends not at all upon youth or beauty and is universally felt,' one observer wrote, 'he will be sure to be proud of her.'[2] The unconventional marriage appeared happy and soon two children followed, Hester and Billy. Annie and Eleanor were close, both modern thinking, highly intelligent and social. Their children were playmates, and their husbands were colleagues in the India Office. Annie had even been given the honour of taking the role of godmother to Eleanor and Lionel's son, Charlie.

Waking to a bright day during their stay, Janie suggested the three ladies and nannies take the children down to the beach. Hester and Billy, Eleanor's sons, Charlie, Ally and baby Michael, along with Godfrey, Dorothy, Oliver and Maud, all splashed and played along the seashore. Annie's children revelled in the seaside, languishing in the cool surf like 'two delicious bunches of seaweed'.[3]

Annie's stay was a pleasant one, full of children's laughter and long, contented days in the sunshine, but it proved to be one of the last happy social occasions that Eleanor and Annie shared as, just the next year, an event occurred that ended the friendship. Just a few months after the trip to Cromer, Eleanor's husband Lionel Tennyson died at the tragically early age of 32 from malaria and pleuro-pneumonia, which had been caught while on a goodwill tour of India with Eleanor, which had been arranged by the India Office.

Annie Thackeray Ritchie in 1870. (Taken from Julia Cameron and Anne Thackeray Ritchie, Lord Tennyson and his Friends *[1893], Heritage Image Partnership Ltd / Alamy)*

With Lionel and Eleanor leading largely separate lives by 1885, and with rumours of infidelity by both partners, it could have been an opportunity to save their unhappy marriage. Instead, the seriously ill Lionel died on the boat home and was buried in the Red Sea and Eleanor arrived home in May 1886 alone. Kindly Annie, who was herself poorly, sent her husband to assist Eleanor, who was struggling with financial affairs and probate. What she did not expect was her friend and husband falling quickly into a passionate love affair. When Annie found out she gave Richmond a choice. He eventually chose Annie and the affair ended but not without considerable damage to Eleanor's reputation, especially when cruel rumours started to circulate, possibly by Annie's friends and family, that Eleanor had danced the night away on deck as Lionel lay dying in the ship's hold below.[4] However, in the summer of 1885, this was all months in the future and the friends enjoyed the nightly dinner parties, company, tennis and parlour games up at Newhaven Court together.

Staying at Newhaven at the same time as Annie Ritchie was arguably the most tragic of all the guests to pass through the house. Twenty-two-year-old, golden-haired Winnie, born in 1863, was the third child of a family of five girls and one son born to Frederic Seebohm, a wealthy Quaker banker, and his wife Mary Ann. The Lockers and Seebohms were friendly, mixing regularly in the same Cromer Quaker family circles and it was in the home of the Barclays at The Warren in 1881 when Winnie had first met the Locker-Lampsons. She liked Janie immediately, but her initial impression of Frederick was not so favourable, describing him as 'very condescending'.[5]

However, in the summer of 1882, aged 19 and following a disastrous and unsuccessful love affair that had left her drained, Winnie had found both Frederick and Janie sympathetic listeners and a reliable source of comfort. She went bathing in the sea with Janie and enjoyed the company of their children, especially Godfrey, who she would take bird spotting. Like many others, she found she soon warmed to Frederick, impressed by his genuine kindness and concern for her, 'I like Mr Locker much better now. One does not notice his affected way of talking when one is used to him, and he is so kind.'[6] Over the winter, Winnie and Frederick kept up their correspondence. They became firm friends and Frederick even arranged a visit for the Seebohms to meet Tennyson. Upon hearing of the death of Sir Curtis in 1885, Winnie wrote to her friends to say she had been thinking of them all.

Winnie was exceptionally bright and had ambitions to attend college. She achieved her dream in the spring of 1885 when she passed the tough entry exam to Newnham College in Cambridge. However, she suffered from an affliction that threatened her plans. She had lived with asthma her whole life, but the condition took a turn for the worse in 1883, possibly compounded by the anxiety from a failed love affair, when it started to become chronic and unrelenting. Frightening symptoms appeared, nervous coughing and a constriction of her jaw and throat that made it uncomfortable and at times impossible to talk or to eat anything but liquids.

In August 1885, she caught a chill and her symptoms accelerated. In September, just a month before she was due to start at college, she was sent to Janie at Newhaven Court for rest and recuperation. At times, Winnie was well enough to sit with Mrs Locker and Annie Ritchie to partake in the afternoon tea ritual, exchanging ideas, opinions and gossip over bread, butter and cake. She read poetry and played games with the little children, took part in parlour games and played the piano for the family and their guests.

On one of the evenings that September, little Godfrey, just 10 years old, sat playing with Winnie on the piano in the lounge. Winnie described what happened next:

> Godfrey and I played duets and then he said solemnly, 'Do you know a Dead March? I love a Dead March.' When I was in the middle of it, I was alarmed to hear him sobbing behind me, but he recovered before the end and thanked me enthusiastically.[7]

Winnie Seebohm. (Hertfordshire Archives and Local Studies, DE/So/F4/19)

Godfrey may have been told how unwell Winnie was or perhaps the intuitive and sensitive boy had looked at how thin and frail his friend had become and worked it out himself. It is reasonable to assume the whole household must have listened to her relentless coughing late into the night and watched her painful struggles to eat.

At other times during her stay, Winnie was too unwell to join in any activities and her attacks, despite Janie's best efforts and care, appeared to be worsening. It was the last time Frederick and Jane saw their young friend. Winnie managed just a month at college before her symptoms became so severe that she was forced to move home to her parents. Devastated, increasingly thin and exhausted from almost constant asthma attacks that would see her up the entire night praying for relief and gasping for breath, her frail body finally gave up. Winnie died on 18 December 1885; tragically, she was just 22 years old.

Augustus Hare crossed paths with Winnie in the September of 1885, invited to stay by Frederick who was always keen to encourage interesting guests. Augustus was a travel writer and a skilled watercolour artist and was 51 when he made the journey to Cromer, a town he called 'charming'. He would often be found on the sea-facing balcony or upper terrace at Newhaven, a slim figure with dark side-parted hair and thick moustache, where he would spend the day sketching the outline of Cromer. He took to wandering through the town to the water's edge to capture beach scenes, or just people watch, observing their oddities.

Augustus was not unsociable, however, and enjoyed the long dinner parties and conversation. He was famous for his vividly told ghost stories, and the guests would look forward to sitting after dinner to listen – even the children were allowed to stay up to hear them. Some were so chilling that the guests and children retired to bed in a tremor.

He found Frederick's company congenial and was much amused at his host's gentle teasing of Janie. He was especially entertained by the story of how Janie had marked a stranger at a railway station as eternally damned for wearing trousers with too broad a check and holding an 'unusually large cigar in his mouth'.[8] For all the teasing, he found the atmosphere delightful and the Lockers very happy. Later in his life story, he wrote of a conversation that he had overheard between Frederick and Janie. '"My winsome marrow," Mr Locker has just said to his wife, "you know I can never go anywhere without you."'[9]

Old friend, the Poet Laureate Alfred, Lord Tennyson, had been invited and was expected that September, although a telegram arrived rather late calling off the visit due to bad weather. He did make the trip in the following August, along with his older son, Hallam. Still grieving for Lionel, the swarthy poet in his sombrero and cape took himself off for long, reflective walks down to the shore, where he strolled along the sands, trousers rolled to the knee and barefoot, with shoes in hand. He was observant on these walks, often returning to look up in books an unfamiliar bird, flower or insect he had encountered on the way.

On other occasions, tired of being recognised, he stayed in the grounds of Newhaven. There, he would be found sitting for periods of time ruminating in the rose garden or taking circular walks around the estate, puffing on his clay pipe. He stayed up late, long after the other guests had gone to bed, sitting behind a closed door enjoying his customary drink of port and mulling over his compositions in front of a log fire.

Tennyson could, at times, be difficult company and certainly Emily Clarke, the companion to Lady Lampson and Janie, found him grumpy and formidable and would try to stay out of his way. It is unlikely that Janie approved of his coarse language, drinking and pipe smoking, but there was something about the poet that endeared him to many he met. Frederick certainly knew the right thing to say to his old friend and, given some cajoling to be social and the right atmosphere, he would outshine the other guests with his clever wit and charm. His dry humour, hearty laugh and kindness always assured him a warm welcome at Newhaven.

To entertain Tennyson and Hallam, Frederick and Janie arranged excursions to local landmarks, including a day sailing on picturesque Wroxham Broad. As the group's sailing vessel glided through reeds, willows and waterlilies in waters alive with bream and pike, Tennyson sat admiring the view. Hallam later remarked that 'the various coloured sails of the wherries made my Father think the whole landscape like a picture of Holland'.[10]

Nothing was more important than family to Tennyson, and Eleanor's boys, Ally, Charlie and Michael, the grandchildren he shared with Frederick, were even more cosseted since the death of Lionel. Tennyson felt threatened and displeased when, in 1888, two years after Lionel's death, Eleanor remarried the liberal politician and author Augustine Birrell.

Alfred, Lord Tennyson, Poet Laureate. (Lebrecht Music & Arts / Alamy stock photo)

Eleanor's new husband was a widower, 38 years old, with a stocky build, fair hair and round glasses that he wore for his poor sight. For he, at least, it had been love at first sight, and Eleanor came to adore him.[11] Despite Tennyson's initial misgivings, the marriage proved to be an exceptionally happy one, leading one friend to describe her as a 'changed being'.[12]

Birrell was eccentric and kindly, and with his love of literature he was a perfect match for the highly educated and intelligent Eleanor, getting on brilliantly with all the family and, in time, he even earned the hard-won respect of Tennyson. Birrell became an excellent stepfather to Charlie, Ally and Michael and two more sons were born to Eleanor, Frankie in 1889 and Tony in 1892.

Augustine Birrell, who fell for Eleanor Locker on first sight. (Family collection)

Wishing to have their own summer home in the area for their growing family of sons and to stay close to her father, Eleanor and Birrell built The Pightle, a large, rambling home on a low, sandy cliff just outside Sheringham village. Sheringham was just over 4 miles from Cromer and, at the time of building, it was a small red-brick flint fishing village. The Pightle was one of the first new houses to be built in the village and in 1889, when the family moved in for the summer, it must have sent some ripples through the town to have such a well-known couple build in the area.

Newhaven was gathering a reputation that lived up to its name, becoming in the following years a place of refuge and relaxation. Indeed, it was a haven from everyday life.

Tennyson was not the only exhausted figure on the beach that summer. Caroline Jebb was a striking, adventurous American socialite who mixed in the same literary circles as the Locker-Lampsons. A quarter of a century before, aged 21 and living in an army fort in Florida with her first husband, Lieutenant Adam Slemmer, Caroline had been present at the beginning of the American Civil War. In January 1861, while left in sole charge of the barracks, Adam was forced to call an emergency meeting with officers when Confederate troops were threatening to seize control of all military forts.

As the men deliberated for hours whether to fight or flee, Caroline, exasperated, jumped up and announced, 'If you men won't fire the first shot to protect our flag, then I will!'[13] Impressed by the heroic enthusiasm of the auburn-haired patriot, the men moved to a neighbouring fort and hunkered down to fight. Slemmer and his men defended the fort until reinforcements arrived.

Back in Washington and dismayed to find her husband had not received a promotion for his efforts, Caroline brazenly made an appointment to see President Abraham Lincoln. Accompanied by her two brothers-in-law, she waltzed into the president's office and placed a hand on Lincoln's shoulder. Having captured the president's attention, she smiled sweetly while making a case for her husband.

Her flirtatious charms worked. Scribbled on a paper listing the officers he wished to promote, Lincoln had written next to Slemmer's name, 'His pretty wife says a Major or First Captain'.[14]

*Caroline Slemmer, later Lady Jebb, 1861. (John L. Magee, lithographer. Library of Congress
Prints and Photographs Division)*

Mᴿˢ. CAROLINE SLEMMER

Wife of the Gallant Lieutenant Slemmer now in Command of Fort Pickens

From a Photograph taken Feb 11ᵗʰ 1861

Published and for Sale at Magee's Cheap Stationery Store and Envelope Manufactory
No 316 Chesnut Street, Philadelphia

Slemmer died in 1868 and Caroline moved to Cambridge, where, in
1874, she married Richard Claverhouse Jebb, a greying and tired classical
scholar, and settled down to a far quieter life. In August, she persuaded her
industrious husband to take a rare holiday to go and stay with their friends
at Newhaven.

Carrie and Dick, as they were known, took the train to Cromer from
their home in Cambridge. She later described the visit:

It was delightful to see how completely for the time he forgot the existence of such things as committees and bills and even Greek texts; how he shared in all the amusements of the large house party. The expeditions by day, the bright talk, the music, the games in the evening and was even one of the chief actors in the charades –wisely taking the benefit of a complete rest from his ordinary occupations.[15]

Richard Jebb was undemonstrative and reserved in company and it is testament to the atmosphere at Newhaven that this quiet man was willing to join in.

Despite her evangelicalism, Janie was genuine fun to be around, and the guests flocked in, coming back year on year. There was a relaxed air at Newhaven; it had a homely feel. Guests would fill the house, but they were often left in peace and there was a distinct lack of servants that might have made the house feel too grand or formal. Regular visitor Emily Lytton, staying at Newhaven for a night in 1889 and finding herself in need of a lady's maid, later wrote, 'The house is full of company, and with an establishment not equal to the occasion, I was aware from experience that I should ring the bell to no purpose. Nobody would have come.'[16]

The dinner parties that Caroline Jebb spoke of were legendary. Guests dressed for dinner in their rooms and then came down to find Frederick waiting by the door of the drawing room, ready to inform them as to where they had been placed at the dinner table and who they would be sat next to. Unpretentious and simple in her tastes, it is unlikely that Janie ordered extravagant meals from her cook and she probably favoured dishes such as boiled beef, mutton or curried veal with seasonal vegetables from the garden. Frederick put thought into the seating plan, purposely inviting those on opposing sides of an argument or opinion and then sitting them across from each other to create a lively debate, making the evenings seldom dull.

With her customary energy, Janie often invited more guests over after dinner, eliciting a groan from the rest of the family, who were often ready for bed. Parlour games filled the later hours, Blind Man's Buff, Charades, Twenty Questions and a game that involved guessing the guest just from their eyes behind holes in a newspaper. Janie would often sing, and music was played. On chilly evenings, guests would gather around the fireplace, where ghost stories, humorous limericks and poems were read. Occasionally, there would be impromptu plays, with all guests encouraged to take part. The more artistically or literary talented would be encouraged to leave an entry in the visitors' book.

Conservative Party politician Sir Edward Bruce Hamley was one such guest. Kindly, silver-haired Hamley was a friend to Frederick of over thirty years and a hero of the Crimean War as well as a talented author, and would entertain the other guests with his lively stories and poems. His final entry, of many, that he wrote inside the visitors' book on 20 October 1892 was a poem he had written, entitled 'The Ghost's Chair – A Legend of Newhaven Court', about an old Elizabethan-era antique chair that was sat by the fireplace, allegedly occupied by a female spectre. The ghost story was just one of many that Hamley entertained the children with. In fact, the old man was a favourite with the children, who found him amusing and fun. He loved animals, was anti-vivisection and had written about the horrors of animal cruelty. He adored the family's pets, and he would often be found in a chair with a happy cat or dog in his lap, surrounded by the children, who were allowed to stay up and listen as he told them a clever story.

If the weather was fine, tennis was played on the lawn or a spot of cricket. Interesting guests who were staying nearby would be invited up to the house to join in the games, and among these was the troubled Irish-born playwright Oscar Wilde, who was spotted deep in conversation with Hamley in the dining room. Major Dent,[17] the local doctor who had been befriended by the Lockers, looked on in curiosity and was shocked by the appearance of Wilde, who, in Dent's words, was now 'an obese man, whose features showed a total loss of character and refinement'.[18]

On the advice of his doctors to take a rest by the sea, Oscar was renting a Norfolk farmhouse for the summer and had been invited up to Newhaven by Frederick, who was eager to befriend the interesting author. Oscar's appearance may have been due to the inner turmoil that he was undoubtedly feeling inside. Though he was married with children, a summer previously Wilde had met and started an intense and passionate love affair with the aristocratic Lord Alfred 'Bosie' Douglas. Spoiled and petulant as Bosie was, Wilde could not keep away from his handsome young lover and Bosie was invited down to visit the farmhouse, on one occasion staying under the same roof as Wilde and his wife, Constance. In an age of intolerance, it was an affair that would ruin Oscar's life and reputation and would ultimately end with a disastrous charge of gross indecency against Oscar and a sentence of two years' hard labour.

Daytime excursions for the guests were arranged, sometimes to the pretty Roman camp on Beacon Hill, nearby Felbrigg Hall to see the Ketton sisters, or to marvel at the eccentric Lady Lothian at the stunning seventeenth-century Blickling Hall estate. Lady Lothian had an obsession for white and proudly showed visitors around the stunning old house with its long library full of wonderful old books, tapestried walls and carved sweeping staircases, before leading them to the radiantly beautiful gardens, where they would be shown all-white cattle, ponies, pigeons and peacocks. One of Janie's guests even claimed to have seen kangaroos in the grounds.

Closer to home, there was always the attraction of the beach for bathing. The more adventurous guests would go sailing on the Broads, before returning to Newhaven for dinner and fun. There was, however, a notable absence of alcohol, Janie being passionately and actively involved with the Temperance movement. One visitor who tried to sneak in half a glass of champagne before her meal thought she had avoided Janie's watchful eye, only to find her wine glass was removed the next evening.[19]

In fact, Janie was active in several moral and worthy causes, often hosting the Band of Hope Temperance Society at Newhaven, and she was also instrumental in campaigning for a new lecture hall in Cromer. An excellent orator, she wrote and read her own lectures, becoming, Oliver later thought, the best female speaker of her time. According to Oliver, she also busied herself in causes further afield, particularly those of missionary expeditions in Africa and the plight of leper colonies.

Kate Greenaway – 'short sight instead of rendering her awkward, rather heightened her charm'. (Courtesy of Michael Dadd)

One cannot mention the 1880s, Cromer and the Locker-Lampson family without including the children's illustrator and author Kate Greenaway. Kate was so much a fixture at Rowfant and Newhaven that she was considered family.

Born in Hoxton, London, in 1846, Kate was the second child of four born to John Greenaway, a talented wood carver and illustrator, and his wife, Elizabeth. Despite his talents, John struggled to make a living. With the family facing severe financial strain, when Kate was still a little girl her quick-thinking mother opened a millinery shop, which sold children's dresses and fancy trimmings. The family lived above the shop and, in time, hardworking Mrs Greenaway turned enough profit to allow her children to follow their passions.

Kate had shown prodigious artistic talent from an early age and due to her mother's sacrifice, she went through several art schools refining her talent. While still at school, Kate received commissions for illustrations and later produced a range of popular greetings cards featuring her characteristic designs of sweet children in historic costume.

With her reputation growing, Kate looked to publish her own book of illustration and verse. Having partially completed the book, she showed it to her father, who offered to mention it to an old friend and colleague, wood engraver and colour printer Edmund Evans. Evans, who now ran a successful printing business, was impressed by Kate's book and introduced it to his publisher associate, George Routledge. Kate's book of pictures and verses *Under the Window* was due for publication in 1878 but Routledge, fearing the verses were weak, suggested they be sent to Frederick – now a popular author of light verse, thanks to the success of his volume of poetry, *London Lyrics* – for consultation.

Frederick showed the work to Janie, and both were much impressed. Always one to champion a young artist, Frederick boldly turned up unannounced at Kate's studio one day to introduce himself. Frederick befriended Kate, who herself was dazzled by his connections, charm and sophistication. It was the start of a lengthy friendship that saw Kate regularly stay at Rowfant and Newhaven with the family. *Under the Window* became a bestseller, and three years later Frederick persuaded Kate to illustrate a new volume of *London Lyrics*.

In 1883, she dedicated the volume *Little Ann* to 'The Rowfant Quartos', her name for Godfrey, Dorothy, Oliver and Maud, which featured a picture of the four little children on its inner page. Now in her late thirties and single, Kate became extremely fond of the four children and took on the role of a favoured aunt, writing the children notes and sketching them amusing pictures as well as encouraging them in their own artwork. Nothing was too much trouble when it came to the children, and Oliver could not remember a time without her. He remembered her as:

> … a dark, quiet little woman, with a profusion of black hair curled up simply at the back and allowed to grow in a long fringe at the front. Short sight, instead of rendering her awkward, rather heightened her charm, causing her to look up wonderingly at those with whom she spoke. In face she was neither pretty nor ugly, with a rather turned up nose, brown eyes, and a small mouth, which she would screw up while she drew.[20]

THE ROWFANT QUARTOS

DEDICATED TO
GODFREY, DOROTHY, OLIVER & MAUD
CHILDREN OF FREDERICK LOCKER ESQ.

'The Rowfant Quartos' – Kate's name for the Locker children. (Taken from Kate Greenaway, 'Little Ann')

Kate loved Cromer and the relaxed atmosphere at Newhaven with the Locker-Lampsons. During her stay at Newhaven, frequent walks were taken to the beach or along the cliffs, walking hand in hand with the children and chatting happily. At times, she stopped to admire the beautiful landscape or to sketch little ones playing on the shore, 'baby boys and girls, mere bundles of tucked up clothes paddling in the sea'.[21] She helped the children to search rockpools and drew them pictures in the sand with the tip of her umbrella, only to sit and watch them wash away by the incoming tides.

Back at the house, she helped bake potatoes in the novelty revolving summerhouse and made the children laugh by pulling silly faces or by darting behind the hedges playing hide and seek. Kate was often the first to suggest and join in with a game of croquet, which on one occasion found her in trouble with Janie for playing a game on a Sunday while many of the family were at church. Unaware that Janie held such strict rules outlawing games on the day of rest, Kate had laughed and played on the lawn while, unbeknownst to her, she was being watched by the matron of the Fletcher Convalescent Home that neighboured Newhaven on its southern boundary. Word got back to Frederick and Janie from the disapproving matron and Janie hastened to dispatch a note of apology.

Kate was mortified. Fiercely loyal and wanting to defend her friend's reputation, she put on her plain little cape and her wide-brimmed felt hat and marched down through the grounds to the convalescent home, where she explained in her lisping voice that all blame should lay upon the players alone.

Kate was in Cromer in 1892 when Janie held a birthday tea party for the twins. Oliver and Maud were turning 12 and Janie, in her usual energetic manner, had arranged games on the lawn. In addition to the house guests, other Cromer visitors were invited up to take part in the fun and games.

'… mere bundles of tucked up clothing paddling in the sea.' Sketch of Cromer beach by Kate Greenaway, 1896. (Family collection, courtesy of Michael Dadd)

Henry Fowler MP was one of many guests who walked up to Newhaven, with his daughter Edith, only to find himself roped into a game of Bat Trap and Ball by Janie. Also coerced into playing was Judge Justice Denham. Both older and reserved, neither man would have normally partaken in such a game, and it is testament to Janie's firmness and insistence that the two men joined in.

Indeed, Janie was the lynchpin at Newhaven around which all activities revolved. Frederick, growing older and wearier, was happy to let his younger wife do what she did best, while he sat back and watched the goings on through his eyeglass.

In just a decade since Newhaven was built, Cromer had expanded dramatically. The red-brick building, which had once stood dominant on the landscape just ten years before, now looked out upon houses that had sprung up all around, many of them guest houses accommodating the influx of summer visitors. St Margaret's Terrace, a row of red-brick, tiled houses, now bordered Newhaven on its northern boundary and in June 1885, Benjamin Bond Cabbell II of Cromer Hall sold sixty plots of building land, nearly all on the Norwich Road surrounding Newhaven Court. Special trains were laid on from London to encourage wealthy city dwellers to buy land to build tasteful large properties and summer houses.

To the east of Norwich Road, landowner Samuel Hoare had laid out Cliff Avenue, capitalising on the town's housing boom. Horse and carriage cabs now stood at either end of Norwich Road, conveying the endless stream of visitors up and down from the station to their boarding houses. Though the family may have been concerned by the constant building works and the clatter of horses' hooves, Sir Curtis had bought a large plot and the maturing shrubs and trees ensured Newhaven remained a haven from the crowds and noise.

NOTES

1 *Horsham, Petworth, Midhurst and Steyning Express*, 24 March 1885.
2 Lady Caroline Jebb, quoted in *With Dearest Love to All* by Mary Reed Bobbitt (1960) p.134.
3 John Aplin, *Memory and Legacy: A Thackeray Family Biography* (2011) p.71.
4 Ann Thwaite, *Emily Tennyson: The Poet's Wife*, p.564.
5 Winnie Seebohm, quoted in Victoria Glendinning, *A Supressed Cry*, p.27.
6 *Ibid.*
7 *Ibid.*, p.73.

8   Augustus J.C. Hare, *The Story of My Life*, Vols 4–6.

9   *Ibid.*

10   Hallam Tennyson, *Alfred, Lord Tennyson: A Memoir*, Vol. II, p.326.

11   Augustine Birrell, *Things Past Redress*, p.110.

12   Caroline Jebb, quoted in Mary Reed Bobbitt, *With Dearest Love to All*, p.237.

13   Mary Reed Bobbitt, *With Dearest Love to All*, p.34.

14   *Abraham Lincoln, Papers*, edited by David C. Mearns (1948) p.594.

15   Lady Caroline Jebb, *The Life and Letters of Sir Richard Claverhouse Jebb* (1907) p.315.

16   Emily Lutyens, *A Blessed Girl: Memoirs of a Victorian Girlhood* (1953) p.26.

17   Four years previously, Dent had gone to India as an army doctor, achieving the rank of major, but a severe attack of malaria and typhoid that weakened his heart meant he was pensioned off due to ill health. Expecting he would not have long to live, Dent took an assistant doctor position in Cromer and was quickly befriended by the sympathetic Locker-Lampsons.

18   Major H.C. Dent, *Reminiscences of a Cromer Doctor* (1923).

19   Jane Ridley, *The Architect and his Wife: A Life of Edwin Lutyens* (2002) p.133.

20   Oliver Locker-Lampson, 'Kate Greenaway, Friend of Children', *The Century Illustrated* monthly magazine, Vol. 75, p.183.

21   *Ibid.*

5

Death Comes Knocking

I hold it true, whate'er befall,
I feel it, when I sorrow most;
'Tis better to have loved and lost
Than never to have loved at all

Alfred, Lord Tennyson

In the closing chapter of his autobiography, Frederick wrote, 'I am fast growing old. The inevitable is upon me … Now and again, during a passing sickness, a shadowy hand seems stretched forth and then withdrawn. I am only waiting for it to beckon me away.'[1] By 1894, Frederick was 73.

In December 1880, he had stood in the pouring rain at Lewes Cemetery in London at the funeral of his friend, the author, Mary Ann Evans, known to the world as George Eliot. Over the following few years, he lost a succession of friends and acquaintances: Randolph Caldecott, the illustrator, was just 40 when he died in 1886; Lady Lampson in 1889; Alfred, Lord Tennyson in 1892; and the following year, the much-loved Edward Hamley died. Always prone to melancholy, and with his circle shrinking, Frederick had lately become more introverted, spending lengthy periods in his specially created strongroom. He often sat alone, surrounded by shelves of valuable and rare books where, among the precious volumes, he wrote letters to friends, worked on his autobiography and constructed verse.

Attuned to her husband's moods, Janie knew when to leave him alone and she was quite content herself to get on with her work in the house or grounds,

Frederick and Janie Locker-Lampson by Edward Clifford, 1892. (Family collection)

conducting Bible classes, entertaining or writing letters of support to her many causes. The children joined her in conversing with the guests or playing the piano to entertain, but all were now beginning to lead their own lives and were around less often. Gone was the time of careless days in the nursery and squabbling over toys; the children were now almost grown up.

Godfrey was nearing 20 and a student at Trinity College in Cambridge. Most like his father, in both looks and personality, the curly haired, eldest Locker was chiefly interested in collecting books, coins and artwork and writing poetry. Godfrey was kind, gentle natured and generous, although he could be awkward and was unusually sensitive for a man of his period, once sending a male friend the unusual gift of a bouquet of roses.

Oliver, confident, bright and headstrong, was more like his American relatives. He was tall and handsome, like his mother, and had a restless, adventurous spirit and natural leadership qualities that were reminiscent of Sir Curtis. At Eton, he was keen to take part in debates, which highlighted his oratorical skills and persuasive charm. Oliver was particularly interested in learning German, and a tutor, Dr Karl Ott, was hired by his parents to encourage him. Oliver was popular and fun and always one of the first boys to join in with school high jinks, once swimming across a river fully clothed in 'toppers and tails' to win a bet against a friend.

(L–R) Dorothy, Oliver and Maud at Newhaven Court. Behind them is perhaps Janie's mother, Lady Lampson. (Family collection)

Dorothy and Maud, now 16 and 14, were still at home, although they were regularly going to organised camps or into London to see exhibitions and lectures together. They were also frequently invited to visit Kate Greenaway at her home in Hampstead. Kate was particularly close to Dorothy, who shared her artistic talent. 'Would you be able to come to tea and see the drawings one afternoon next week – and bring Maud?' she wrote to Dorothy in 1893.[2]

Every time they went away, Frederick missed the girls terribly. In February 1895, Frederick wrote to Maud, who was staying away with Dorothy with friends in London. It is a letter touching in its sincerity and love, 'The house is most extraordinarily quiet, and all the doors are shut! [Frederick used to playfully tease Maud for leaving doors open.] All this makes me very dull and wish you may soon come home.' He signs the letter off with a postscript, 'Love to Dorothy. Tell her not to be in a hurry unless it is to <u>come home</u>!'[3]

Both girls were intelligent, well-educated and pretty. Dorothy was petite but had striking dark eyes, shiny hair that she wore swept back from her face and a trim figure. Maud was a talented musician and endearingly short sighted. Her dark curls were already turning heads. When Maud attended a family open day at Eton with Oliver in the summer of 1895, she was 'the most attractive thing there, gazed upon by all'.[4] The young men swarmed around her, leading her to fend them off with a volley of clever rebukes.

Conway Fisher-Rowe at Eton, 1897. (Family collection)

In fact, both girls had already picked the men that they would later marry. Maud, at just 14, was head over heels in love and secretly engaged to Conway Fisher-Rowe, the golden-haired, athletic and handsome son of Edward Fisher-Rowe and his wife, Victoria (née Liddell). A talented cricket player, Conway, who was the same age as Maud, lived at Thorncombe Park, a large manor house in Surrey with his parents, siblings and servants. Conway's father, late captain of the 4th Dragoon Guards, had been at Balaclava during the Crimean War. The Fisher-Rowe and Locker-Lampson families mixed in similar social circles and Conway was at Eton with Oliver, which is likely to be how the young couple met.

Dorothy had her eyes firmly fixed on John Delmar-Morgan, known to all simply as Jack, the quiet, intelligent, inventive son of explorer Edward Delmar-Morgan and his wife, Bertha. Jack lived at Effingham House in Copthorne, just a few minutes down the road from Rowfant. The two families were friendly neighbours and Dorothy and Jack, being of a similar age, found themselves thrown together on social occasions and dinner parties. It soon became clear that they were very attracted to each other. However, both Dorothy and Maud were too young to wed and admiring glances and regular correspondence would be the limit to their prospective relationships for the next few years.

In the lead up to Christmas 1894, Janie and the girls had noticed that Frederick had seemed more tired than usual, worn down from a series of severe colds, rheumatism and neuralgia, as well as the gastric trouble that had tormented him for so long. When Oliver arrived home from Eton for the holidays, he found that instead of joining the family for dinner, food was being taken to his father in his rooms. Janie and the children took turns to keep him company. It was a quiet Christmas, but pleasant all the same with games around the Christmas tree, long walks, horse riding in crisp frosts and adventures onto the lake on Oliver's homemade canoe.

Although she tried to hide it from her husband, Janie was concerned. Despite her energies, Janie suffered from a nervousness that we would now call health anxiety. Much of her worries centred around her family's well-being. Oliver later described her unusual fears:

Her main dreads were draughts, drains, thunderstorms, tramps, mad dogs and mumps. She taught me to spit – not furtively but with ostentation – if I met a smell. I went round muffled to the ear tips against winds; for her an open window – like an open drain – led straight to the grave. Every cranny of our rooms was sealed against the demon draught. Scarlet fever was also one of her manias.[5]

To ward off mad dogs and tramps, Oliver was armed at the age of 12 with an American revolver. Unbelievably, Oliver took his six-shooter to Eton, where it was kept in plain sight on his bureau. Along with the revolver, he was also sent back to school with 'silver in one pocket and gold in the other, and new coins by preference', as Janie feared copper 'was the coinage of the infected'.

As the children grew older, they began to tire of her nervousness. In a letter from Maud to Oliver, written while she was away at a summer camp, she asked him to thank their mother for her letter and 'tell her not to worry about me as I am taking enormous care of myself'.[6] In advance of a visit to a family friend over Christmas 1897, Oliver felt the need to write to Maud:

Don't let me have any letters or telegrams about illness etc. It will make me excessively angry and will do no good! Also, I should prefer no letters being sent to Mrs Butler to shut the windows when I come and to ask the Doctor if there are any cases of leprosy in the village.[7]

As winter slowly turned to spring and as snowdrops and daffodils emerged from the earth, all started looking forward to their Norfolk summer. From his little bedroom at Eton, Oliver wrote to Kate Greenaway, 'When I feel tired, I always think of Cromer – somehow it comes with its wide grey sea, and sands with shining pools – and the crash of the waves coming in – don't you love the sound as the waves break?'[8]

Janie began to prepare for the Cromer season, hoping that the sea air and sunshine might help Frederick to feel better. She wrote to the overwinter caretakers, Mr and Mrs Simmons, to prepare Newhaven for a June arrival. Little did she then know that the family would next arrive at Cromer missing their paterfamilias and altered forever.

One bright spring morning in May, Oliver was suddenly taken out of his class at Eton College and told to go to the head tutor. The tutor closed the door and proceeded to tell him his father was terribly ill and he must go home immediately. Oliver left for the train and arrived back Rowfant to find the house unusually quiet, Janie pale and anxious and his father in bed.

Frederick had suffered a stroke a few days before. Medical help was summoned but as the stroke had left Frederick unable to swallow even water and the nurses could do little for their patient. Meanwhile, word had reached the family's friend and neighbour Wilfrid Blunt at Crabbet Park, 2 miles away. Hearing of Frederick's desperate plight, dashing Wilfrid, 'black bearded and magnificent upon an unshod horse without bit or bridle', came galloping over the fields to dispense some invaluable advice.[9] Having travelled extensively in the Middle East, Blunt had seen sick Arabs who could take nothing else but were able to swallow warm milk, straight from the animal. Immediately, a cow was brought to the house, where Dorothy conveyed pails of hot milk up to her ailing father. Frederick rallied, but within days, two more doctors had arrived for consultation.

Oliver later described his mother's anguish as she waited for the doctor's verdict:

> She could not rest but must jump up and walk to the window and sit down and jump up afresh many times and now and again she would half kneel against the sofa and offer up, as we knew, little secret prayers for a good report from the doctor.[10]

Despite receiving only guarded, neutral replies, desperate Janie remained cautiously optimistic, and Oliver was sent back to school.

Within days, it was clear that Frederick would not recover. In his final hours, he had asked for his autobiography, 'My Confidences', to be brought to him. In a spidery, weak hand, barely legible, he scrawled in the margin, 'St Pauls master is mine, and I look to him.'[11] Frederick's faith had always been weak and the message, we assume, was a last act of love to reassure Janie as to his religious leanings.

Frederick Locker-Lampson breathed his last on 30 May 1895, a day after his 74th birthday. His last wish was to be buried with the poor and by the poor. Two days later, six men from the estate arrived, dressed in the best mourning clothes they could muster, to carry Frederick away. Frederick was taken by wagonette to Worth Churchyard, and after a service filled with love, flowers and tears, he was laid to rest in a plot next to Sir Curtis. Around his grave his children gathered along with Augustine Birrell and extended family, including several Lampson nieces and nephews. Notable literary figures like Kate Greenaway and Wilfrid Scawen Blunt were there, as well as prominent neighbours like Edward Delmar-Morgan, the father of Dorothy's beau, Jack. The Buxton family and Lady Battersea sent floral tributes.

Janie, just 48, was now a widow. Maids cried as they laid out the customary traditional widow's weeds, heavy black dresses, crepe black bonnets and weeping veils, for Janie and the girls. Frederick had not wanted the family to fall apart after he was gone, writing, 'Do not grieve when I go. Be occupied, be cheerful, be gay; nourish a tender recollection',[12] but all the children and Janie missed him terribly.

Godfrey and Oliver went back to Eton and Cambridge and finished their summer terms in a kind of shock, while the girls felt the loss and the empty space keenly. Janie felt distress but was comforted by her faith and pragmatic in her grief. She decided the diversion of Cromer would do everyone good, so they pressed ahead with plans for the new summer season.

NOTES

1   Frederick Locker-Lampson, *My Confidences*, p.416.
2   Kate Greenaway to Dorothy Locker-Lampson, 20 July 1893 (family collection).
3   Frederick Locker-Lampson to Maud Locker-Lampson, 1895 (family collection).
4   Stephen Locker-Lampson, *Nothing to Offer but Blood*, p.54.
5   Stephen Locker-Lampson, *Nothing to Offer but Blood*, p.4.
6   Letter from Maud Locker-Lampson to Oliver Locker-Lampson (Towle).
7   Letter from Oliver Locker-Lampson to Maud Locker-Lampson (Towle).
8   Oliver Locker-Lampson, 'Kate Greenaway – Friend of the Children', *The Century Illustrated* monthly magazine, Vol. 75 (1907–08).
9   'Recollections of Frederick Locker-Lampson' by Oliver Locker-Lampson, p.44 (family collection).
10   *Ibid.*, OLL.
11   Unpublished copy of Frederick Locker-Lampson, 'My Confidences' (family collection).
12   Frederick Locker-Lampson, *My Confidences*, p.415.

6

Janie Starts Again

From London's storm and stress, we came
to seek a calm New Haven.
We found it, and its kindly name
is in our hearts engraven.

W. Algernon Locker – September 1896

By late July 1895, Frederick's will had been finalised. With affairs now in order, Janie decided there was comfort in routine and ordered the Rowfant household to pack for their Norfolk summer. A large horse-drawn omnibus was hired to transfer the towering piles of luggage along with some of the staff to Liverpool Street Station in London. The family, still dressed in their black mourning attire, travelled in a separate carriage. As Janie left Rowfant, she must have felt sadness at the vacant carriage seat beside her, once occupied by Frederick.

The group arrived half an hour before the train was due to depart to find that, although the station was heaving, a flock of porters swarmed around ready to help unload the piled-up omnibus, eager for a tip. On boarding their reserved carriage, the lunch basket of sandwiches and sponge cake was placed on the rack and newspapers unfolded and all sat down ready for the journey to Cromer.

As the engine trundled along, the scenery changed from the busy streets, grand brick houses and businesses of London to Norfolk, where flint churches and windmills jutted out from the flat landscape. As farmers and cows stopped in their fields to stare as they steamed by, Janie stared blankly back at them, thinking quietly of her husband. The emotional upheaval of the last few months had been trying and all were keen for a change of scenery and the diversion and distraction of friends.

As they pulled into Cromer Station, Emily Clarke, who had been a trusted companion of Lady Jane Lampson, helped Janie from the carriage and accompanied the group up to Newhaven Court. Emily was always a step ahead and was there to ensure everything was comfortable for the grieving family.

To commemorate a new chapter in her life, Janie had ordered a new visitors' book to start that summer. The first page of the book was illustrated by Kate Greenaway, who had travelled up to see her friends. Among her carefully drawn fairies and dancing girls, family friend, the poet and biographer Austin Dobson had written a few lines of greeting.[1]

Two of the first signatures in the new visitors' book in August 1895 were those of 20-year-old Emily Lytton and her best friend, Judith Blunt. Judith was the daughter of the Locker-Lampson's poet friend, Wilfrid Scawen Blunt, Frederick's neighbour, who had ridden over the fields to help his dying friend just a couple of months before.

The dashing and charismatic author Wilfrid Scawen Blunt, described by Emily Lytton (Lutyens) as 'the handsomest man I have ever met, and I think the most physically attractive'. (KGPA Ltd / Alamy stock photo)

Wilfrid was a few weeks shy of 55 but still strikingly handsome with dark eyes and a magnetic charm. His controversial stance on issues such as Irish Home Rule, faith and imperialism made him even more daring and attractive and he was never short of female admirers. He and his wife, Lady Anne Blunt, the granddaughter of Lord Byron, were known for travelling in the Middle East. From there, they brought back rare Arabian horses for breeding at their home in Crabbet Park, just a thirty-minute walk from Rowfant. Being such close neighbours, the couple had been friends of the Locker-Lampson family for many years, even gifting them a fine dark mare they called 'Mansura', after the Egyptian city. Just a month prior, Blunt had been at Frederick's funeral.

Wilfrid and Anne, despite doting on the horses, did not dote on one another. Anne was snubbed by her husband, who had many affairs and lovers. They had just one surviving daughter of the marriage, Judith.

Judith, who was 21 when she came to stay at Newhaven, was as striking as her father with thick, dark hair, full lips and a straight nose. She was athletic, excelling at tennis, and was fond of shooting, vaulting over gates and wrestling with her friends. Her best friend, Emily, was clever, shy and pretty with long, curly brown hair, blue eyes and a beautiful voice but she was also passionate with an easily aroused temper. She was especially impatient with her mother, the Countess of Lytton, and her siblings, brothers Victor and Neville and sisters Betty and Constance. Writing in her later years, Emily herself talked of suffering from 'moods of black melancholy for no apparent reason'. She found it, at times, impossible to control her temper, once biting her brother Victor on the shoulder in a rage and 'boxing' her grandmother with 'a resounding smack'.[2]

Emily lost her father, former Viceroy of India Robert Bulwer-Lytton, in 1891, whereupon the family fell into reduced circumstance. The Locker-Lampsons were kind and sensitive to their friends, and when they stayed at Cromer, not a morning would pass by before an invitation of some sort came from Newhaven. Janie invited Mrs Lytton and the girls for dinner and Frederick often turned up on their doorstep to invite the girls out to a play. To Mrs Lytton's horror, Frederick occasionally tipped Neville or Victor a £1 note, an action which was kindly but only served to highlight the family's impoverished state.

Being of a similar age, the Lytton and Locker-Lampson teenagers, along with Judith Blunt, were all friends and spent time together at Newhaven. Victor Lytton was particularly friendly with Godfrey, although when Victor was in a temper, he could turn spiteful and cruel. Despite the rebuttals, Godfrey still spent much time with his fiery friend at Cromer.

Neville Lytton and Oliver were schoolfriends at Eton and Neville often came to stay at Newhaven during the summer holidays. They would often be found down on the beach together, swimming or watching the sea that was dotted with passing vessels and fishing boats. After a particularly happy stay at Newhaven in 1897, Oliver returned to Eton and swam in the pond there. 'The bathing was not bathing compared to Cromer. How I enjoyed the last bathes!' he wrote to his mother.[3]

Constance, older sibling of Victor, Emily and Neville, was more reclusive and often found alone or playing the piano in the sitting room. Heartbroken, having been forbidden by her mother in 1892 to marry a man of a 'lower social order', Constance never considered another and remained single. The rebellious spirit seen in all the Lytton children appeared later in Constance. In 1908, she became a militant suffragette activist and in the following years she was imprisoned four times and forcibly fed, which caused her permanent damage. During one spell in Holloway Prison in 1909, she began to carve, 'Votes for Women!' into her chest, only to have to stop after the 'V' in fear of contracting blood poisoning.

Emily was often invited to the Blunts at Crabbet Park, where she would find herself in the company of Judith's father, Wilfrid. The two had undeniable chemistry and their flirtation took the form of teasing insults that would shoot back and forth between them. Although he found her fascinating, Wilfrid took advantage of the young girl, sensing her naivety, vulnerability and unhappiness. He constantly endeavoured to find time with her alone, asking her to ride unaccompanied with him in his carriage or suggesting walks where, out of the gaze of onlookers, he would profess his love and kiss her in hot embraces. He wrote her poetry and gave her a ring, declaring that she was now his Arabian wife. On one occasion, he asked if he could come to her room. Though she refused this offer, she was wildly attracted to him, calling him in a letter to her friend and confidante, the Reverend Elwin, 'the handsomest man I have ever met, and I think the most physically attractive'.[4]

Judith Blunt. (Taken from Lady Wentworth, Toy Dogs and Their Ancestors [1911] /wikicommons)

The love affair came to a culmination in the summer of 1895 at Newhaven Court. On the evening of 3 August, after a day at Cromer beach, Emily and Judith were enjoying dinner at Newhaven when Wilfrid turned up and joined the party. Under the table, he held Emily's hand and during the after-dinner games, looked at her longingly. Passions were running high on that warm summer evening as, on retiring to bed, Emily felt it prudent to lock her bedroom door. Perhaps a mutual understanding had passed between the two and then she had nervously changed her mind or, more likely, Wilfrid was willing to chance a nocturnal visit in the hope of spending the night in Emily's bed. Despite her obvious feelings for him, Emily was not a fool and understood that if they were caught, her reputation would be ruined.

The smaller rooms at Newhaven ran along a corridor and in the middle of the night she heard the soft tread of approaching footsteps, followed by a rattle of her bedroom door handle. Emily pretended not to hear and Wilfrid, disappointed, skulked back to his bedroom and left early the next morning.

Though still not yielding to Wilfrid, Emily could not keep away. When he left for the Middle East, she showered him with love letters. Eventually, she found it impossible to contain, and the whole story, including Blunt's nocturnal attempts in Cromer, spilled out to Judith, who had been unaware of the intensity of the relationship between her father and best friend. Judith replied by telling Emily that Wilfrid had recently fathered a child with a mistress. Emily was furious, having naively believed Blunt had eyes only for her.

Judith, in tears of shock and disgust, confronted her father. He denied any serious moral wrongdoing until Judith mentioned him trying Emily's door during the night at Cromer, at which he stammered and became speechless at the accusation that he could not defend. It was the end of a tumultuous love affair.

Judith, rocked by the news and already prone to to melancholy, found herself without an anchor. In 1899, snubbed by Emily's brother Victor and on the rebound, Judith turned her attention to Neville, the youngest Lytton sibling, who worshipped her. They married in 1899. Neville was just 19 and Judith 27. Upon hearing of the engagement of his school friend, Oliver wrote to his mother, 'I suppose you see Neville's engagement? If one must marry, one might marry at a reasonable age. Marriage at any time is ludicrous but marriage at 19 is absurd!'[5] The rebound marriage was doomed from the outset and the couple later separated.

Emily was back as a guest at Newhaven in 1896, along with her sister, who was now Betty Balfour, having married Gerald, brother of the future prime minister Arthur Balfour, in 1887. Emily also returned in 1898, 1899 and 1900, but this time with her husband, the blue-eyed, talented and fashionable architect, Edwin Landseer Lutyens.

Edwin, known as Ned, was born in 1869 as one of thirteen children to an Irish mother and a soldier-turned-painter father. Although his illustrious first and middle names had been tributes to his father's artist friend, Edwin Landseer, hardworking and grounded Lutyens found the privileged company at times trying and he found Janie overbearing. A letter he wrote to Emily's sister, Constance, has a little sketch of himself with his head in his hands and Janie standing over him. Below the sketch, Ned has written, 'Mrs L, more desperately irritating than ever'.[6]

Although happy to accept an invitation, Emily could be a critical guest and, at times, found Janie grating. She did not hold back her feelings from her husband, telling him that Janie was 'next door to an idiot'.[7] There is a clue the feeling may have been mutual, although both women were too polite to acknowledge it. Emily was a vegetarian, and this irked Janie, who would only give her potatoes to eat. This led Emily to remark in a letter that there was 'an element of hostility behind her kindness'.[8] However, in contrast to the chain-smoking, workaholic Ned, Emily loved holidays by the sea and Newhaven was a convenient and free place to stay during the summer months, especially once she had had their first child, Barbara, known as Barbie.

It was also an excellent place to network and create some opportunities and commissions for her husband. Using his quick wit with a little well-placed flirtation, Ned gained a reputation as a perfect guest and commissions came from his efforts. Ned saw the wealthy visitors he met over dinner as fair game and privately he conversed with Emily as to how much money he could make from them.

Close friends aside, the summer of 1895 was reserved for friends and family, who rallied around Janie. The Birrells were nearby in Sheringham and in August, Frederick's nephew, William Algernon Locker, and his wife Edith came to stay. William was the son of Frederick's brother, Arthur Locker, who had once sailed off to join the gold rush but had returned to the UK as editor of *The Graphic* paper. William had followed his father into journalism and was appointed in 1895 editor of *The Morning Post*. Oliver, who had shown the family flair for writing, encouraged his mother to invite the couple, in the hope that one day he might get a permanent job writing for the paper.

Frederick had stayed close to his family, especially to his older sister Ellen, who had married Herbert Dobie, a major in the East India Army, and now resided in Cumberland. Ellen, fair haired and slim, had six children, who all seemed to have inherited the gene for artistic talents and literary flair, especially her daughter, Mary Dobie, who drew illustrations for publication in her Uncle Arthur Locker's paper. When the children came to stay, Frederick introduced them to his many and varied friends, including taking them to dinner with Lord Tennyson.

Sadly, tragedy was to strike in the Dobie family, and when Ellen first visited Newhaven, it was without her talented daughter, Mary. Ellen had undertaken a voyage to New Zealand in the autumn of 1877 on the ship *The May Queen*. Accompanied by her two adult daughters, Mary and Bertha, the trio were going for an extended stay to visit Herbert, their much-loved son and brother, who had been residing in the colony for some time, building the new railways. Herbert was engaged to be married to Charlotte Gilfillan and the trio aimed to arrive in time for the wedding. In a manner not dissimilar to their Locker-Lampson cousins, the brave and adventurous women took the opportunity to visit not just New Zealand but as much of the South Pacific as possible, revelling in travelling off the beaten track and priding themselves in not showing weakness or fear in the face of some quite perilous conditions. Bertha caught the eye of a soldier, Forster Goring, married in June 1880 and settled down to life in the colony. Mary sketched everywhere she went, often walking out with her little dog and unaccompanied, sending back the pictures for inclusion in her uncle's paper.

Group portrait of the Dobie family in 1866. Standing: Ellen Slater (née Dobie) holding baby Alice, John Bedwell Slater, Bertha. Front: Mary, Ellen (née Locker), Herbert and Hugh, with Stanley raised on one knee. (Auckland Libraries Heritage Collections, 1342-Album-244-11-5)

Mary Dobie in 1879, the year before she was murdered in New Zealand. (Auckland Libraries Heritage Collections, 1342-Album-244-133-5)

In November 1880, just a few days before they were due to set off back for England, Mary and her mother went to stay for a farewell visit with Bertha and her new husband. On a warm afternoon, 29-year-old Mary, with her dark hair and refined jaw jutting out from underneath a straw sunhat, took the fateful decision to go for a stroll by herself to sketch the local area around the picturesque local beauty spot, Te Namu Bay. When she had not returned by dusk, the alarm was raised, and a search party was sent to look for her. It was not long before Mary's lifeless body was found 'a little off the main road, amongst the flax, with her clothes in great disorder, and with her throat cut – her head being nearly severed from the body'.[9]

A 20-year-old local man known as Tuhi eventually confessed to the crime. Drunk and broke, he had met Mary by chance on the road. He insisted that initially he just wanted what money Mary had, but when she had threatened to later report him to the authorities, he panicked and attacked her. He was quickly sentenced to death and hanged in Wellington that December. One can only imagine how Ellen must have felt, travelling back to England alone, having lost one daughter to marriage and a second in the most dreadful way imaginable.

Ellen accepted the invitation to stay with Janie at Newhaven in September 1896, enjoying family dinners with her nephew William Algernon and Ethel, as well as her sister-in-law. It is unlikely anyone mentioned Mary and talk of her murder seems to have been a taboo subject. In their later written reminiscences, neither her mother, brother nor sister even mentioned her name. Perhaps it was too painful or simply her awful end was just so dreadful that it was hidden away. The younger children must have known of their older cousin's grisly end and were probably warned not to mention the subject.

A second grieving figure to end up seeking refuge at Newhaven was Alice Bligh, daughter of the Earl and Countess of Darnley, of Cobham Hall, who came to stay in September 1898. Two years previously, her family had been at the centre of most unwelcome column inches and society whispers over the apparent suicide of Alice's sister, Lady Mary Bligh.

On a quiet Sunday afternoon in July 1896, the tall, pretty, 28-year-old Lady Mary went for a walk through the picturesque gardens of Cobham Hall and down to the ornamental Waterhouse Pond, a few hundred yards from her home. From there, she calmly took off all her clothes and folded them into a neat pile, which she left by the water's edge. Desperately unhappy and feeling there was no way out of her present misery, poor Mary proceeded to wade into the freezing murky pond out of her depth, purposely taking in deep breaths of the cold water to drown herself. The alarm was raised when she did not appear, and later that night two maids found her floating lifeless in the centre of the pond.

On hearing the news, shocked villagers turned their attention to Lady Mary's recent infatuation with a young barrister who she had set her heart on marrying. The Darnleys had refused the match. At the inquest, it was confirmed that Mary had been very melancholy of late and the last person to see her alive had been Earl Darnley's valet, who had seen her looking downcast. The verdict was suicide in a fit of temporary insanity.[10]

The earl was devastated at the loss of his beloved daughter and the circumstances of her death. Despite an increasingly compassionate view of suicide, it still meant endless and unwelcome 'talk'. Desperate letters were sent to newspapers by Darnley refuting the claim of suicide, stating instead that his daughter had been suffering from 'pains in the head'. The earl never recovered from the shock and died just five months later. On a freezing December day, with snow lightly falling on the mourners, Darnley was laid to rest alongside Mary in the family vault.

Alice Bligh found peace at Newhaven and a refuge away from London society gossip. Janie assured a friendly welcome and warm understanding and when Alice's mother, Lady Darnley, visited with her in 1899, Janie sensitively made her the principal dinner guest. Alice became a regular fixture at Newhaven, returning nearly every summer until the outbreak of the First World War.

Newhaven was not just a refuge for the down of heart, however. Most of the visitors were there for fun, company and frolics. Blanche, Countess of Rosslyn was one such figure. Socialite Blanche was eccentric, kind and Janie's greatest friend. After losing her second husband in 1890, Blanche became a welcome and regular visitor to Newhaven, sometimes accompanied by one of her beautiful daughters.

Her eldest, Frances, was known as Daisy and later became the Countess of Warwick. It has been rumoured that Daisy's unconventional lifestyle, affairs, being mistress to Edward VII, and her championing of women's cycling was the inspiration for the popular music hall song, 'Daisy Bell (Bicycle Built for Two)'.[11]

Blanche dressed to reflect her personality and Oliver recalled that on one visit, Blanche wore a fashionable picture hat, silk stockings and scarlet high-heeled shoes. She could not pronounce her 'r's, which became a great source of amusement for the family. They all loved having her to visit and the fun she brought along with her, and Janie enjoyed her company. The two women spent hours talking or walking down into Cromer town to attend sermons together at the Lecture Hall. The few maids and coachmen at Newhaven were pleased when she came to visit as when she came to stay, she was fond of taking down a cup of tea for them herself.

Janie was coping well with widowhood, refusing to slow down in her grief and throwing herself into her causes. In 1897, she invited 45-year-old Bishop Oluwole from Lagos in Nigeria to talk to her guests about the Anglican Mission in Western Africa. The drawing room at Newhaven was packed with Janie's friends and neighbours, including Lady Buxton, a close ally. Later that month, the Bishop of Minnesota, Henry Whipple, was at Newhaven. Whipple was a humanitarian and known as an advocate for the Native Americans. The visit of these two men, both working on the side of the underdog, may have permanently influenced Oliver, who would later fight doggedly for persecuted minorities.

As well as visitors from overseas, Newhaven was also a destination for more local gentry. The Ketton sisters lived at Felbrigg Hall, a large country house just a forty-minute walk, or a short carriage ride, away. Marion and Gertrude, both in their early forties and single, lived together with their younger, unmarried brother Robert in the rambling mansion, surrounded by beautiful beech trees, an orangery and a charming walled garden.

Marion was short but full of vitality and a perfect host to the many and varied guests that filled the house during the summer months, and Gertrude was the tall, graceful beauty who welcomed them. Felbrigg was a frequent destination for those at Newhaven and the girls would often return the visits and head to Cromer.

The sociable pair were fond of joining the Locker-Lampsons in hosting croquet and riding parties as well as music evenings, picnics on the lighthouse cliffs and bathing in the sea. In common with Newhaven Court, Felbrigg Hall was subject to a frequent battering by a chilly easterly breeze, leading one guest to refer to the house as 'one of the coldest houses in England'.[12] Despite every room being open to them, the unheated house was often so cold that the girls decided to sleep in a small attic bedroom with a fireplace that they jokingly called 'The Balcony Hotel'.

Unfortunately, when Marion visited Newhaven in September 1896, she came alone and bereft. Gertrude, her beautiful and adored sister, had died in July 1895. Her early death, after several exhausting months of influenza-type symptoms, is believed by some to have been caused by the toxic Paris green shade of fashionable wallpaper that covered the attic walls in the room where the girls slept.[13] The pigment used to colour the paper contained arsenic, prolonged exposure to which could cause all manner of serious and alarming ailments, including darkened skin, cancer and heart disease.

In April 1898, just under three years after following her sister's coffin to the Felbrigg family vault, Marion came back from a walk in the garden and ascended the stairs to her bedroom to change for luncheon. Shortly after, she was found by her servants lying dead on her bedroom floor. One newspaper reported she had been under medical care for some time. Perhaps her unrelenting and non-specific symptoms could also be attributed to chronic arsenic poisoning?[14]

In the last year of the twentieth century, news began to filter downwards of escalating political tensions in South Africa caused by disputes over land and the ownership of several gold mines. The following conflict, known as the Boer War, began in October 1899. The war would go on to cause upheaval and heartache to the settled equilibrium at Newhaven – and particularly to young Dorothy, now known as Dolly to most of her family and friends.

Dolly was now 21 and deeply in love with Jack Delmar-Morgan. Privately, the couple felt they were destined to wed, but there had been no announcement as Janie considered her daughter still too young. Dolly was horrified when, just after Christmas 1899, Jack signed up to fight in the South African conflict. He was not alone. Despite the terrible early losses, young men signed up in their thousands, looking for adventures in foreign climes. Jack was appointed to the Imperial Yeomanry, along with his friend Basil Napier. Both were required to have their own horses to be allowed to volunteer.

Dolly was convinced he would be wounded and immediately took it upon herself to learn basic nursing. In fact, her premonitions of injury came

Jack Delmar-Morgan (right) with Basil Napier. Both men were required to own their own horse to enlist to fight in the South African Boer War. (Family collection)

true. Throughout 1900, Jack saw action and fought bravely in several battles at Vrede, Reitz, Bethlehem and others. He had so far avoided injury.

However, in November 1900, Jack's mother, Bertha, received a letter from Basil Napier explaining that Jack had been wounded. Their unit had been on the road when they encountered thirty to forty Boers ahead, who all began to fire heavily. For five minutes, fire rang back and forth. Suddenly, Basil Napier heard Jack calmly call out that he had been hit. He looked around to see Jack 'half crawling, half rolling down to the horses'.[15] Another soldier went for an ambulance and, a day later, surgeons operated.

Jack had been lucky. The bullet had gone through his right cheek, just missing the eye and from there into his shoulder, where it hit a small artery but missed all the bones. Doctors told him the arm would be stiff and his vision affected for a few months but he would recover with time.

Jack was taken to Ladysmith, a South African town that was then besieged by the Boers. With luck, he was transported out with other wounded soldiers on the last armoured train to the Cape to leave Ladysmith before the siege closed in completely. He took with him a Mauser sniper rifle that he had captured from a Boer, which he proceeded to carve with the names of the battles he had fought.

In January 1901, Jack arrived home a hero and Dolly rushed to his side. Having mostly recovered by August 1901, Jack went to stay for two nights at Newhaven. It is likely he was there to ask formal permission for Dolly's hand in marriage, because just three weeks later, the engagement was announced. Dolly was introduced to Jack's wider family, including his 91-year-old grandmother, Louisa Thomas. Louisa took immediately to Dolly, writing in her diary, 'I am most pleased with my future granddaughter. She is very nice and sensible and agreeable and has lovely eyes.'[16] After the visit, she sent Jack £20 as an early wedding gift, announcing the couple had every prospect of happiness.

At dinner with Jack at Newhaven that August in 1901 was Kate Greenaway. Jack must have noticed immediately that something was very wrong with his fiancée's friend. Kate had been diagnosed with breast cancer in November 1899, but decided to keep it a secret, explaining away her fatigue and illness to her friends as severe colds, rheumatism or influenza.

After a much-delayed operation was performed in the summer of 1900, doctors delivered the terrible news that the cancer had spread throughout her chest and was incurable. In shock, she retreated to Newhaven Court, where she sought comfort from Janie and the children. She struggled on through the next year, following her doctor's orders of medicines, alcohol and a special diet but by summer 1901, the cancer had spread to her lungs and by the time she met Jack at Newhaven, she had lost weight and was clearly in great pain and discomfort and unable to sleep.

Probably guessing the gravity of her friend's situation, Janie watched Kate struggling for breath and tried her hardest to help. As well as suggesting long beach walks and hearty meals, she ordered local workmen to bring up seawater in buckets suspended from yokes on their necks up the steep cliff walkways and back to Newhaven. The water was heated through to make Kate a hot seawater bath, which was thought to be beneficial to health. In the evenings, Kate was given prime place in front of the roaring fire.

The summer of 1901 was Kate's last visit to Newhaven Court, and it appears she knew it would be. Before she left, she added a melancholy poem to the visitors' book:

> When I am dead, and all of you stand round
> And look upon me, my soul flown away
> Into a new existence – far from the sound
> Of this world's noise, and this worlds night and day
> No more the inexplicable soul in this strange mortal body
> This world and it in severance eternal:
> No more my presence here shall it embody,
> No more shall take its place in time diurnal
> What beauteous land may I be wandering in
> While you stand gazing at what once was I?
> Why, I may be to gold harps listening
> And plucking flowers of immortality
> Why, Heavens blue skies may shine upon my head
> While you stand there and say that I am dead![17]

Kate died, aged just 55, on 6 November 1901, just a few weeks after leaving Newhaven. In contrast to Janie, Kate spurned organised religion. She believed God would not be found in turgid sermons in stifling churches but in the beauty of nature. With a characteristic minimum of fuss, she was cremated after a short service and her ashes laid to rest alongside her parents in Hampstead Cemetery.

NOTES

1 Henry Austin Dobson was Poet Laureate from 1896–1913.
2 Emily Lutyens, *A Blessed Girl*, p.6.
3 Oliver Locker-Lampson to Hannah Jane Locker-Lampson, 1897 (Towle).
4 Emily Lutyens, *A Blessed Girl*, p.228.
5 Oliver Locker-Lampson to Hannah Jane Locker-Lampson, 1899 (Towle).
6 Jane Brown, *Lutyens and the Edwardians: An English Architect and his Clients* (1996) p.94.
7 Jane Ridley, *The Architect and his Wife*, p.133.
8 *Ibid.*, p.133.
9 *Taranaki Herald*, 26 November 1880.
10 *Leeds Times*, 11 July 1896.
11 The popular music hall song 'Daisy Bell (Bicycle Built for Two)' was written by Harry Dacre in 1892.
12 R.W. Ketton-Cremer, Felbrigg: *The Story of a House*, Introduction by Wilhemine Harrod, p.vii.
13 Alida Sayers, www.thehotelbalcony.com – National Trust-Felbrigg Hall
14 *Norfolk Chronicle*, Saturday, 9 April 1898.
15 Letter from Basil Napier to Bertha Delmar-Morgan, November 1900 (family collection). Basil was killed in action just a few weeks later on 28 December 1900.
16 Helen Allinson, *Louisa Thomas of Hollingbourne: The Journal of a Victorian Lady*, p.390.
17 Kate Greenaway, 'Newhaven Court Visitors' Book', courtesy of Michael Dadd (family collection).

7

A New Century Dawns

Cromer in Norfolk's a pleasant resort
And the best thing in Cromer is Newhaven Court!

Austin Dobson

On Wednesday, 14 May 1902, Dolly arrived at Copthorne Church in Crawley on the arm of her brother Godfrey.[1] Audible chatter came from the pews within, where Jack was waiting to make Dolly his wife.

Dolly was dressed in white satin, trimmed with lace. Following behind her and holding her full court train were Jack's sisters and Maud, with five little girls all dressed to match in white satin and blue chiffon shoulder knots, with feathered, biscuit-coloured straw hats. Pinned to Dolly's dress was a magnificent Russian diamond brooch from the court of Tsar Alexander I, which had once belonged to Jack's great-grandmother.

As Godfrey escorted his sister into the prettily decorated church, light shone down from the stained-glass windows, many bearing dedications to the Lampson family. At the end of the aisle was Jack, who stood at the flower-strewn solid oak altar beaming with happiness and pride. The couple were deeply in love. Augustine Birrell, who had to decline his sister-in-law's invitation, wrote to say that while she was getting married to the man of her heart, he would regretfully be working but he wished them all happiness. He had no doubt that she and Jack would 'always be lovers'.[2]

Although Birrell was absent, the interior of the church was crowded with family and friends, who all celebrated the young couple's union. After the ceremony, Janie invited guests back to Rowfant for a lavish reception. The Delmar-Morgan and Locker-Lampson families, who had long been friends and neighbours, worked together to impress and entertain. Janie had characteristically thrown herself into organising the event. 'I think everything went off extremely well,' wrote Dolly, two weeks later, to Oliver from her honeymoon in Wales, 'mother had taken such infinite trouble and pain'.[3]

Jack's mother Bertha was 47, but still a stunning woman with dark hair and eyes. She dazzled in fashionable green satin in contrast to Janie who, according to Jack's sisters, was badly dressed. The American ambassador was so taken by Bertha that he asked her to dance, much to his wife's chagrin.[4] Not so happy on the day was 21-year-old Maud, who sat looking glum but beautiful in her bridesmaid dress. Although she wished every

Dolly, around the time of her wedding.
(Family collection)

happiness for her sister, she pined for Conway. Dolly added in her letter to Oliver, 'Poor Maud at the wedding! I felt that it was the thought of Conway that upset her – the thought of how far off her wedding would be.'[5]

Dolly was the first of the Locker-Lampson children to wed and she was keen for Jack to quickly become one of her tight-knit family circle. 'You will only gain by my marrying,' Dolly reassured Oliver, 'for you will be able to look upon Jack quite in the light of a brother, I hope.'[6] In fact, Jack and Oliver would become firm friends and, within a few years, business partners.

Jack was kind, intelligent and a gifted inventor and brilliant engineer, as well coming from a cultured and interesting family. Jack's father, Edward, known as Delmar, was an explorer, translator and author, who had lived in St Petersburg as a child and was fluent in Russian and French. The family had links to the very highest social circles both in Russia and England and through his work on the council for the Royal Geographical Society, Delmar became friends with the giants of the polar exploration expeditions, including Sir Clements Markham, who launched the polar career of Robert Scott.

Scott, later to become a household name as heroic Captain Scott of the Antarctic, was friendly with the Delmar-Morgans, having been a fellow

Royal Navy lieutenant alongside Jack's older brother, Edward, on HMS *Majestic*. Young Edward met a tragic end when he threw himself off the topmast of the pre-dreadnought battleship while suffering from delusions. He was killed instantly.[7] Scott attended Edward's funeral and afterwards returned to the Delmar-Morgan family home, where he stayed for a night. It was here he met Jack's sister, Woodbyne, who was a talented artist. Family legend suggests that Scott proposed to Woodbyne, who subsequently turned him down.[8] Jack's parents and Woodbyne, as well as his brother, Stephen, all stayed at Newhaven in the first decade of the new century, suggesting the families were more than just in-laws but real friends.

All of Janie's children were now grown up. Dolly swiftly moved up to Scotland, where Jack had found engineering work. By 1903, she had given birth to their first child, a dark-haired little son named Edward after Jack's brother. Maud was still at home but unofficially engaged and desperate to wed. Godfrey was working in the Foreign Office and Oliver was busy in study at Trinity College in Cambridge.

Janie must have felt the loss of Dolly keenly. She began to spend increasingly long summers at Newhaven, the home in which she felt most comfortable and happy. There were genuine friends in Cromer too, especially the Birkbecks, Gurneys and Constance, Lady Battersea, nearby at The Pleasaunce in Overstrand, who shared so many of Janie's interests. Increasingly, however, Oliver was using Newhaven to invite his own friends and acquaintances to Cromer.

A regular and enduring visitor to Newhaven, who came to stay for a month every summer before the outbreak of the First World War and for decades of summers afterwards with Oliver, was Karl Ott. Born in the winter of 1873 near to Lake Bodensee, a strikingly beautiful expanse of water in Germany near to the northern edge of the Alps, Karl studied history and languages before moving to England to work as a personal tutor. The man who Oliver would later describe as becoming 'our tutor and best friend' had first been employed by the family back in 1895 after Oliver showed a particular aptitude and interest in learning German.

Janie had initially been unimpressed when Ott turned up for an interview with a bandaged brow. Janie, who abhorred drink, assumed he had been in a fight. When Ott gently explained he had been caught square in the eye by a rogue ball while playing the very English game of cricket, Janie laughed and hired him on the spot.

Ott stayed for a month almost every year, and he was treated as one of the family, joining in the fun and games on their boat *Mansura*,[9] swimming and going for walks down to the beach or along the new pier that appeared in 1901, replacing the old timber-built jetty. Ott adored the countryside around Cromer and the German would often be seen by locals on his bicycle, grey hair flowing in the wind, stopping occasionally to stand on the cliffs to breathe in deep gulps of the salty sea air. He enjoyed walking to the local pub for a glass of beer or cycling to Sheringham to the woods full of beech, oak and fir trees. On other occasions, he left his cycle to walk for miles through the bracken-covered undulating uplands.

Karl Ott, who Oliver described as 'our tutor and our best friend'. (Family collection)

Ott was a lover of literature and he must have been delighted when, in August 1904, he arrived at Newhaven to find that the following day, 42-year-old ghost story author Montague Rhodes (M.R.) James was expected for the weekend. 'Monty' James, a direc-tor of the Fitzwilliam Museum, medieval scholar and later Provost of Kings College, Cambridge, was very much a guest of Oliver's, the two men having met in the university town.

Bachelor Monty came mourning a dear friend, Cambridge scholar and artist James McBryde, who had died following an appendix operation just two months prior. Married McBryde, ten years Monty's junior, has been said by some to have been the great love of the author's life and his death left him broken-hearted. For the previous decade, Monty had gained a reputation in Cambridge for entertaining students with his frightening tales, and the two men had been working together to publish a volume of ghost stories with illustrations by McBryde when the latter became ill and died.

The collection of these spine-tingling terrors, *Ghost Stories of an Antiquity*, is a volume of distinctive and chilling tales whose style of combining con-temporary settings with building creeping dread redefined the genre for the new century. With only four plate illustrations, the book feels curiously unfinished, but instead of hiring another artist to finish the works, Monty left the four by McBryde as a memorial to his great friend.

Despite his loss, Monty was naturally genial and humorous and Karl Ott, along with the other guests that weekend, was assuredly treated to a story or two from the book by the light of the fire, animatedly told by the bespectacled James himself. Staying in a large, atmospheric house, James may have chosen to read 'The Mezzotint'. The story follows a museum curator who buys an engraving of a grand house, only for a sinister figure to appear on the lawn, who, on each view, is creeping and crawling ever closer to the house. The story is particularly frightening, and we can be sure the guests would have gone to bed unnerved. The collection was published for Christmas 1904 and sold well.

Monty clearly enjoyed his time at Newhaven as he returned the following year and stayed for a fortnight. Before leaving, he left a lengthy entry in the visitors' book, playfully written in a Gothic old-word style, extolling Newhaven Court and the virtues of his host.[10]

Staying at Newhaven for a fortnight in August 1904, alongside Ott and M.R. James, was Conway Fisher-Rowe. Throughout their long engagement, Maud and Conway had never lost their passion for each other and they were mutually delighted when, at the end of his stay, Janie eventually gave her consent for them to wed. Conway spent time with Dolly and Jack and was introduced to the wider family, including Maud's half-sister Eleanor Birrell and Eleanor's youngest boys, Frankie and Tony. All took turns to function as chaperones while the young couple, both now 23, took long carriage rides, turns around the garden and picnicked on the lighthouse hills. 'How glad I am that you are going to announce the engagement. That is splendid. Hurrah!' wrote Dolly to Janie on returning home.[11] An engagement photograph was commissioned, and Dolly, Maud and Janie began to arrange wedding plans.

One guest's view of Cromer, taken from Newhaven Court. (Author's own)

An engagement portrait of Maud and Conway. Behind the couple stands Oliver; the other figure is likely to be one of Conway's brothers. (Family collection)

Maud was not the only Locker-Lampson to become engaged. On 24 August, just after Conway had left, Sophy Félicité de Rhodes, of Barlborough Hall in Derbyshire, was invited to stay. Sophy, known to her family as Lalla, was there for Godfrey.

Godfrey and Lalla had much in common. They were both lovers of literature and kind, quiet and good natured. She was also the same age as Godfrey, 29, and from an ancient wealthy and distinguished family. The pair must have enjoyed the company of French-born Hamilton Aide, a fascinating member of the London literary set and an accomplished and popular author of novels and romantic melodies, who was staying with them at Newhaven during that late summer. Though a lifelong bachelor himself, Aide may have witnessed the young couple falling in love, because before he left, he drew an etching in the visitors' book entitled 'Moonlight on the terrace'. Aide had drawn a couple deep in conversation on the balcony of Newhaven under a romantic night sky. Perhaps he had been thinking of Godfrey and Lalla.

Lalla returned to Cromer the following month, where it is likely Godfrey proposed. Seeing it was an excellent match, Janie wholeheartedly gave her consent. On a chilly day in early January 1905, Godfrey, assisted by Oliver as his best man and Maud as the only bridesmaid, married Lalla near her home in Derbyshire.

Four months later, Maud finally married Conway. Carrying a shower bouquet of roses, ferns and lilies, Maud walked down the aisle on the arm of Oliver. Guests marvelled at her beauty and her stunning wedding dress of 'pearl white duchesse satin, trimmed with old lace, and arranged round the skirt with true lover's knots in the same satin, with a tulle veil over a tiara of orange blossoms'.[12] After a reception at Rowfant, the new Mr and Mrs Fisher-Rowe left for a Paris honeymoon. Maud was held in such high esteem by the household servants of Newhaven Court that they collectively gifted her a large chiming clock in an oak case.[13]

Unlike his siblings, Oliver had no intention of marrying anytime soon, although he certainly would not have been short of female attention. In the year Godfrey and Maud wed, he was 25, good-looking and confident with dark hair, a prominent profile, striking eyes and olive skin. He was charismatic and extremely generous, with a persuasive charm and the ability to turn heads when he entered a room.

Fiercely patriotic, imperialistic and an ardent royalist, he also believed in the notion of class order and a paternalistic duty to the working classes;

he was particularly known in later years for championing the underdog. He had enjoyed his time at Cambridge, where he had been president of the Amateur Dramatic Society and demonstrated his literary abilities as the editor of *Granta*, the university paper, where he used his connections and persuasive influence to convince prominent writers of the day to contribute.

After Cambridge, he studied law and spent a year in a solicitor's firm before being called to the bar, where, as marshal, he accompanied Mr Justice Bingham, Lord Mersey, on circuit. Oliver was an excellent administrator, but he craved fun, adventure and attention that a staid law career could simply not provide. Describing himself as 'penniless', although he was far from that, Oliver decided to try his hand at journalism, where he showed a natural talent, before following Godfrey by turning his attention to politics.[14]

In late June 1905, clearly thinking of a way to get his name known in political circles, Oliver cleverly organised a garden party in the grounds of Newhaven Court for the Cromer and District Conservative and Unionist Working Men's Club. Ever supportive, Janie threw herself into helping organise the event. It was an enormous success. The weather was glorious and by the afternoon, over 300 guests milled over the grounds, basking in the warm sunshine, enjoying the party, band music, tennis, croquet and games organised by Oliver and Janie that ran well into the evening. The evening ended with Oliver and Janie giving out the prizes for the games earlier in the day. This gave Oliver a perfect opportunity to demonstrate his excellent ora-torial skills and he gave a short speech about the importance of the club and his support for the Unionist division before he characteristically rounded off the party with a rousing chorus of the national anthem.[15]

Over the next couple of years, Oliver made Cromer his home and became more involved in the local Conservative Club, where meetings were held in the town's lecture hall. Although only still in his mid-twenties, he became known for his confidently delivered, eloquent and rousing patriotic speeches and was often received with loud applause.[16] By November 1907, he was unanimously adopted as the prospective Unionist candidate for North Huntingdonshire, with a local paper declaring that the party had been:

> … most fortunate in finding such an able champion. Mr Locker-Lampson is a fluent and convincing speaker with a dash of natural wit that will do much to enhance his popularity on the public platforms. He strikes one too, as a candidate who will fight to win.[17]

Alongside his party popularity, he became well-liked by the electorate, helped somewhat when, in 1908, he organised a marathon race and gave all the proceeds to Huntingdonshire County Hospital.

Just before the election in 1910, Oliver was on his way to speak at a meeting when his driver misjudged the width of a bridge and flipped the car upside down into the river. Thankfully, both men were uninjured and Oliver, undeterred, sourced some clothes from a local vicar and still attended the meeting. The *Peterborough Standard* reported:

> Thus, it was that Mr Locker Lampson in a pair of trousers nearer his knees than his ankles, without a collar, with a red scarf and a pair of carpet slippers, addressed an enthusiastic gathering at Broughton, within two hours of the accident. The audience carried him shoulder high.[18]

The accident made him more popular than ever with the electorate and after the 1910 General Election, Oliver was overjoyed when he took the liberal stronghold by a margin of 435 votes.

Top Row, L–R: Godfrey, Jack, Conway and Oliver. Bottom Row, L–R: 'Lalla', Janie, Dolly (with Edward) and Maud (with Victor), Newhaven Court c. 1906. (Family collection)

In February 1910, fresh from his election success, Oliver decided to head back to Newhaven. He had always felt a strong attachment to Cromer and genuinely thought of the little town as his home. He and the rest of the family were well known and liked and when officials and townsfolk found that Oliver was due to arrive in Cromer on an evening train from London, a touching torchlit procession was organised to accompany him from his train to Newhaven Court. He was drawn through the town on a carriage to Cromer Church, from where he addressed the cheering crowds from the balcony of Rust's Wine Stores. Oliver told the crowd that he had grown up among them and thanked his many friends, irrespective of party, for the hearty welcome, before adding that he would strive to worthily represent his new constituency but would also seek to always do his best for Cromer.[19]

It was through his emerging political career that Oliver met and became friends with Ernest Shackleton. The explorer who was to become famous for leading three Antarctic expeditions was born in 1874 to an Anglo-Irish middle-class family. He had an unremarkable education at Dulwich College, before leaving to join the navy at 16. The young man had a restless spirit and was itching for adventure. When in 1901, he heard of a national Antarctic expedition being organised in London to be led by naval man Robert Falcon Scott, he used an acquaintance to gain an audience with the chief financial backer to gain himself a place on the boat.

The Discovery Expedition of 1901–04 achieved a furthest south record and made Scott a hero and household name, as well as laying the ground for a serious attempt at reaching the pole. Shackleton, who had become seriously ill on the march south, was sent back to New Zealand early by Captain Scott on the relief ship.

After a period of convalescence, Shackleton tried to settle on land, taking temporary naval posts and buying shares in a speculative company. Becoming increasingly restless, he then tried his hand at politics, standing unsuccessfully as Liberalist Unionist candidate for Dundee. His heart, however, was in his passion for the Antarctic, and he became determined and relentless in his quest to return.

In 1907, Shackleton secured funding for an expedition south. The Nimrod Expedition, as it became known, was a resounding success, with the party securing a new furthest south record, just 112 miles from the pole. Shackleton, with his broad shoulders, weather-worn features and striking voice, sailed back to England the epitome of an Edwardian hero. When he arrived in London in June 1909, the city 'erupted into a near frenzy of hero worship'. Papers were full of praise, with the *London Telegraph* stating that Shackleton had helped 'breath new inspiration and resolve into the British stock throughout the world'.[20]

Rugged, dark, craggy and charismatic, Shackleton was a man in demand. In July alone, he attended thirty events, speaking engagements, appearances and celebratory public appearances. It is testament to his friendship with Oliver that, in August 1909, he made the time to stay at Newhaven Court for a long weekend. Oliver moved to action and organised a talk at the Cromer Conservative Club so the explorer could regale the audience with tales of his Antarctic exploits. At the meeting, Oliver took the chair to introduce Shackleton to the crowd. 'Though the south pole might be cold,' he told the audience, 'Cromer was warm, warm in its reception for Lieutenant Shackleton.'[21] The room erupted in cheers. After the talk, the two men left for Newhaven Court, but not before Oliver begged all to rise and sing 'For He's a Jolly Good Fellow', followed by three loud cheers.

Heroic explorer, Sir Ernest Shackleton, with Oliver outside Newhaven Court. (Family collection, courtesy of The Hon. Alexandra Shackleton)

Before leaving Newhaven Court, Ernest Shackleton wrote his poem 'Erebus' in the visitors' book. (Family collection, courtesy of The Hon. Alexandra Shackleton)

Back at Newhaven, Janie had organised a dinner party. Maud and Conway, Edmund Gill (E.G.) Swain, author of ghost stories, as well as Chad Waldstein, a Cambridge-based archaeologist, with his wife Florence, had been invited to meet the explorer. Over dinner, Shackleton introduced New Zealand journalist Edward Saunders to the other guests.

Shackleton had employed Edward to ghost write an account of the Nimrod Expedition, based on his dictation. Janie told the two men that a private hut in the grounds of Newhaven was available for their sole use during the weekend visit and gave the order that they were not to be disturbed. The two men worked tirelessly in partnership on the book, no doubt helped by the solitude and privacy of their hut. Shackleton's conversation and descriptions proved so vivid that Saunders was able to get a clear picture of the Antarctic scene and the resulting book, *Heart of the Antarctic*, was released later that year to huge commercial success.

Shackleton's wife Emily joined her husband on 8 August. Before they left, the following day, Shackleton wrote the words of 'Erebus', a poem inspired by his southern journey, in the visitors' book, before posing for a photo at the front door. The explorer appreciated Janie's hospitality. 'Kindest regards to your mother,' he wrote to Oliver the following week.[22]

Most of those present at the club meeting subscribed a small sum, which Oliver collected, and with the fund were purchased a pair of gold links with a white enamel circle and a blue enamel centre. Oliver sent the links to Shackleton with a letter explaining the symbolism:

> The heart of the enamel we hope may serve to keep in your memory Cromer's sky and sea, when you were a visitor here; the pale outer of enamel is meant to recall the white wastes of Southern snow and ice, with which your name is for ever identified; and the gold setting in which the whole is cast we venture to think is somehow symbolic of those sterling qualities of bravery, enterprise and faith.

Shackleton was stunned by the thoughtful gift. 'They will always be a remembrance of my pleasant visit to Cromer,' he wrote back.[23]

The two men kept in contact and the friendship deepened when, in the middle of 1910, Shackleton moved his family from Edinburgh to a furnished property in Sheringham, just a few miles from Newhaven. Again, Oliver organised a talk at the town hall for Shackleton to give his lecture 'Nearest the Pole'. To honour the explorer, Oliver organised a surprise torchlit procession preceded by a band to accompany Shackleton as they walked out of Newhaven and down the hill to the town hall.[24] Shackleton spoke to another enraptured audience, including Lady Battersea and Godfrey, who had come down to Cromer for the occasion.

Following Shackleton's first visit in 1909, Jack and Dolly came to stay for the last week of August. As well as a social visit and a chance for Dolly to catch up with her mother and siblings, Jack was there to discuss his business partnership with Oliver. Following a flurry of meetings and talks in 1908, Oliver, Jack and a distant connection to them both, Granville Duff, founded the motor company Duff, Morgan & Vermont. It was presumed that Oliver, wanting to keep his part in the venture silent and his name away from an association with trade, used the USA state of Vermont, from which Sir Curtis had hailed, as his contribution to the new business. However, it is equally likely that 'Duff, Morgan and Locker-Lampson' was just too long and cumbersome to be a viable name.

The company had a base in London and one in Norwich, next to the now demolished Victoria Station. Completed cars conveniently came by rail and, if not already complete, the engine and chassis were similarly delivered, and the coach work added to customer requirements by the company. Others arrived dismantled in crates to be reassembled at the garage. A fourth family member, Charles Hore-Ruthven, joined the company in 1911 as chairman. The venture was successful from the outset and the company would later play a significant role in Oliver's exploits during the Great War.

Family was core to everything at Newhaven. The Locker-Lampson children, their spouses and their extended families were all given an open and welcome invite to come and stay whenever they wished. Conway's sister Ethel and their brother Guy both stayed at the house, as well as Jack's siblings. Lampson cousins popped in and out along with Eleanor, Birrell and their boys. Sometimes, Eleanor's eldest Tennyson sons, Ally and Charlie, joined the happy group.

Godfrey, Dolly and Maud returned year on year, often staying for weeks on end with their mother and Oliver. Jack regularly drove up to Cromer when he was at the Duff Morgan branch in Norwich to have long lunches in the garden with Janie and her guests.

The happy marriages soon produced growing broods of children. Dolly and Jack were delighted in 1907 when they had a daughter, Rachel, to join Edward, and the following year a second son, Curtis, known as Ben. Godfrey and Lalla had three pretty little daughters in quick succession, Felicity, Stella and Betty, born in 1906, 1907 and 1908. Maud and Conway had a son, Victor, in 1906, followed by Hermione in 1908. 'Large dark eyes, dark skin and a wonderful mop of black hair,' wrote Conway to Janie following the birth of Hermione, 'a wee gypsy girlie to couple with our young Samson'.[25]

It was a golden period for the family, full of happy laughter and the running footsteps of the children that rang through the house. Tennis and games were played on the lawn, picnics were taken at the beach and sometimes the children would ride a pony around the gardens. 'Very many thanks for a happy holiday at Cromer. What fun we had!' wrote Godfrey to his mother after a summer stay in 1911.

Janie was a loving mother and grandmother, always on hand to help her children and their young families. She was generous to a fault, forever trying to give them money. 'Thanks so very much for the cheque, but I wish you would not always be sending something, I know you have so many expenses on such limited means,' wrote Maud to her mother. Following a visit to Dolly from Janie and Oliver, who came laden with baskets of herring and plaice, as well as presents of furnishings and a beautiful rug, Dolly wrote to Janie, 'You so overwhelmed us with gifts that us both were blown away.'[26]

In 1912, Jack built a petrol-electric hybrid cabin cruiser called *Mansura*, with an innovative design 100 years before its time. As he and Dolly hosted parties on the boat and sailed regularly to the Continent, they often left the children at Cromer with Janie and the nannies, where they felt they would benefit from a holiday by the coast. On one return, they were surprised to find little Rachel's hair had grown curly from the salty sea air. On other occasions, the whole family would head out on the little boat, sailing around the Norfolk Broads, through waterlilies and bullrushes, passing stooping cattle and little thatched cottages in the sunshine, laughing, chatting and sharing lunch under the bright red awning.

The most prominent pre-war guest to visit Newhaven was arguably Winston Churchill. Then First Lord of the Admiralty, Churchill was a friend of Oliver. The two men had first met through political connections but hit it off immediately. They certainly had similarities. Both were engaging orators and writers and they shared views on empire and monarchy, as well as both being resilient and energetic. They also had mothers from prominent American families.

Just a year previously, Churchill had defended his friend in the Commons after a practical joke by the notorious prankster Horace de Vere Cole resulted in a mortified Oliver having to explain himself at a police station. Cole, who was a school friend of Oliver, had become headline news when, as a Cambridge undergraduate in 1905, he had posed as the uncle of the Sultan of Zanzibar, making a ceremonial visit to his own college. Other outrageous pranks followed, including tricking the captain of the Royal Navy's flagship HMS *Dreadnought* into thinking he and his friends, including the young Virginia Woolf, were Abyssinian delegates.

In 1911, he met Oliver in London and challenged him to a race to the nearest corner, giving him a 10-yard start. What Oliver did not know was that Horace had slipped a gold watch into his pocket. As Oliver ran down the road, Horace called, 'Stop! Thief!' to a passing policeman. Oliver was caught and Cole tried to explain that it had all been a joke, at the same time playfully waving his stick at the officer. Unimpressed, the policemen arrested them both.

Although Oliver was subsequently released without charge, it had been an embarrassing incident. The arrest was raised in the House of Commons. Churchill spoke to dispose of any notion that Oliver had been to blame in any way, resulting in a loud cheer of support.[27]

Oliver and Winston were on such friendly terms that in August 1912, Churchill arranged with Oliver that he and his wife, Clementine, would make a private visit to Newhaven Court. The couple planned to arrive on the Admiralty yacht *Enchantress* for a long weekend in Cromer.

Janie and Oliver took the visit very seriously and decided his entertainment would need to be carefully planned to the last detail. As Winston had expressed a desire to play golf during his stay, Oliver asked his private secretary, Stanley Monard, to be present at the golf links on the Monday morning at ten o'clock. It was not enough for Oliver just to provide a fellow golfer for Churchill, he wanted to rig the game to ensure Winston would win. 'I should not think you are very good at this game Monard, but neither is Winston,' Oliver reportedly told his secretary. 'But he likes to win. So, if you find you are likely to win, which is probable, you must lose your ball, your clubs or even yourself before you permit him to lose.'[28]

Though it was summer, the weather had been unusually poor and, on the Saturday, when Churchill's yacht was due, Cromer townsfolk woke to a dull, rainy day and a choppy, grey sea. The ship dropped anchor about a mile north of Cromer and at about 10 a.m. the stately vessel first loomed out of the drizzling haze. Word had spread around the town that the Churchills were expected, and the pier was full of onlookers as well as a group of militant suffragettes who were there with the intention of making a scene.

At 1 p.m., as planned, Oliver, his friend Geoffrey Knights, Jack, Dolly and Maud drove down to the shore, where they boarded a little surf boat to take them to the yacht for lunch. In drizzling rain, Maud and Dolly were seen carrying baskets and bunches of flowers as gifts for their hosts. Over lunch, the weather progressively got worse and by 3 p.m., dense fog and drizzle blocked the yacht from the view of the crowd on the pier.

Onlookers were further disappointed when the small party, along with the Churchills, returned in the little boat, landed east of the pier and quickly departed in a vehicle that had been waiting on the cliff. The driver motored them to Birrell in Sheringham for a flying visit, before heading back to Newhaven Court.[29]

Janie and Oliver had planned a large dinner party to mark the beginning of the weekend's events but due to the weather, plans were downscaled to a light tea reception. Fifty-four-year-old American-born retail and department store magnate Harry Gordon Selfridge had been one of the guests invited to dine with Churchill, along with Lord Fisher, a retired admiral of the fleet.[30]

The Churchills were driven back to the boat at 5.45 p.m., where they departed to the sound of cheers from those gathered on the pier. Monard never got the opportunity to throw his game of golf.

The weather that had rained off the dinner party that weekend was a portent of what was to come. Around dawn on the Monday after Churchill's visit, a prolonged spell of rain accompanied by strong north-westerly winds lasting for over twenty-four hours drenched already saturated soil and flooded large areas. Norfolk was severely affected, with Norwich completely cut off by flooding, and roads out to coastal towns, including Cromer, became impassable. Farmers found their crops devastated and lost acres of land as well as thousands of pounds.

In his unpublished autobiography, Oliver claimed to have been the only MP to lobby the Lord Mayor to raise funds for the flood victims in his constituency. He later wrote that he raised over £6,000.

The following summer was quiet in comparison, with just the family and a few select guests enjoying the peaceful atmosphere at the house. Little were they to know that it would be the last normal summer for them all before the world would be turned upside down.

NOTES

1 The modern church had been picked in tribute to Dolly's grandparents, Sir Curtis and Lady Lampson, who had donated money for its construction in 1870.
2 Letter from Augustine Birrell to Dorothy Locker-Lampson, 1902 (family collection).
3 Letter from Dorothy Delmar-Morgan to Oliver Locker-Lampson, 25 May 1902 (Towle).
4 Helen Allinson, *Louisa Thomas of Hollingbourne: The Journal of a Victorian Lady*, p.393.
5 Letter from Dorothy Delmar-Morgan to Oliver Locker-Lampson, 25 May 1902 (Towle).
6 *Ibid.*
7 Edward Delmar-Morgan, naval service record, National Archives.
8 Interview with Jane Fowler, 2021.
9 Sailing vessel owned by Jack Delmar-Morgan, named after Dolly's Arabian horse, 'Mansura'.
10 'Newhaven Court Visitors' Book' (family collection).
11 Dorothy Delmar-Morgan to Hannah Jane Locker-Lampson, 28 August 1904.

12 *Surrey Mirror*, 7 April 1905.

13 *Derbyshire Times and Chesterfield Herald*, 8 April 1905.

14 Godfrey unsuccessfully contested Chesterfield at the 1906 election.

15 *Eastern Daily Press*, 23 June 1905.

16 *Norfolk Chronicle*, 11 May 1907.

17 *Peterborough Standard*, 16 November 1907.

18 Quoted from *The Czar's British Squadron* by Bryan Perrett & Anthony Lord (1981).

19 *Eastern Daily* Press, 4 February 1910.

20 Michael Smith, *Shackleton: By Endurance We Conquer* (2014) p.228.

21 *Eastern Daily Press*, Tuesday, 10 August 1909.

22 Ernest Shackleton to Oliver Locker-Lampson, 1909 (family collection).

23 *Norfolk News*, 11 September 1909.

24 *Norfolk News*, 20 August 1910.

25 Conway Fisher-Rowe to Hannah Jane Locker-Lampson, 1908 (Towle).

26 Dorothy Delmar-Morgan to Hannah Jane Locker-Lampson, 3 September 1908 (Towle).

27 Despite the incident, Horace remained on good terms with Oliver and later acted as godfather to Oliver's niece, Jane De Vere Delmar-Morgan.

28 *Portsmouth Evening News*, 6 September 1958.

29 *Eastern Daily Press*, 26 August 1912.

30 Newhaven Court Visitors' Book (family collection).

8

The War to End All Wars

The war that will end war.

H.G. Wells

In May 1914, after a tiring session in the House of Commons, Oliver decided to take leave to go on a short holiday to visit his old friend and tutor, Dr Ott in Baden, south-western Germany. The weather was glorious and presented a perfect opportunity for traversing the countryside on foot. Nearing the end of his stay and with the warm sunshine on his back, Oliver stumbled across an open plain where stood a large hangar sheltering a Zeppelin. Using his persuasive charm, along with some financial incentive, Oliver persuaded the crew to take him up in the air. As he sat on the plush, red-trimmed seats in the aluminium saloon of the monstrous airship, admiring the view down onto the countryside below, he asked the pilot to call on him should he ever come to England.

'We will meet again in England, but sooner than you think,' came the calmly spoken, ominous reply.

More forbidding was the German lawyer who Oliver sat with on the train home, who told him that there was 'a limit even to the Fatherland's patience' and 'every cog wheel in the military machine was ready oiled for "The Day"'.

There had been rising tension with Germany for some time, but it had been decades since England had faced a Continental enemy and not many in England that summer truly expected war.[1]

❄ ❄ ❄

Back home, life was continuing in happy equilibrium. Both Dolly and Maud were pregnant and enjoying home life. Jack was busy with his engineering work; Conway was working in the City Stock Exchange and Godfrey and Lalla were hectic with constituency administration.

By 1914, Janie was nearing 67 years old. Although still fretful and anxious about health, she herself was beginning to show signs of age. In somewhat of a role reversal, her children were now constantly asking her to take care. Janie was struggling to sleep, going to bed too late, and uncharacteristically spending the afternoons lying in the drawing room.

However, she must have heeded some of their advice to try and get to bed earlier and to minimise guests. 'I am glad you are really taking care – it is worth it. You are much too precious to us all to run any risks of making yourself ill,' wrote Dolly.[2]

Janie's life revolved around her children, with a loving focus on her grand-children. Edward was sent crates of apples to Eton and the other children were sent strawberries and eggs from Rowfant. All were always welcome at Cromer for holidays, love and fun.

A day before the assassination of Archduke Franz Ferdinand, an event that would light the match of the Great War, Dolly and Jack sent Rachel and Curtis to Janie at Newhaven in advance of the imminently expected birth of their fourth child. Janie was delighted to hear from Jack a fortnight later announcing the birth of a healthy daughter. 'Doll goes strong and the babe also,' he wrote to his mother-in-law.[3] The new baby was named Jane after Janie and given the middle name of De Vere after Horace de Vere Cole, the infamous practical joker who had been asked to be Jane's godparent.

Baby Jane had been born into an increasingly uncertain world. A com-plex network of interlocking alliances meant that the assassination in Serbia prompted full-scale deployment of troops around Europe. Within a few weeks, Germany found itself facing imminent war with both Russia and France. Germany's strategy was to concentrate troops in the west, hoping to quickly overrun France before the Russian giant could fully mobilise.

Germany declared war on France and invaded Belgium on 3 August. The invasion of Belgium pushed the UK to declare war on Germany the follow-ing day. The system of alliances that had been designed to keep the peace had taken years to establish; it only took days for them to lead to war.

On hearing the news, in a mood of electric patriotic fervour, men all over the country swamped hastily erected recruiting offices, many desperate not to miss the prospect of an adventure in a war that most thought would be over and won by Christmas. In a remarkably foresighted move, and spotting an opportunity to win hearts and minds, Oliver rushed out and bought up a large supply of flour from local traders. He sold a small portion at such a profit that he was then able to distribute a bag of flour to each cottage in his constituency. 'Locker's Flour Fund', as it became known, made 33-year-old Oliver extremely popular.[4] Meanwhile, through the summer, he was considering his best options for war service.

The Belgian Army had used armour-plated and machine-gun-mounted cars from the outbreak of war, chiefly employed to aid reconnaissance missions and to rescue downed pilots. Churchill, then First Lord of the Admiralty, had seen the success of the vehicles and subsequently made the decision to form an Armoured Car Division of the Royal Navy. In his unpublished autobiography Oliver mentions his talks with Winston and, soon after, Churchill decided to base the new Admiralty Armoured Car Headquarters at 48 Dover Street, Piccadilly, which also happened to be the London branch of Duff, Morgan & Vermont. Perhaps Oliver influenced Churchill, or the Admiralty simply felt the firm's draughtmen to have valuable experience in design, but the work was a boost for the company. A classified Admiralty document discovered in 1999 states that the Admiralty cars were 'entirely designed by and the manufacture arranged through the firm'.[5]

Considering his business links with Duff, Morgan & Vermont and his friendship with Churchill, Oliver saw the Armoured Car Division as the natural choice to concentrate his efforts. The navy also held a certain amount of prestige and glamour and offered the best chance for the adventure that Oliver so desperately craved. In October 1914, he wrote to Churchill and offered to form and pay for an armoured car squadron. Guaranteeing £27,600 of his own funds, he then used his network of contacts and his personal relationship with Sir Edward Carson MP and the Irish Unionists to fund the extra £10,000 required. He recruited many men from Cromer and his Huntingdonshire constituency, as well as troops from the Ulster Volunteer Force. In December 1914, Oliver was commissioned as a lieutenant commander in the Royal Navy Volunteer Reserve, forming No. 15 Squadron.

Oliver was not the only member of his family to jump into service. As early as August 1914, Dolly mentions Jack taking officers on *Mansura* on 'dangerous' secret service. By September, Jack was commissioned as a lieutenant in the Royal Navy, serving on HMS *Undaunted*. Godfrey joined the Royal Wiltshire Yeomanry.

'I hope you won't see any German ships at Cromer,' wrote Godfrey's little daughter, Stella, to her grandmother, 'Salisbury is full of soldiers. I wish we could send you some.'[6] Conway, who had previously served in the Grenadier Guards during the Boer War, had remained in the special reserve. The moment war was declared, he immediately re-joined his regiment, where he waited an imminent call to fight. 'I feel very useless after these years as a civilian,' he wrote to a brother officer, 'and hope I shan't shape up too badly.'[7]

As Conway waited for call-up, terrible news flooded out of Belgium. On the eve of war, German soldiers demanded passage through Belgium to invade France. When the Belgian king refused, there were terrible repercussions. Houses were ransacked, cities burned and civilians murdered in the streets. Terrified Belgian refugees began to flood to the UK.

Oliver and Janie characteristically set to action to help in the best way they could. In early September 1914, Oliver wrote a letter that was published in the newspapers, suggesting a scheme for householders to take in Belgian refugees, going on to offer an office of his in London to function as a clearing house. Letters flooded in from all over the country with offers to take in the refugees. 'I am a poor country vicar (married); but we gladly do what we can to help,' wrote one. 'As a patriot, I am willing to do my share,' wrote another.[8]

From Newhaven Court, Janie organised a fund for the support of the refugees, and many initially gave willingly. She raised over £300 with the aim to keep forty refugees in Cromer until the end of 1914 and, after Oliver's letter appeared in the paper, offered sanctuary herself to several Belgians, who came to stay with her at Newhaven Court.

By January 1915, the fund had run dry. Janie appealed directly to Cromer through the local newspaper. In a letter to the *Eastern Daily Press* the same month, Janie asked the readers for money and gifts of clothing, stating, 'Many of these poor people are in great distress and any sacrifice we can make for them will be infinitely valued.'[9]

Subsequent scheduling of Norfolk as a prohibited county meant the transfer out of the refugees. One person who was not sad to see them go was Maud. A small minority, including Maud, were concerned that the Belgians were not as innocent and helpless as they appeared. In October, she wrote to her mother:

I hope everyone is being very careful about the Belgians, a lot of them are German spies and I think nothing ought to be discussed or told before them. I hope they are carefully watched and everyone aware. Please be v.v. careful, this is no fairytale, I can assure you.

Although Maud was unfairly cautious regarding the Belgians, she proved to be correct about the duration of the war. While most were optimistic for a short, sharp war, Maud envisaged a long struggle. 'I feel certain this war will last a long time. Oliver thinks two [years] and you know how optimistic he is,' she wrote to Janie in late October. 'It is far better to brace oneself for a long arduous struggle than to busy oneself up with false hope.'[10]

The wait for Conway was over in September after monstrous casualties hastened his call-up. He was given twenty-four hours' notice to leave for the front. On hearing the news, his sister and mother both rushed to his side. One can only imagine how anxious and bereft Maud felt as she kissed her husband goodbye, knowing that their unborn child might never meet its father. A couple of weeks later, letters arrived from Conway at the front, reassuring Maud that fellow officers had been sent to the front line but he was presently safe, having been left in charge of the junior men.

He had a naturally sunny temperament and his easy-going personality and military experience made him popular among the men. Conditions, however, were tough. Conway found it hard camping out at night in increasingly cold temperatures and he was exhausted from marching up to 15 miles a day.

Dolly was worried about her pregnant sister and wrote letters to her mother asking her to try and persuade Maud to stay at Newhaven for the summer. However, she declined, presuming the house and Janie would be busy with the refugees.

Maud gave birth to a little girl named Ruth nine days before Christmas in 1914. Just three months later, terrible news came that Conway had been wounded at the Battle of Neuve Chapelle in northern

Conway Fisher-Rowe, 'I feel very useless after these years as a civilian and hope I shan't shape up too badly.' (Family collection)

France, where he was serving as an adjutant in the 1st Battalion, Grenadier Guards. The battle was the first planned offensive strike upon a German trench system by the British Expeditionary Force and Conway had found himself serving alongside his older half-brother, 48-year-old Lieutenant Colonel Laurence Fisher-Rowe, who had taken charge of the 1st Battalion in November 1914.

At dawn on the fresh, bright, spring morning of 10 March, a massive artillery bombardment began pounding German lines, signifying the start of the battle. Laurence was coming up with the companies in support when he was struck in the head by a bullet and later died of his wounds. Shortly after, in the same battle, with shells roaring overhead, Conway was injured in the thigh in an act of bravery that earned him the military cross at a time when the decoration was only given for gallantry in the field. Conway recovered and, as soon as he was able, he bravely returned to the front to avenge his brother's loss.

Over the first winter of war, Oliver had proved himself to be a natural leader, taking a firm but friendly attitude with the ratings and a harder line with his officers, expecting nothing less than his own exacting standards. After basic training at Wormwood Scrubs and Whale Island in Hampshire, in the spring of 1915 the squadron was sent to East Anglia to counter a possible invasion threat. There had been a zeppelin raid in January 1915, which had caused damage in Sheringham and fatalities in nearby Great Yarmouth.

Happily, the squadron was posted to Cromer, where Oliver was able to use Newhaven Court as the base. Officers were billeted in the house and other men in nearby boarding houses. The troops mustered in the grounds, learning drill, first aid and self-discipline in the shadow of the big house. Troops sat on the grass outside, listening to lectures on the effects of gas and life in the trenches. The croquet lawn was turned over to make a training trench and the armoured cars were kept in garages to the side of the house.

The nearby golf links were used as a shooting ground and the people of Cromer got used to Oliver and his men rumbling through the streets of Cromer in the heavy vehicles or parading in the town. Oliver even gained permission from the council to anchor a boat at sea to use for target practice by the men shooting pistols from the shore. When Dolly came to stay, Oliver took 12-year-old Edward off in an armoured lorry to shoot at the sea with three-pounder guns. The excitement of having the unit in the town prompted more local men to join the squadron.[11]

Rolls-Royce armoured vehicle laden with Cromer naval ratings, Newhaven Court, 1915.
(Cromer Museum/Norfolk Museums Service, CRRMU: 1979.41.10)

The early months of the war proved to be an exciting interlude for Oliver, with the future full of adventure and promise, but others were struggling with food shortages and a general feeling of anxiety that pervaded the town. Despite her generosity to others, for the first time in her life, Janie was struggling for money. There were always minor maintenance works to pay for, such as the bell wires that continually broke because of the damp. Prices were rising everywhere, and the extra cost of housing Belgian refugees meant several household staff, including a footman, were given notice.

In March 1915, Oliver wrote to Godfrey to tell him that Janie had been rendered hard up by the war. To relieve her of another wage bill, he took on Thomas 'Tug' Wilson, previously Janie's chauffeur, as his driver. Forty-one-year-old Tom and his 39-year-old wife, Maude, were familiar faces at Newhaven, having worked for the family for over a decade. The couple and their young children lived in a cottage on the grounds and functioned as general secretaries, gardeners and caretakers when the family were absent as well as looking after the animals and chickens. Oliver also advised Janie to fell some trees to sell the chopped timber at a high price.

On the very day that Conway's brother Laurence was shot and killed in a remote corner of northern France, in London, Eleanor Birrell also breathed her last. Birrell was devastated by the loss of his wife, but grateful that Eleanor had finally been put out of her misery. For the previous three years, Eleanor had suffered from an inoperable brain tumour that gradually affected her sanity, and lately she had slipped into a coma. Subjected to a barrage of cruel and unnecessary treatments by her doctors, including the removal of all her teeth, her death came as a relief.[12]

Birrell took comfort in the company of his sons, but just a month after Eleanor's death, he was saddened when one of his sons, Frankie, left for France along with his lover David Garnett (later of the Bloomsbury group), where the two found work with the Friends War Victims Relief Mission. Frankie was a conscientious objector and after working to restore a ruined village, the two joined the Friends ambulance unit, where they bravely worked on ambulance convoys under the jurisdiction of the British Red Cross.

Just weeks after the news of Conway and the death of Eleanor, the family was dealt another devastating blow when, on Saturday, 15 May 1915, Janie suffered a sudden seizure at Rowfant, which left her seriously ill and in considerable pain. She rallied for a few days before her strength failed and she died early on Wednesday, 26 May. The news was sudden and shocking. She had been in Cromer just a fortnight before and had been planning to go back imminently for the summer season. Newspapers paid tribute to Janie and letters of condolence flooded in, especially to Oliver, who everyone knew would feel the loss of his mother particularly keenly.

One of the very first letters to arrive was from the Everetts' household staff at Newhaven, who wrote on the very evening of Janie's death to Oliver in London expressing their shock and sending condolences. Blanche, Countess of Rosslyn, who had brightened many a day at Newhaven, wrote, 'I recall the old days and I shall never forget her kindness to me,' and the Bishop of

Norwich, also a frequent guest in Cromer, wrote, 'How sad for you it is! You were so much to your mother and your life was bound up with hers, it will be very lonely for you without her.'

Other letters came from the nanny of Maud's children, Clara Lowe, who had spent whole summers with the children under Janie's roof, 'Your beloved mother had always a kind word for me while I have been in the family.' Constance Battersea, neighbour from The Warren and friend of Janie's for so many years, spoke touchingly of her kind and loving friend and how much she had cared for her. A few weeks later, there came a long letter from the headmaster of Eton College, Edward Lyttleton, who mixed in the same circles as Janie in Cromer:

> It makes a big gap in our lives at Overstrand. She was one of those whose minds are habitually set on high things and high aims, and a character of rare and unfailing consideration for others, with a great gift for friendship.[13]

Janie was laid to rest with her father and Frederick in Worth Churchyard.

Janie's death and the advent of war marked the end of an era. Rowfant went to Godfrey and Oliver inherited Newhaven and £30,000. Dolly and Maud were left a generous allowance.[14]

Oliver had little time to process his mother's death. In June 1915, he received a letter that his squadron was likely to be called into action in Belgium by the end of the following month. Oliver was told to weed out delicate or incompetent personnel and to kit the cars and men in khaki. Knowing he was likely to be away for some time, he wrote to Godfrey from Newhaven:

> Tell Lalla I expect you and her to come to Cromer whenever you want to while I am away, if the house is not let. I particularly want Lalla and the children to come. It would give me great pleasure.[15]

Oliver was also eager to assure Dolly and Maud that the house would always be theirs to use whenever they wished. With departure imminent, Oliver decided to throw a farewell ball for the troops at Newhaven. Food was plentiful and the men partook in much dancing with the ladies in their silk dresses and satin shoes. However, on the evening came news of a breakthrough at Ypres and emergency orders for the squadron to despatch immediately for Dunkirk. Within two hours, Oliver, his men and cars had left Cromer for Dover and their expedition overseas, piled high with food from the ball, given to them by the disappointed ladies.

Oliver and his squadron were sent to the front line in Flanders, a Dutch-speaking region in the north of Belgium. Armoured cars are best suited to chasing down an enemy on retreat and the deadlock of trench warfare put the cars virtually out of action, useful only for short runs to the line to 'worry the enemy'. By the end of summer 1915, it became apparent that the unit might be disbanded. As Perrett and Lord write in their book, *The Czar's British Squadron*, the threat of disbandment caused a personal crisis for Oliver, who was set to lose his prestigious appointment.

Commander Oliver Locker-Lampson outside Newhaven Court. (Courtesy of Mike Rogers)

However, always an opportunist, Oliver turned the changing situation round to his advantage. Over dinner one evening with a senior Russian officer, talk turned to the armoured cars. The Russian suggested that Oliver volunteer his squadron to fight on the Eastern Front, where there was far greater scope for adventure. Oliver put his request to transfer his squadron as an alternative to disbandment in writing, and he soon heard that the Admiralty had agreed to send a complete division. They also promoted Oliver to commander.[16]

Shortly after, Oliver was back in the UK on leave. He headed for Cromer, where Dolly was staying with the children. Like many who had been in France, Oliver came back unwell. Dolly cared and cooked for him, and the siblings enjoyed a happy interval together. 'The holidays were delightful,' Dolly later wrote to Oliver. 'I so enjoyed seeing so much of you.'[17]

Edward took the opportunity to capture some impressive photographs of his uncle in full uniform, which Oliver later had reproduced. Oliver left soon after for war work in London, but Dolly stayed on for an extra fortnight. She was keen to keep the children safely in Cromer away from the sporadic Zeppelin raids that had been attacking the capital. 'It seems a pity to take the children back to London where there are prospects of further raids,' Dolly wrote to Oliver's secretary. Dolly had also been arranging a rental of the flats, Oliver's Newhaven Court accommodation, and was pleased when the rental was finalised to begin at the end of September 1915.[18]

Oliver travelled back to London to interview extra men as potential volunteers for his Russian expedition. He was not short of candidates. Men flooded in from as far away as Australia, incentivised by the prospect of adventure with the charismatic Locker-Lampson. From his London office in Dover Street, Oliver gave each potential recruit a grilling interview. He did not sugar coat what was on offer, excitedly thumping the table while promising no women, glory or medals but the grim realities of a wartime mission abroad. It was a distinctive style and one that shocked recruits into a stunned silence, but it was delivered with such panache that the men became even more eager to join up.

The squadron left for Archangel in Russia on 1 December 1915 with a farewell message from King George himself. He wrote to Oliver:

> Tell the men under your command how glad I am that they have been placed at the disposal of His Imperial Majesty the Emperor of Russia. I know they will uphold that high reputation which they have already earned in the Western Theatre of War.[19]

A message came from Rudyard Kipling, friend of the Locker-Lampson family, wishing them good luck, along with a specially designed waistcoat for each man as a gift from Princess Marie of Schleswig-Holstein.

Not all of Oliver's friends were as optimistic about his expedition. Over dinner with Oliver, presumably shortly before the departure, Churchill had tossed a rifle over the table to his friend, telling him to take it to Russia as he was 'going to need it'.[20]

Danger and death lay ahead, but it was the start of a unique adventure and one of the most unusual and little-known operations of the Great War. Over the next three years, Oliver and his men saw service in Russia, Bulgaria and Romania as well as the area around the Black Sea in modern-day Ukraine, Georgia, Turkey and the Gulf of Bakon on the Caspian Sea.

During his time in Russia, Oliver engineered a meeting with Tsar Nicholas II, in the guise of handing over a personal letter from his cousin, the English King George. The Tsar was of medium height, charming and courteous, but weak in character, and Oliver went away with the distinct impression that he could have 'induced him to agree to many things which he might have felt obliged to withdraw from afterwards'.[21]

Fiercely patriotic, loyal and a committed royalist, Oliver had dinner with the Tsar at the Stavka (Russian army headquarters), where he met and joked with the Tsarevitch Alexei.[22] In 1917, Oliver was in the middle of St Petersburg during the February Revolution where, under fire in a hotel, he rescued Princess Toumanova as well as helping nurses and others escape.[23]

Following the first revolution, the Tsar and his family were placed under house arrest. Oliver hatched a plan to rescue the Tsar by sending in one of his men, of the same size and stature as the Tsar. Out of the guard's view, the plan was for the two men to swap clothing and the Tsar, dressed in khaki, would walk out in plain sight. The plan failed to come to fruition, however, when it became apparent that the Tsar would never leave his family behind.[24]

Following the overthrow of the Tsar, Kerensky, a leading figure in the revolution although opposed to violent social revolution, came to power. Under Allied pressure to continue the war, he accompanied Oliver to the front line to launch a great attack. Despite the bravery of some Russian soldiers and Cossacks, as well as the squadrons of armoured cars sent to assist, the revolution had sapped the soldiers' loyalty and the armies melted away, leaving the army in retreat.

In November 1917, in a Bolshevik Party coup led by Vladimir Lenin, the moderate provisional government was overthrown and Lenin placed as dictator in the world's first communist state. Civil war ensued. Oliver was surrounded and the armoured cars confiscated by the Bolsheviks (although not before the men rendered the cars unusable) and the men were successfully evacuated. Oliver later recounted the horrors of what he witnessed in Russia during the civil war, including the murder of nuns on the streets.[25]

❋　❋　❋

While Oliver was busy in Russia, life at Newhaven and Cromer continued at a sedate pace. Dolly had stepped in to help Thomas Wilson and Oliver's secretary, Miss Fowler, with the general administration of Newhaven, dealing with accounts, repairs and staff. In April 1917, Dolly and the Secretary of State signed an agreement to lease Newhaven Court, fully furnished, for the use of the 193rd Infantry Brigade for the duration of war. Maud came down to help Dolly turn out the strongroom and put all the valuable papers, contained in a myriad of boxes, tins and cases, into the locked schoolroom to keep them safe during the military occupation. Initially, the £7.70 per month rental money was very welcome but it was not long before Dolly was writing to Oliver's accountant requesting reimbursement for replacing damaged items, claiming that 'the military have broken and spoilt everything'.[26]

The rented flats on the estate lay vacant, having been damaged by a small fire in 1916. Oliver did not wish them rented again and kept them free for visitors to use. Maud came regularly to Newhaven with the children and nannies to enjoy the memories and peace, but it was impossible to avoid the conflict entirely. Following a visit down to the beach in August 1917, Maud's eldest, Victor, excitedly wrote to Oliver from Newhaven Court, 'Do you know that yesterday a bit of the fleet came up and about ten destroyers? After that I saw following seven submarines and an enormous ship!'[27] Occasionally, Oliver would join his sister. Maud became a familiar figure in town and a regular member of the church.[28]

By early 1918, Oliver and most of his men were safely home in England. Exhausted and traumatised by his exit from Russia, Oliver was suffering from an illness that was severe enough to effectively end his active war service. Brenda Stibbons, in her book *The Baker Brothers: Diaries from the Eastern Front 1914–1918*, floats a theory that he had contracted tuberculosis. He may have even had influenza, one of the millions who became ill in the Spanish 'flu pandemic of 1918–20.

Whatever the illness was, it was severe enough for Oliver to write to Godfrey at the end of March 1918 informing him that an ambulance was taking him to Cromer to get well. He was taken back to Newhaven Court for recuperation and rest, and by summer 1918 he was well enough to be sleeping in a tent on the Roman camp (a pretty wooded area on Beacon Hill, west of Cromer), felling trees and chopping wood.

Some of the locals were shocked at Oliver's appearance. He had suffered from a serious bout of pneumonia in Russia a year before, and he

(L–R) Ruth, Hermione and Victor at Newhaven Court, August 1918. (Family collection)

had become ill again in the spring. In a time before antibiotics, it may have been that he was simply suffering from the lingering effects of these severe respiratory illnesses exacerbated by the exhaustion of his campaign. A photograph dated August 1918 shows Oliver at the camp with axe in hand, taken by Maud, who had come to stay for the summer with the children. He looks tired but physically quite well.

Maud and Conway endured a tough war. Having recovered from the thigh wound sustained in the battle that killed his brother, there is evidence that Oliver may have tried to get him a job in a less dangerous area of war, but to his credit, Conway went back out, serving as adjutant to the brigade major. On three separate occasions he was badly gassed, three times mentioned in despatches and three times recommended for the DSO.[29] Having survived the gas attacks and bullets, at the very end of the conflict a shell exploded near to him and knocked him out, leaving his health permanently impaired.

Oliver chopping wood at the Roman Camp, near Cromer, 1918. (Family collection)

For the remainder of the war, Oliver was attached to an intelligence organisation, responsible for interpreting developments inside Russia. In December 1918, there was a General Election and Oliver was returned with a clear majority. In 1919, he was appointed Parliamentary Private Secretary to Austen Chamberlain, then Chancellor of the Exchequer, and was present at the Versailles Peace Conference. In attendance at the conference was Queen Marie of Romania, who dazzled in her flamboyant 'hats, veils, brocades and furs' and was feted in the newspapers as an anti-Bolshevik pin-up.

Oliver had met British-born Marie, a granddaughter of Queen Victoria and Prince Albert, when his armoured car squadron had spent the unusually frigid winter of 1916–17 in the country. The Romanian Army, recognisable for their 'chocolate box soldier' sky-blue uniforms, was large but inexperienced in modern warfare and the country had quickly been overrun by the enemy. Oliver found the queen clinging on in a last remaining fragment of unoccupied Romanian territory in the Palace of Yassi. Spotting an opportunity to introduce himself, he personally rushed up to the palace to pay a courtesy call. Finding the royals short of food, he sent a much-appreciated gift of rations, which ingratiated him to the family.

Marie, who, in her early forties, was five years Oliver's senior, simply blew him away. He found the combination of hereditary prestige, brains and beauty irresistible. His later writings leave no doubt as to his attraction to the strong-willed and dark-haired queen. Paragraphs are devoted to her radiant beauty and her fine dress sense but also her fierce resilience in face of adversity, and he was deeply impressed by her devotion to her country and the wounded Romanian soldiers. The two shared similar defiant and patriotic qualities, Marie grabbing headlines in early 1918 by stating, 'We must fight to our last man!'[30]

Oliver spent an increasing time at the palace, becoming, as he put it, one of the family. Eldest son Prince Carol was absent with the army, but Oliver soon became acquainted with the other children, Princess Elisabeth – later to become Queen of Greece, Princess Maria, Prince Nicky and Princess Ileana. Oliver and Marie must have spent time together in Versailles. It is unknown whether anything physical or romantic passed between the two or whether her status put her on an untouchable pedestal that only made Oliver admire her more but, in any case, the friendship lasted through the war and in the decades after, Marie's children would all enjoy a warm welcome at Newhaven.

The following August, Oliver accompanied Prime Minister Lloyd George on a holiday to Lucerne in Switzerland, where they stayed in a private chalet among breathtaking scenery. On their return, local papers reported that Lloyd George was to be Oliver's guest at Newhaven Court for a few days before the new parliamentary session. One can imagine the two men in the dining room at Newhaven on the warm, late summer evenings talking politics and discussing the future of the country, which had been beset by strikes and unrest. Undoubtedly, talk must have turned to 'the red threat'. Oliver's episode in Russia had left him with a deep-rooted fear of revolution as well as an absolute hatred of communism, which would determine the rest of his career.

Above left: *Queen Marie of Romania around the time she met Oliver. He was dazzled by her beauty and dedication to duty. (GL Archive/Alamy stock photo)*

Above right: *The two central figures are Lloyd George and Oliver Locker-Lampson, Switzerland, 1919. (Family collection)*

✳   ✳   ✳

Like many who returned from war, Oliver had seen death and was left with renewed purpose and imbued with a spirit of *joie de vivre*. With his mother gone, Newhaven was now his and as a wealthy and popular war hero, he was determined to enjoy his new status as a minor celebrity. With war over, there was now time for Oliver to make his mark on Newhaven. Quickly he set about updating the 40-year-old property and making it his own.

The first substantial change he made was to install electric lighting through the whole house. Records from the Cromer Electric Company show the wiring cost him £100 – a few thousand today. He also spent £27 on two new circulators in the main house and for another £45 he updated the boiler system in the converted stable accommodation to give him hot water on demand.

There was significant wear and tear damage from the military occupation and local handyman George Lines was given a list of jobs to do. Lines got to work converting the old carpenter's shed into accommodation, fixing the broken peach and green houses, waterproofing the tower bedroom and redecorating the rooms on the upper floors. Tom Wilson, with the help of his teenage son Kenneth, functioned as Oliver's assistant, relaying instructions to Lines, looking after the tenants and organising the maintenance work.

Tom also sought to save his employer money. Newhaven had always had animals on the estate – horses and domestic cats and dogs – but during the war, out of pragmatism and necessity, Tom had been looking after farm animals. There were now over 100 chickens, an old pig and goats who grazed on the long grass on the boundary of the estate. The chickens guaranteed eggs all year round and enough for Tom to sell on the surplus to locals for extra income. Chopped timber from the estate was bundled for sale and goats were sold at market.

Tom was a friend as well as an employee and Oliver was fond of his wife and their children. 'How I wished I could have been with you all,' wrote Oliver after the Christmas of 1919.[31]

Oliver certainly had his hands full. Now nearly 40 and until this point a bachelor, he was soon to meet the person who would share his burdens and change his life for the better, and as a team, the pair would usher in a new era at Newhaven.

NOTES

1   Stephen Locker-Lampson, *Nothing to Offer but Blood*, p.100.
2   Dorothy Delmar-Morgan to Hannah Jane Locker-Lampson (Towle).
3   Jack Delmar-Morgan to Hannah Jane Locker-Lampson, 1914 (Towle).
4   *Eastern Daily Press*, 27 August 1914.
5   Classified Admiralty document dated 26 May 1919, referenced in booklet, *History of Duff Morgan* by David Barratt (2009).
6   Stella Locker-Lampson to Hannah Jane Locker-Lampson (Towle).
7   Conway Fisher-Rowe obituary (family collection).
8   Letters to Oliver Locker-Lampson, Norfolk Record Office, OLL3383/1-48,759X7.
9   *Eastern Daily Press*, 19 January 1915.
10 Letters from Maud Fisher-Rowe to Hannah Jane Locker-Lampson (Towle).
11 Brenda Stibbons, *The Baker Brothers: Diaries from the Eastern Front 1914–1919*, p.12.
12 Charles Tennyson, *Stars and Markets*, p.121.
13 Letters of condolence (Towle).
14 Will of Hannah Jane Locker-Lampson, 1915.
15 Oliver Locker-Lampson to Godfrey Locker-Lampson, Norfolk Record Office, OLL2713/1-55,323X5.
16 *The Czar's British Squadron*, Bryan Perret and Anthony Lord, p.28.
17 Dorothy Delmar-Morgan to Oliver Locker-Lampson, Norfolk Record Office, OLL2723/1-79,323X5.
18 Dorothy Delmar-Morgan to Miss Fowler, Norfolk Record Office, OLL2723/1-79,323X5.
19 *Archangel Herald*, printed onboard SS *Umona* for the men of the RNAS Russian Expedition, 14 December 1915.
20 Recounted to Julian Delmar-Morgan.
21 Stephen Locker-Lampson, *Nothing to Offer but Blood*, p.125.
22 Stavka was the general headquarters of the Imperial Russian Army.
23 Report by Oliver Locker-Lampson, The National Archives, FO 371/2996.
24 Tsar Nicholas II and Tsarina Alexandra, the four grand duchesses and the Tsarevitch Alexei, along with their doctor and a number of servants, were shot and killed by the Bolsheviks in Ekaterinburg in the early hours of 17 July 1918.
25 Report by Oliver Locker-Lampson, National Archives, FO 371/2996.
26 Dorothy Delmar-Morgan to Miss Fowler, Norfolk Record Office, OLL2713/1-79,323X5.
27 Victor Fisher-Rowe to Oliver Locker-Lampson (Towle).
28 After the war, Maud decided to purchase a house that she named Puck's Hill in Roughton, just a few miles from Cromer and her brother.
29 Distinguished Service Order – a military decoration awarded for distinguished service by officers.
30 Tessa Dunlop, 'Romania's Wartime Queen', *History Today* (6 November 2018).
31 Oliver Locker-Lampson to Tom Wilson, undated, Norfolk Record Office, OLL3183/1-75,324X2.

9

Oliver and Bee

With war over, Cromer's summer visitors gradually returned. In guesthouses all over town, sheets were washed, tablecloths laid, cutlery polished and staff hired as they reopened their doors for holidaymakers eager for the normality of a sunny holiday by the beach. Guidebooks extolled the virtues of the Cromer air and advertised all manner of exciting activities for visitors. On offer were motor excursions to Felbrigg and Sheringham, concerts in the Olympia Gardens, the marvellous beach, golf and tennis facilities and the brilliantly illuminated pier where, six afternoons a week, a band entertained the crowds.

With Oliver, Jack, Godfrey and Conway home, life for the family began to settle down once more. Now in his early forties, Oliver was going by the name Commander Locker-Lampson and enjoying his status as a popular and respected war hero and trusted MP. He quickly opened up the refurbished Newhaven Court to his family.

Though left with a permanent and serious respiratory weakness from his wartime gas injury, Conway was well enough to enjoy holidays to Newhaven with Maud and the children. He found the sea air a tonic and he enjoyed his outings to the Royal Cromer Golf Club, where his considerable skills as a scratch golfer still won him prizes.

Jack, who had escaped the war unscathed, took the family sailing on *Mansura* around the Norfolk Broads under wind-beaten clouds. The older children played tennis together on the lawns, indulged in a little photography or took themselves off on bicycles, loaded up with picnic baskets and bathing costumes. The sound of happy laughter rang out from Newhaven once more.

In addition to family, Oliver invited a new wave of visitors and friends, often those in the upper echelons of society. With electric lighting and hot running water, the house would have been a haven of luxury.

One good friend who would not be returning to Newhaven was Sir Ernest Shackleton. The Antarctic explorer had died, aged 47, of a heart attack in the cabin of his ship at Grytviken, South Georgia, while leading an expedition south in January 1922. The world had lost a hero. Shackleton was buried on the island at the request of his widow, Emily. A memorial service in March was held at St Paul's Cathedral. Oliver was there to support Emily, riding to the service in the car alongside her and sitting with her through the service along with Ernest's three children.[1]

Oliver's extensive network of social and political ties now extended to royalty. Princess Marie-Louise of Schleswig-Holstein, a granddaughter of Queen Victoria, came to stay as Oliver's guest in the summer of 1921 and again the following year. Eight years Oliver's senior, Marie-Louise, known as 'Louie' to her family, married for love in 1891 to Prince Aribert of Anhalt just a few weeks after first meeting. For Louie, it was a sad case of marry in haste, repent in leisure, for when the newly married couple settled in Germany, it quickly became apparent Aribert had no feelings for her, instead preferring the company of men. Increasingly lonely, she suffered with poor mental health, lost weight and became ill with bouts of pneumonia.

In 1900, Aribert was allegedly found in the embrace of another man, possibly a servant, and Louie fled. To cover the scandal, the poor princess was bombarded with a range of extremely personal accusations from her father-in-law, who used old German laws to have the marriage annulled.[2]

Louie found comfort from an unusually sympathetic Queen Victoria and once freed from the disastrous marriage, she started to recover. The rest of her life was dedicated to promoting the arts and her many philanthropic causes. Oliver had probably met Louie through his friendship with other interconnected members of royalty and they became firm friends. A smoker and drinker and fond of music and dancing, Louie made an interesting guest and, importantly for Oliver, she hated the communists, who she held accountable for the murder of several of her Russian cousins, including the Tsarina Alexandra Feodorovna and her family, in 1917.

Oliver had put personal wealth into his Russian expedition, which was never returned to him, the armoured cars and other assets having been confiscated by the Bolsheviks. Following the war, he found the mounting costs of running Newhaven Court as a private country retreat and the large maintenance and staff bills increasingly difficult on his decent, but not exorbitant, MP's wage. Using the increasing amounts of time he spent in London and his new Birmingham constituency[3] as a reasonable excuse to keep his financial struggles private, Oliver took a bold step and converted Newhaven into a private hotel ready for the summer of 1922. He added extra chalet accommodation in the grounds for workers and a new dance pavilion for guests. Oliver ordered a printed and illustrated souvenir and advertisements were placed in the papers, one of which read:

> A charming country home converted into a private hotel, offers the most perfect holiday in the world. Standing in its own ten acres of gardens and grounds, it is in the midst of everything yet 'far from the madding crowd.' Wonderful golf, splendid tennis, gorgeous sands, beautiful drives, bracing air.[4]

Princess Nina Georgievna, who married Prince Paul Chavchavadze in 1922. Nina was the great-granddaughter of Tsar Nicholas I of Russia. (The History Collection / Alamy stock photo)

It was a pragmatic move, ensuring he could keep his country estate while making some extra money. It also meant he could still host his own friends and family to stay whenever he wished.

A month after Princess Louie's visit in 1922, Oliver hosted more royalty at Newhaven Court. Arriving in Cromer with her new husband, Prince Paul Chavchavadze, was Nina, the tall, slim, dark-haired 21-year-old daughter of Grand Duke George of Russia. After the war, Oliver had maintained contacts with anti-communist 'white Russians' exiled in the UK and when Nina married in September, he generously offered Newhaven Court to the handsome young couple for their honeymoon.

Princess Nina, a granddaughter of Tsar Nicholas I of Russia, had left her native Russia in 1914 when, in a thinly veiled attempt to distance herself from her husband, her mother had moved herself and her daughters to England on the pretence that the girls would finish their education there. When war broke out, it was too dangerous to go back and then revolution made it impossible. In 1919, along with other Romanov relatives, Nina's devoted father was rounded up and shot by a firing squad of Bolsheviks.

Prince Paul's family had suffered a similar fate. Paul had fled Russia in 1918, aged 19, going first to Romania and then on to England. His father was not so fortunate and was later shot by Bolsheviks in the 1930s.

The year after their stay at Newhaven, the couple celebrated the birth of a son. Shortly after, the family of three started a new life in America. Nina became an artist and Paul an author, and neither were known to mourn the loss of their early riches.

It may have been a worsening cough, a temperature, or a new and severe pain in his chest that first prompted Conway to seek help, or perhaps it was Maud who spotted the signs first and called a doctor. Already weak from the gas attacks he had sustained during the war, which had weakened his lungs, when the doctors confirmed pneumonia in the spring of 1923, it was a profoundly serious diagnosis. The infection soon spread to the linings between his ribcage and lungs, causing acute respiratory distress. In an age before antibiotics and with little reserve to fight the infection, Conway quickly became extremely ill.

His youngest daughter, just 8 years old, was sitting with her father when he said in a quiet, reflective voice, 'Ruthie, I'm so tired.' Conway slipped away shortly after, aged just 42, another tragic casualty of the Great War.

Maud was utterly heartbroken at the loss of her childhood sweetheart and the children, Victor aged 16, Hermione, 14, and Ruth, were devastated at the loss of their good-natured and much-loved father. Maud fled to the comfort of Newhaven and Oliver. In a picture taken by Dolly on Cromer beach that summer, Maud cuts a forlorn figure, sitting in a deckchair hidden under a hat and behind a dark pair of glasses, sadly looking off to the side while nanny sits with the children around her.

It may have been his severe bout of illness or the recent and sudden loss of Conway at the same age as himself that made Oliver revaluate his life, or maybe the loss of his mother left a hole that no number of friends in the world could fill, but in late July 1923, Oliver changed his opinion on marriage. To the great shock of his friends, family and fellow Members of Parliament, he announced his engagement.

His intended was 23-year-old Bianca Jaqueline Paget. Although described by excited journalists as a Californian, Bianca had been born in Llandudno, Wales, in September 1899. She was the daughter of errand-boy-turned-grocer Arthur Wilfred Cadle Paget and his wife Winifred (née Sweetland). In 1907, Bianca was joined by a younger sister, Blanche. Arthur's grocery business must have seen some success as in 1911 the family were living in a substantial five-bedroom house in Southport.[5] If, or when, the family moved to California is uncertain.

It is likely that the couple met when Bianca assisted in Oliver's last election campaign. Oliver must have been blown away by Bianca, who was the very definition of post-war chic, glamorous, modern and effortlessly elegant. She enjoyed dressing in the latest styles, which suited her slim frame, as well as sporting an on-trend dark, bobbed haircut that she often wore under a close-fitting cloche hat. Bianca was a talented artist, interested in the arts and Egyptology, and contributed pieces of writing to Oliver's newspaper, *The Empire Review*.

Following the shock engagement announcement on 31 July 1923, a paper featured pictures of the couple in the grounds of Newhaven. Oliver is dressed casually in sweater and trousers, leaning on a wooden tennis racquet or relaxing in a chair in the gardens, while Bianca stands in front of an easel painting her fiancé. Like Oliver, she had personality and the gift of making friends easily. When Oliver introduced Bianca to his family, they hit it off immediately and soon she was known simply as Bee.

Oliver and Bee at Newhaven Court. (Family collection)

Bee stayed at Newhaven during the month of August and assisted with some of the events and dinners Oliver had planned. It gave her an ideal opportunity to mingle with local people and it is likely she dazzled and impressed. On the evening of 3 August, Oliver opened Newhaven for a charity event in aid of the local hospital and parish church funds. Paying 7/6 a ticket, guests arrived in fancy dress to dance on the newly built pavilion to the latest tunes played by the Alex Wainwright Band, hired by Oliver for the occasion. Later in the evening there were competitions, and prizes were presented to the best fancy-dress costumes and dancing couples. Bee proved a natural and popular hostess. Later in the month there were tennis competitions with both Oliver and Bee joining in the fun and games.

It was a short engagement, and the wedding took place just a month later in Cromer Church on Thursday, 30 August. Sensitive to Maud's loss, it was a low-key affair with no choir and no big white dress, bridesmaids or reception. Bee wore a simple yet becoming grey crêpe de Chine dress and sable fur, with a matching grey velvet hat with an ostrich feather at the back. Pinned to her dress was a diamond and pearl brooch, a present from Oliver. In the absence of Augustine Birrell, who had been due to give Bee away but was called away unexpectedly, Oliver's friend Sir John Henniker Heaton stepped in.

The wedding was not without glamour, however. The Bishop of Norwich officiated over a church full of friends and family, including some local members of the armoured car squadrons, Dr Ott, Dolly, Jack, Maud, Godfrey, Lalla and all the nieces and nephews. Outside the church, enthusiastic Cromer locals crowded the main street hung with flags and bunting for the occasion. Bee and Oliver left by motor car, dragged on ropes by the local men of the armoured car squadron amid a shower of rose leaves, confetti and cheering crowds. From Newhaven they took the evening train to Rowfant, where they spent a ten-day honeymoon before returning to Cromer.

Although missing a grand reception themselves, just after Christmas 1923, Bee and Oliver offered Newhaven for the wedding reception of Henrietta Levine, daughter of local Jewish couple Mr and Mrs Louis and Barbara Levine of Dun Robin House in Cromer. Oliver had felt deeply for the Levines, who had lost two sons during the war – Cyril, who had died at Arras in 1917, and Myer, who was just 18 when he died in a mid-air collision during training in 1918. Guests commented on the 'tastefully decorated' interior and the evening of dinner and dance passed off extremely well.[6]

That summer, Oliver and Bee hosted another charitable fancy dress dance and in November of the same year they held a dance, with the funds going to the National Trust for the purchase of the Roman Camp.

It soon became clear that the couple made a dynamic duo and Bee's presence at Newhaven brought the house back to life. With her flair for artistic interior design, she set about making changes to the house, breathing new life into the dark interiors. She updated the dusty Victorian furniture by buying new soft furnishings and drapes and designing signature pieces herself.

Procession in Church Street, Cromer, Norfolk, after the wedding of Commander Oliver Locker-Lampson to Miss Bianca Paget in August 1923. (Cromer Museum/Norfolk Museum Service, CRRMU: 1979.41.9)

We can be certain Bee would have taken inspiration from the latest interior fashions of the time. Excess clutter would have been replaced with block colour spaces with one striking feature piece of artwork. Cocktail cabinets might have occupied the space where Frederick's treasure cabinets once stood, perhaps topped with mother of pearl or tortoiseshell cigarette boxes and ashtrays or vases of exotic ostrich feathers. Strong, streamlined pieces of furniture took the space of old Victorian plush sofas and a new radio set was brought in.

Bee also worked her magic on the exterior and instructed that the grounds and ballroom be illuminated by strings of pretty multicoloured lights. The couple hired a new ballroom instructor, Eileen Pidcock, previously a judge at world dancing competitions, who directed twice-daily ballroom dancing sessions at the house with backing by Bensons 'Mayfair Three', as well as a gala night every Friday from 9 p.m. until the early hours.[7]

In August 1925, Queen Marie of Romania asked Oliver and Bee if she could leave her 16-year-old daughter, Princess Ileana, at Newhaven for 'some seaside air and sports'. To give his young guest some appropriate company, Oliver invited Dolly, Maud and all the children to Newhaven, as well as the sons of the MP, William Bull.

He organised activities for the teenagers, including a treasure hunt around Cromer. One of the clues was on a lifebuoy 100 yards from the shore, requiring the group to swim out to retrieve it, and the last clue was hidden in one of six tennis balls left innocently by a racquet on one of the tennis courts. Ileana and Hermione, Maud and Conway's daughter, jointly found the treasure – £4 in copper coins.[8] The girls, both the same age, sat piling up their loot in the afternoon sunshine.

A few days later, Cromer was 'given over to revelry and merriment'[9] when Oliver and Bee oversaw the first illuminated fete on the pier. Costumes were hastily made and arrangements finalised, and the day before the fete, Ileana had been one of a party from the house dressed in disguise who had gone out selling tickets for the following day. Driven about town in Oliver's car, nicknamed the 'yellow peril', the princess was selling tickets not realising that a placard with her name was pinned on her back and everyone knew who she was.

The grand carnival started at Newhaven Court after a spectacular fancy-dress opening ceremony. Ileana was the star of the show, captivating and resplendent as the fairy princess. She wore a stunning rose gown with a golden crown and beautiful pearls. Thick-set 63-year-old Sir William Bull MP played the King of Neptune and received the princess, while Edward, dressed as a medieval musician and wearing a bandana, played a banjo behind them. Rachel was dressed as a court herald, complete with trumpet, Ruth and Jane, just 10 and 11, waddled along in penguin outfits with heavy papier mâché heads. Bee, in heavy dark eyeliner, wore a stunning robe of leaves and Hermione looked beautiful dressed as a fairy attendant.

Journalists and photographers stood on the lawn watching the ceremony and taking notes while a cameraman filmed the occasion for British Pathé News.[10] The group drove to the pier in Oliver's decorated car, where they found a cheering crowd of over 5,000 waiting for the princess to officially open the fete.

The event was an enormous success. The entertainment laid on included a fancy-dress party, fireworks, an orchestra and a band employed to play for the large crowds.

Ileana was happy to join in the fun and games. She loved Newhaven and the friendships she had made with the other teenagers. Back at the house, the happy party spent time together, running barefoot and wild in the gardens, horse riding or handling Ileana's exotic pet kinkajou, which she had brought with her to Cromer. On the long summer evenings, they danced to gramophone records, chatted over long dinners and listened to one of Ileana's ghost stories.

Above: *Princess Ileana of Romania (left) counting her winnings with Hermione Fisher-Rowe in the gardens at Newhaven Court, August 1925. (Family collection)*

Below: *The spectacular fancy-dress opening ceremony of the Cromer Carnival, Newhaven Court, 1925. (Family collection)*

Princess Ileana outside Newhaven Court with Oliver's nieces, Jane Delmar-Morgan and Ruth Fisher-Rowe, 1925. (Family collection)

The atmosphere was raucous, and the fun lasted well into the night. On one particularly lively evening, they angered a prominent MP's wife by keeping her awake playing 'rugger' with a melon in the corridor outside her bedroom door, leading her to remark that Newhaven seemed 'more like a nursery than a hotel'. Ileana stayed until early September before returning reluctantly to her governess in London.[11]

In May 1926, a general strike crippled Britain. The roots of the strike lay in the economic distress of post-war Britain combined with a revolutionary wave sweeping Europe, but the immediate trigger lay in the coal-mining profession, where miners were asked to work longer hours for less money. The Trades Union Congress called a strike. In solidarity with the miners, substantial numbers from other industries followed suit, including bus, rail and dock workers, as well as others in jobs supplying gas and electricity.

On the first full day of the strike, armies were called in when up to 1.75 million workers downed tools, causing the transport network to collapse and food deliveries to be held up. In Cromer, bus drivers joined the strike, demonstrating with placards. In London, tussles broke out between strikers and the armed forces, and volunteers offering to drive the buses were attacked.

Prime Minister Baldwin appealed for calm and nine days later, the strike was called off without a single concession made to the mining men. It was a huge relief to those who had genuinely thought that Britain had stood on the cusp of revolution.

The strike was enough to intensify Oliver's fear and hatred of communism and push him to form a new right-wing political movement. Within a few months, Oliver launched his reactionary 'Clear out the Reds!' campaign and began to organise anti-communist protest rallies across the UK. They were hugely popular, attracting thousands, who would listen enthralled to Oliver's rousing oratory.

However, within that tumultuous summer of 1926, Oliver made time to come back to Cromer to host another royal visitor.

King George of Greece had acceded to the Greek throne in late September 1922 but, following a failed royalist coup in 1923, was exiled to Romania. When Greece was proclaimed a republic in 1924, George was stripped of his Greek nationality and sent into exile, along with his wife of three years, Elisabeth of Romania, the daughter of Queen Marie and sister of Ileana. The couple courted much sympathy from Oliver, who saw them as victims of revolutionaries, and especially Elisabeth, who he had known for many years. In his own words, Oliver and Bee ambitiously organised for the King and Queen of Greece, 'a monster celebration which enabled the King to be put on the map again'.[12]

George and Elisabeth arrived at Newhaven Court in early August 1926. Newspaper photographers, probably tipped off by Oliver to give the couple maximum exposure, captured images of the pair sitting casually on the grass with Bee. Looking stylish in a leopard print tight-fitting dress and cloche hat, Bee outshone the frowning Elisabeth. The Greek princess, who was only in her early thirties but looked considerably older, was wearing a shapeless dress in the loose fashion of the day that did nothing to hide her overweight frame. Other photos showed them with tennis racquets after a game on Newhaven's courts or placed in front of a car that had been put aside to motor them to see friends and explore the local area. Elisabeth and George had gained a reputation for their cool demeanour, a trait evident in some of the pictures where they stare wearily at the camera.

'The monster celebration' that Oliver had planned was similar to the massive event he had organised for Elisabeth's sister the year before – an illuminated fete on the pier. Again, he gathered his friends and family to play the parts in a historically themed fancy-dress grand reception. William Bull MP was King Canute, handing the king and queen an address from the citizens of Cromer. William's sons, Peter and Stephen, were Beowulf and Hereward the Wake. Edward played Ethelred the unready, Curtis was Horsa, and Hermione and Rachel were ancient Britons. Jane and Ruth, along with others, played little Saxons, Danes and Jutes.

The party stood either side of the steps in front of the house as George and Elisabeth descended to the waiting car. Behind them, in a train, followed Hermione and Bee in a calf-length, fitted print dress.[13] On the pier and promenade, over 6,000 revellers enjoyed a fancy-dress parade, two orchestras, exhibition dancing by Captain Dudley and his partner, dancing competitions and a thrilling finale event, which saw Professor Kenna dive in flames into the sea from the top of the pier pavilion.

Elisabeth and George gave out prizes for the winners of the various events, before they and the family retired, exhausted, back to Newhaven Court and their comfortable room in the royal suite. Shortly after, the couple left for a stay with Lord and Lady Birkenhead, friends of Oliver and Bee. Some of the older children were glad to see them go, considering the couple 'boring and hard work!'[14]

Rehearsing for the carnival in the grounds of Newhaven Court in the summer of 1926. (L–R) Oliver, King George of Greece, Bee, Queen Elisabeth of Greece and Sir William Bull, MP. (Cromer Museum/Norfolk Museums Service, CRRMU: 1981.80.91)

Newhaven Court was briefly named The Royal Cromer Hotel. (Author's own)

George was eventually reinstated as king in 1935, but without Elisabeth, who had initiated divorce proceedings against him. She cited desertion from the family home, the marriage having failed from the toll of years in exile, extramarital affairs and financial difficulties. Spotting an opportunity to use the royal visit to their advantage, Oliver and Bee renamed Newhaven the Royal Cromer Hotel.[15]

One week after the Greek royals left for the Birkenheads, another exciting event of the summer occurred at Cromer. Locals were enthralled when four RAF Supermarine Southampton flying boats came to town, the first stop in a publicity tour of seaside locations by Sir Samuel Hoare, the 46-year-old, bright-eyed Air Minister who owned Sidestrand Hall in Norfolk. For four hours in light rain, the planes were seen cruising over the sea or moored at the end of Cromer pier. They were watched by hundreds of spectators, who had rushed to the promenade and cliffs to catch the best view.

A select party of thirty distinguished guests were invited to view the boats before the group were taken back up to Newhaven Court for a special lunch. Packed into the dining room, wealthy and influential guests such as Russell Colman and John Gurney listened as the minister put forward the suggestion that the heavily armed boats, able to fly up to 110mph, might make a valuable contribution in the future defences of Britain's far-flung empire. Hoare envisaged a day, long in the future, when 'nothing would be thought of flying yachts that would take one as quickly to Constantinople, Stockholm or Naples as an LNER from London to Cromer'.[16] He ended his speech by paying tribute to his friend, Oliver, calling him the 'Beau Nash' of Norfolk and eliciting cheers and laughter from the guests.[17]

After lunch, Samuel offered to take Oliver flying in one of the boats. Honoured, and never one to turn down the prospect of an adventure, Oliver joined Samuel and together they flew to Great Yarmouth. Waiting on the jetty in the neighbouring seaside town was the Mayor of Yarmouth and other dignitaries. When the flying boat had landed, a craft was sent over to retrieve Samuel and Oliver. Hoare made a speech to the crowds who had gathered along the seafront, before he and Oliver climbed back into the craft and headed home, to Cromer.

It had been such a busy summer that Oliver and Bee decided to stay on at Newhaven well into the autumn. They were still there on 11 November when, at dusk on that chilly afternoon, a caretaker walked the grounds checking on the buildings for the evening. At 5 p.m., he passed the wooden 'Shackleton Hut', just 50 yards from the main house and all looked quiet.

By 5.30 p.m. the hut was destroyed, the whole structure having burst into flames. Nothing was left, not even the tablet within describing how Shackleton had drafted his book there. Fire engines were called but they could do nothing. Journalists arrived at the house and interviewed Oliver, 'No one sits in the hut in this weather,' he said, 'and as there is a public footpath just behind it anyone who might have set fire to the place could easily slip away.'[18] Although agreeing that the circumstances were suspicious, a police investigation brought no leads and the case was closed.

The mid-twenties were a heyday for Newhaven. The ivy-clad house was full all summer with visitors attracted by the spacious, updated rooms and the two covered tennis courts, built at a cost of £10,000, that permitted all-night play. Guests enjoyed French cuisine directed by a first-class London chef using ingredients grown from the kitchen garden in the grounds. In the evening, there were dances in the magnificent ballroom, where guests whirled around the dancefloor, entertained by a special London orchestra.

It was so busy that Oliver and Bee decided to build a small timber-framed cottage in the grounds in which to live during the busy season. The design and materials of the cottage were bought from Norwich manufacturing firm Boulton & Paul, who also supplied the builders at a set cost of around £900. Located just inside the brick-pillared, gated entry off the Norwich Road, the gravel-drive-facing four-bedroom house was of a very pretty design, with a Norfolk reed thatch roof, central brick chimney, lead-glazed casement windows and a veranda with rustic posts.[19]

The staff who were hired to run the hotel were housed in similar but more basic wooden outbuildings in the grounds. There was almost a disaster on a warm Monday evening in August 1928, when two of the wooden buildings caught fire. A handcart and hose were quickly dispatched to fight the blaze and Boy Scouts rushed to the scene to help push away a section of huts, stopping the blaze from spreading. A large crowd gathered to watch the close escape. The two waiters who occupied the huts escaped unharmed but lost all their possessions.

Between events at the house, Oliver's anti-communist rallies and his work as an MP, it was a busy time for the couple. Oliver found Bee to be the perfect companion and one who supported him in every aspect of his life and career. She often helped in constituency visits, where her 'vivacious personality and charming manner won all hearts'.[20]

Though no children came, it was an incredibly happy marriage. They were sociable, hosting parties at their North Street address in London, inviting the best political, literary and artistic minds of the day. They spent long holidays with their friends the Birkenheads in Nice and Madeira and attended weekend house parties, where Bee was the life and soul of the party. But all this cost money, something Oliver just did not have enough of. One of his nieces later commented, 'Oliver didn't have any money, but he enjoyed spending it.'[21] Indeed, he had inherited a considerable sum from Janie, but running two houses, throwing lavish parties, generous gatherings and regular foreign holidays had drained his funds. He had also lost a considerable amount in his investment in the armoured cars.

Having been brought up in a solidly wealthy family, Oliver had little sense when it came to budgeting. When invited to dinner parties at Dolly's house on Tite Street in Chelsea, Oliver would get a taxi to wait for him for hours outside while he leisurely dined, with no thought to the amount racking up on the meter. He was also generous to a fault, which did not help matters.

The rounds of rallies, parties, Parliament and entertaining continued, and on 1 July 1929, Oliver and Bee cleared their busy calendar to attend the wedding of Rachel de Visme Delmar-Morgan, Jack and Dolly's eldest daughter, to Harold Ellis Richards, who worked in the African Civil Service. Oliver and Birrell signed the certificate as witnesses.

As Rachel left on honeymoon, Jack and Dolly went down to Cromer with the rest of the family for a holiday, staying at nearby Overstrand. Since Conway's death, a few years before, Maud had spent much time with Dolly. Their children were as close as siblings, especially Jane and Ruth, who were the same age as well as the best of friends. It was gloriously warm and despite almost all the children being grown up, much fun was had on Cromer beach, playing, swimming and sunbathing. It was to prove to be a last happy family gathering before an awful event that no one in the family could have predicted.

A few days before Christmas, on Sunday, 22 December, Bee was enjoying dinner at the Birkenheads' home when she was suddenly struck by excruciating stomach pains, sickness and a fever. The illness escalated with frightening speed. Quickly, she was rushed to a Westminster nursing home, fluttering in and out of consciousness. Doctors diagnosed severe acute pancreatitis and operated to remove tissue from the damaged organ. Despite rallying for a brief time, Bee developed sepsis and organ failure and at just past seven on Christmas Day, with Oliver at her bedside, she died. She was just 30 years old.[22] Oliver was absolutely devastated.

Rachel de Visme Delmar-Morgan (R) with Bee at the Newhaven Court stables. (Family collection)

Just three days later, a few personal friends, as well as Godfrey, Lalla, Jack, Dolly, Maud and the nieces and nephews gathered around Oliver in the church at Worth, which had been decorated by lilies from Rowfant. There was a short but moving service, before six pallbearers, all Cromer ex-servicemen of Oliver's armoured car squadron, carried Bee in an oak coffin decked with white chrysanthemums and adorned with a silver tablet, inscribed with words by Robert Louis Stevenson chosen by Oliver, 'Steel true. Blade straight. The great artificer made my mate.'[23] Oliver placed a handful of parma violets on the coffin, Bee's favourite flowers, before she was laid to rest in the family plot, alongside Sir Curtis, Janie and Frederick. Floral tributes were sent from far and wide, including a bouquet in 'affectionate memory from the old boys at Cromer' and another from the staff at Newhaven Court.

On the following Monday, a memorial service was held at the Russian Church in London for those who could not attend the funeral. As the diverse congregation assembled, each were given a candle that was lit by an attendant through the moving service as a symbol of a young life that had ended. The last were extinguished in a final prayer, before an exhausted Oliver left on the arm of his friend, the one-legged General Baratoff, who had fought in the Caucasus with Oliver's troops and had flown in from Paris especially for the ceremony.

In the words of one mourner, 'In her short life, she scattered much happiness'. In her six-year marriage, bright and handsome Bee had come in like a whirlwind, modernised Newhaven and brought youthful vitality and energy to the house and the family, and with her death, a little bit of Oliver and Newhaven died with her.

NOTES

1   *Staffordshire Sentinel*, 2 March 1922.
2   Jenni Wiltz, 'Marie-Louise: The Princess of Nowhere' (girlinthetiara.com, 2021).
3   Oliver was the MP for Birmingham Handsworth from 1922 to 1945.
4   *Peterborough Standard*, 28 July 1922.
5   1911 UK Census, Ancestry.com.
6   *Eastern Daily Press*, 28 December 1923.
7   *Eastern Daily Press*, Friday, 5 June 1925.
8   Over £200 today.
9   *Western Gazette*, 27 August 1925.

10 The British Pathé footage, 'A Real Fairy Princess' (1925), can be viewed on youtube.com.

11 *The Tatler*, 2 September 1931.

12 Stephen Locker-Lampson, *Nothing to Offer but Blood*, chapter plan, p.8.

13 British Pathé footage, 'Ex-King George and Queen Elisabeth of Greece' (1926), can be viewed on youtube.com.

14 Interview, Jane Fowler, 2021.

15 Although it was used for the following few years, the name never stuck and was eventually reverted to Newhaven Court.

16 *Eastern Daily Press*, 7 September 1926.

17 Celebrated eighteenth-century dandy and fashion icon.

18 *Newcastle Evening Chronicle*, 11 November 1926.

19 Boulton & Paul Catalogue, 'Live in Beauty', Norfolk Record Office, ACC1997/146/55/16.

20 *Peterborough Standard*, 27 December 1929.

21 Interview, Jane Fowler, 2021.

22 Death certificate of Bianca Locker-Lampson.

23 *Peterborough Standard*, 3 January 1930.

10

Game, Set and Match

During her short life, Bee helped oversee the most ambitious and best-remembered addition to Newhaven Court, the construction of two huge, indoor covered tennis courts that so many in Cromer still fondly remember today. The game of lawn tennis had always been a favourite pursuit of those staying at Newhaven Court. During the early years, the family and guests enjoyed the outside grass courts, marked out on the flattened land on the sunny, wind-sheltered southern side of the house. These could be accessed through the dining room and adjoining library room, which opened out onto the paved area and court. On clear days, a net was erected, wooden racquets were brought out of the storeroom and invitations to play sent out to friends in Cromer.

With a degree of mischief, Frederick enjoyed bringing together those of differing social classes and opinions. Local doctor, Herbert Dent, was often invited up to Newhaven for tennis and later remembered how his host engineered a tennis match in this way:

> He delighted to bring men together of opposite opinions; and I remember his joy one day when he arranged a set of tennis between Wilfrid Scawen Blunt and Arthur Balfour on one side of the net and Lord Houghton and the retired surgeon on the other.[1]

Balfour and Houghton had lately been responsible for the incarceration of the outspoken and charismatic Blunt for his part in political scuffles over his support of home rule for Ireland. Frederick undoubtedly sat and enjoyed watching the awkward interchange with glee.

Since its rules had been regulated in the 1870s, tennis had become all the rage. Many a party at Newhaven was centred around a day's play, followed

The sunny southern lawns of Newhaven Court, c. 1910. (Author's own)

by dinner, or an al fresco light lunch of tea, cakes, bread and jam and more play until twilight.

It was a pleasant and entertaining way to see friends. Generally, the younger men could not wait to get outside, although occasionally an interesting guest kept them enraptured for long enough to let their dinner go down. Edith Hamilton, writing in her reminiscences of her MP father, Henry Fowler, recorded one such occasion when several young people had been invited to lunch and to play tennis afterwards:

> My Father went into the smoking room directly lunch was over. The afternoon drew on and still the lawn was deserted, and there was no sign of the white flannelled figures. At last, the library door opened and slowly and reluctantly the young athletes passed out on to the sunny lawn – with that sigh of disappointment which children heave on the completion of a fascinating tale. Sir Henry Fowler had been talking, they said, and they could not tear themselves away.[2]

The younger guests and family members were especially fond of the sport that even the girls could join in with and one that promised competition, fun and an opportunity to flirt. Mixed sexes games were encouraged, and it was often a good opportunity to meet and attract potential suitors, although in the early years, girls were too often hampered by their long, heavy dresses and bustles to show off too much athletic prowess.

Everyone was encouraged to join in and even Godfrey, not generally a sportsman, was fond of tennis. He competed against friends and guests as well as Oliver and their athletic brother-in-law, Conway. On one occasion in 1912, Godfrey jumped to hit a ball too enthusiastically and landed badly, twisting his knee and tearing a ligament, leading to weeks out of action as well as bruising his ego. When Godfrey and Lalla returned to Salisbury, Lalla responded reassuringly to an anxious letter that came from Janie enquiring of the injury:

I made him lie on a sofa all day Monday and Tuesday and hop into meals on a stick we had made. He was very cross about it, but it was much better, and he could now go off bandaged up.[3]

After the Great War, the younger generation of nieces and nephews took over the court, socialising with friends, playing matches and practising trick shots. Teen cousins Edward and Victor wandered down to the court with their camera, spending time experimenting with making hoax photographs to fool the adults.

When Newhaven opened as a hotel in 1922, the advertisement boasted, 'Wonderful golf, splendid tennis, gorgeous sands, beautiful drives and bracing air'. However, on arrival, some guests found the tennis facilities at Newhaven inadequate and some walked down to the grass courts at the nearby Cromer Lawn Tennis Club, situated a few minutes' walk from Newhaven on the other side of the Norwich Road.[4]

By 1924, Oliver was happily married to Bee. Seeing their guests wandering off site to use the tennis club facilities, the couple decided to build two covered courts, which would allow all-year-round indoor play. Ever the shrewd opportunists, the couple knew the construction would put themselves and Newhaven in the spotlight and attract extra guests to the hotel. Having previously used the Norwich steel manufacturing company Boulton & Paul to purchase prefabricated wooden huts and outbuildings for the grounds, including the gatehouse cottage, in 1925, Oliver and Bee commissioned the company to design the courts. The enormous detached, rectangular steel and glass structures, costing £10,000,[5] proved to be a huge addition to the hotel's prestige and the town's reputation as a centre of tennis in Norfolk.

An early advertisement for the Newhaven Court Hotel. (Family collection)

The courts were constructed in the north-west corner of the grounds, backed by a wooded path that ran down to the town behind the house on one side and against the brick boundary wall that ran adjacent to the sea on the other. Access for cars was created in the corner where the path and brick wall met. Situated on an incline above the town, it was said that the glare from the sun glinting off the double-apex glass roof was visible to the Cromer fishermen far out to sea, who used it as a reference point.[6]

Inside, the courts were laid out side by side with numbered seating around the edge on carefully constructed balconies giving a splendid view down on to the play below. Four sets of moveable shutters protected the players from the dazzling sun and electric pendant lighting ran in four rows across the length of the courts, allowing play to continue well into the evening. Situated around the courts were separate ladies' and gentlemen's dressing rooms, bathrooms and a player's lounge with wooden bench seating.

The enormous cost was restrictive, but clearly Oliver and Bee expected to recoup some of the expense with increased visitor numbers and by hosting large tennis tournaments. They also had investment through their best friends, the Birkenheads, and Admiral Lord Jellicoe, and in a syndicate formed the Newhaven Tennis Club, which they hoped would encourage return visits. Under the auspices of the Cromer Club, Oliver and Bee immediately began to plan a tennis tournament to take place in the autumn – one to rival not just the existing Cromer summer tournament but to also create a similar buzz to Wimbledon.

In the autumn of 1925, when French tennis champion Suzanne Lenglen arrived at Newhaven, she was 26 and at the top of her game, having won both Wimbledon and the French Open Championship that summer. Suzanne had caused a sensation at her Wimbledon debut in 1919, throwing off the traditional long-sleeved, bulky girls' sportswear in favour of a thoroughly modern silk, calf-length, sleeveless dress and a headband that held back her dark, bobbed hair. Suzanne went on to win the Wimbledon Championship that year and for the next four consecutive years, as well as two gold medals in the 1920 Olympic Games, which helped cement her place in 1921 as the number one ranked female tennis player in the world.

There was something captivating about Suzanne, a certain *je ne sais quoi*. Thousands flocked to watch her matches and marvel at her prowess and finesse on court. Newspapers fed the public interest, poring over every detail, from her distinctive off-court style of fur coats, red lipstick and painted nails

The Newhaven Court indoor tennis courts, commissioned by Oliver and Bee in 1925 for the vast sum of £10,000. (Taken from Newhaven Court Hotel brochure, courtesy of Roy Boyd-Stevenson)

and rumoured numerous love affairs to her eccentric antics on court, where she was said to suck sugar cubes soaked in brandy or cognac between sets, which were thrown down to her from her father in the stands.

Oliver had approached Suzanne that summer and in his most persuasive and charming manner requested that she come to Cromer to take part in the new tournament. Attracted by the indoor red-clay, hard-court surface, which suited her style, she agreed. Due to her late acceptance, it was reported that Oliver had 'aeroplanes and Daimler cars' requisitioned to bring her from the South of France to the courts in time.[7] It was nothing less than a coup for Oliver and Bee, and Newhaven Court remained the only tournament outside London in which Suzanne took part.

Oliver and Bee met Suzanne and fellow tennis star, impressive Parisian Jacques 'Toto' Brugnon, at Victoria Station, London, before driving on to Cromer. Probably alerted to her arrival by Oliver, reporters swarmed Newhaven with cameras, eager to capture a quote and a shot of the superstar. Oliver and Bee, the latter looking tiny in a fitted dress and cloche hat, posed

(L–R) Bee, Jacques 'Toto' Brugnon, Suzanne Lenglen and Oliver at Victoria Station, 1925. Oliver reportedly moved 'aeroplanes and Daimler cars' to get Suzanne to Cromer. (Trinity Mirror/ Mirrorpix/ Alamy stock photo)

outside the front door in the sunshine with Suzanne, complete with her tennis racket, as cameras snapped and film cameras rolled, capturing the three sharing a joke and smiling in conversation.[8] There was a gala dinner in the dining room before chairs were brought out to the front of the house, where the entire group assembled for a photo to mark the momentous occasion.

To house the considerable number of expected spectators, the Cromer Club had gone to considerable expense to erect additional galleries that could hold 1,500 people. Seated tickets were priced from 2 shillings on the first day up to 15 shillings on the day of the finals and a standing room ticket could be acquired from the Newhaven Court ticket office for as little as 1 shilling. Parking spots were reserved on the estate to encourage those from further afield and refreshments were set up in the dance hall. Play was to begin at 9 a.m. and continue until 9 p.m., or even later, if required.

The tournament was a tremendous success, although Lenglen disappointed some when she pulled out of the singles tournament in favour of the doubles, partnering with Brugnon in the mixed doubles and Dorothea Lambert Chambers in the ladies doubles. English player Dorothea was over twenty years Lenglen's senior and a veteran player, but the 1908 gold medal-winning Olympian wowed the crowds and reached the final to cheers of delight. To the later disappointment of the spectators, Lenglen and Chambers won the tournament by default when the fellow finalists pulled out due to injury.

Eileen Bennet took the ladies title, curtsying to Lord Birkenhead as the cup was presented to her. Colonel Henry G. Mayes took the men's title. Born in the same year as Oliver, Henry was 45 but still in peak physical form and a favourite with the ladies for his dark, dapper good looks.

Suzanne Lenglen and Oliver watch Lord Birkenhead present Eileen Bennet with the ladies' singles trophy, Newhaven Court, 1925. (Taken from a pre-war Newhaven Court brochure, author's collection)

Tennis stars assemble outside Newhaven Court, 1926. Wearing pinstripes on the back row is Bunny Austin. Bee sits bottom left; Dorothea Chambers is third from left; and next to Oliver on the front row is young Betty Nuthall. (H.H. Tansley, Cromer Museum / Norfolk Museums Service, CRRMU: 1998.30.15, courtesy of the Tansley family)

A second covered-courts tournament was arranged for the following autumn. In September 1926, following a sold-out one-day exhibition match the same month, a Cromer tennis fan wrote to his local paper about his trouble getting hold of a ticket. Oliver responded with an apology, stating that demand had been so high that the event had sold out three days before. He had reduced prices so 'even the most humble lover of tennis' would be able to afford a visit. He committed to enlarging the seating to hold an extra 300 seated tickets and increasing standing room for the October tournament.[9]

Demand for tickets in October proved as furious as in 1925. Lenglen was not scheduled to play, having turned professional that year, but Oliver had secured other prominent players, leading fashionable paper *The Tatler* to claim in bemusement just prior to the tournament, 'Commander Locker-Lampson seems able to attract a big crowd of celebrities wherever he chooses'.[10] Jean Borotra was among the men signed up to play. The Spaniard, known as 'The Bouncing Basque' for his trick shots, was an exciting addition. His on-court antics, which included wearing coloured berets that he changed throughout play and kissing the hands of ladies in the stands, made him a favourite among the spectators. Good looking and fair haired, the fashionable young Wilfred 'Bunny' Austin, was another hot ticket.

Twenty-one-year-old Senorita 'Lili' De Alvarez was the standout ladies star. Lili had been born in Italy during a short holiday taken by her affluent Spanish parents but brought up in Switzerland. She showed considerate athletic talent from an early age and won her first tennis tournament at just 14. Considered a pioneering athlete in Spain, Lili was proficient not just at tennis but skiing, skating, equestrianism and car racing. Daring and with a rebellious streak, she was a perfect partner in the hoax that Oliver had planned for that year's tournament.

During the 1926 Saturday finals, in a practical joke reminiscent of his friend Horace de Vere Cole, Oliver walked onto court to announce to the crowd that an exhibition match would be played between four gentlemen players, Wallis Myers and Henry Mayes on one side against Mr Summerson and the newly arrived mysterious 'Senor Alonso' on the other. On walked the four players to much cheering from the crowds.

The more observant in the crowd thought Senor Alonso, in his peaked cap and immaculate white flannel trousers, a little odd, being so short and shapely, but were nonetheless impressed by the skill displayed. It was not until the match was over that the real identity of Senor Alonso was revealed, and the cap pulled off to reveal the dark, bobbed hair of Lili. 'It was one of the best practical jokes I have ever played, and I have played many of them,' laughed Lili, when questioned by the press.[11]

Colonel Henry Mayes won the men's single tournament that year, and while throwing a dinner party for the players, Oliver asked them all to sign their names in the visitors' book to mark the special occasion.

In 1927, on her way to a one-day tournament at Newhaven Court, Lili and her mother were involved in a frighteningly close escape when the small plane that was taking them from Paris to England developed a fault during take-off. The aircraft failed to rise before crashing back down into sand dunes, throwing Lili and the other eighteen passengers forward from their seats. Although none were badly hurt, all were badly shaken. Two hours later, passengers bravely put aside their fears and took off on a different plane, eager to get to Cromer. Lili proved she was unaffected by her experience, taking the mixed doubles title with her British partner, Gordon Crole Rees.

An advertisement for the 1929 championship. (Author's own)

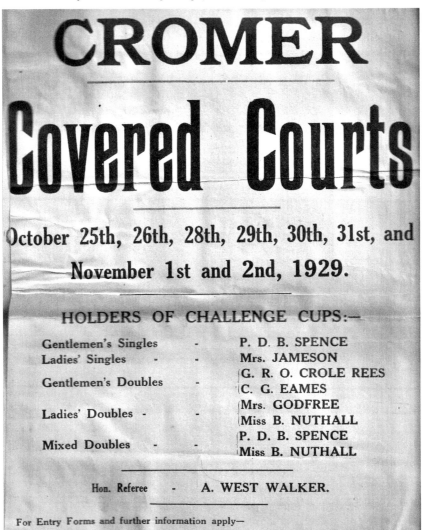

CROMER

Covered Courts

October 25th, 26th, 28th, 29th, 30th, 31st, and November 1st and 2nd, 1929.

HOLDERS OF CHALLENGE CUPS:—

Gentlemen's Singles	-	P. D. B. SPENCE
Ladies' Singles	-	Mrs. JAMESON
Gentlemen's Doubles	-	G. R. O. CROLE REES C. G. EAMES
Ladies' Doubles	-	Mrs. GODFREE Miss B. NUTHALL
Mixed Doubles	-	P. D. B. SPENCE Miss B. NUTHALL

Hon. Referee - A. WEST WALKER.

For Entry Forms and further information apply—

Secretary, Covered Courts Club, Cromer.

The tournament of 1930 was difficult for newly widowed Oliver. Having formed and hosted the tournament with Bee from its inception in 1925, her loss was keenly felt. Hermione, Maud and Conway's glamorous eldest daughter, a good all-round athlete like her father, stepped in to help, assisting her Uncle Oliver in hosting the tournament and partnering him to events.

Stockport-born Fred Perry's first love had been table tennis and by the age of 20 he was World Champion of the sport. However, in 1930 he was approached by the Lawn Tennis Association, who offered him a place on a four-man US tour that kick-started his tennis career. In contrast to the privileged backgrounds of most of the players, Perry was the son of a cotton spinner and the crowds loved him for it. Women adored him, and high-profile romances, including one with stunning superstar actress Marlene Dietrich, made him a household name. Perry signed up for the 1931 covered-courts tournament where, in splendid form, he raced to the finals before winning the tournament in straight sets.

By the middle of the decade and until the outbreak of the Second World War, Newhaven was trading on its reputation for tennis in Norfolk. Advertisements now placed the tennis facilities as the top billing, boasting twenty-one courts, on both hard and grass surfaces. The annual tournament was still popular but, sadly, by 1935 sales dropped and were reported as disappointing.

With the advent of war in 1939 came a hiatus in the famous autumn covered-courts tournament. Although it resumed in October 1946, it never quite recovered its glamorous pre-war status. In the same year, Newhaven appropriately hosted the first organised conference of the Lawn Tennis Professional Association, with Dan Maskell as chairman. Dan, who would later be known as the BBC 'voice of tennis', presided over the meeting, where important decisions were made about coaching and the reintroduction of championships post-war.

Tournaments continued until 1949, after which followed a six-year break until they resumed in 1955, the year that 35-year-old polish star Władysław Skonecki took the men's title. Skonecki was an interesting and passionate player to watch and his reputation for gambling, women and late-night dances must have preceded him onto court.[12]

Despite changes in ownership, tennis at Newhaven remained so important to the locals that when, in 1958, the US Air Force moved into the empty Newhaven Court, a clause in the contract assured that the townspeople could continue to use and have access to the courts. However, a devastating fire in January 1961 at Newhaven, just two years before a fire destroyed the hotel, wrecked the indoor courts, which were never rebuilt. The loss to local and national tennis was described as 'severe' by a local paper and the loss to the town greater still.

NOTES

1   Major H.C. Dent, *Reminiscences of a Cromer Doctor*, p.16.

2   Edith Henrietta Fowler, *The Life of Lord Wolverhampton* (1912) p.636.

3   Sophy Locker-Lampson to Hannah Jane Locker Lampson (Towle).

4   The club had been opened on 13 June 1908 to much fanfare by local town tennis advocate Mrs Bond Cabbell, the Cromer landowner who had donated the plot. Clementine Churchill, wife of Winston, was among them, playing at the club in 1923.

5   The equivalent of approximately £650,000 (2021), Bank of England Inflation Calculator.

6   Interview with George Baker, 2021.

7   *Gentlewoman*, 14 November 1925.

8   British Pathé footage, 'Incomparable Suzanne' (1925), can be viewed on youtube.com.

9   *Eastern Daily Press*, Saturday, 11 September 1926.

10 *The Tatler*, 6 October 1926.

11 *Londonderry Sentinel*, 2 November 1926.

12 Taken from information found at www.historiapolskiogotenisa.pl

11

The Commander

And all at once, summer collapsed into fall.

Oscar Wilde

Bee's sudden death at the brutally young age of 30 devastated Oliver and left a chasm of grief in its wake. Newhaven had lost its mistress and Oliver his young vivacious wife. Bee had been a partner who had supported him so fully in his many adventures, assisted his parliamentary work, boosted his popularity with his constituents, and used her glamorous style to maintain the couple's connections and active social life. Without her, life seemed empty, and the light that burned so bright in Oliver dimmed to a low glow.

Oliver filled his time with family whenever he could, often dining with one of his sisters at their homes in artistic Tite Street, Chelsea. He was close to his grown-up nieces and nephews, especially Hermione – slim, dark-haired, beautiful and glamorous – who became a fine replacement for Bee at social occasions. She was often seen with Oliver partnering as a hostess at the many events and gatherings to which he was invited.

On a holiday with her widowed uncle to the mountain village of Murren in Switzerland in January 1930, she was introduced to Captain Patrick Ellison of the Grenadier Guards. The attraction between the good-looking couple was instant and when Hermione suddenly came down with chickenpox and had to isolate in her cabin, Ellison climbed through the snow to her sickroom window to make a proposal. Bemused, Hermione refused, but the pair remained friendly and by May, Ellison's persistence had paid off

Hermione Fisher-Rowe with Captain Patrick Ellison, Murren, Switzerland. (Family collection)

and Hermione accepted his proposal. After her marriage in October 1930, Oliver relied heavily on lady secretaries to run his household.

A newspaper from the same year captured Oliver chopping logs for firewood in the grounds of his London home. Although he was clearly still slim and fit at the age of 50, his face seemed etched with loneliness. Two accidents within the space of a month – falling in a deep ditch and breaking a rib in September 1931 and a taxicab collision the following month – wounded his pride and embarrassed him, especially as a man who prided himself on physical strength.

In the same month as his accident, Oliver retreated to his bungalow in the grounds of Newhaven Court. But he faced further humiliation when he was asked to prove that he still owned enough of the property to retain his resident parliamentary and local government voting rights in Cromer.

Oliver no longer owned Newhaven Court outright. The huge expense of running several households, his busy social life, entertaining and foreign holidays, as well as the enormous bill for the tennis courts and hosting royal visits had prompted him in June 1927 to form the Newhaven Court Syndicate, a limited liability company, to run the hotel.

Investors grouped together to buy the house, furniture, stock and books, releasing a large sum of money for Oliver and easing some of his financial difficulties. Mindful of his future ability to vote in the town, when the hotel became part of the company, Oliver retained just under an acre of freehold land that the tennis courts had been built upon, ensuring he remained a property holder. In 1931, he was questioned by council inspectors as to when he stayed at the property and it became clear that between his visits, the hotel was occasionally empty. Oliver's interest had waned significantly since the death of Bee and in 1930 he had spent just Easter and some of the autumn in Cromer.

Oliver earned a good wage as an MP and his income was boosted by various schemes and occasional pieces for newspapers, but he was no longer a wealthy man. There had been poor investments and money was occasionally borrowed from wealthier family members, causing friction, made worse by his habit of spending what money he had recklessly and running up enormous bills. 'I do feel unhappy about the money you have spent,' wrote Dolly to Oliver, a few years before. 'You never have any for yourself and you really should not be spending so lavishly on others.'[1]

He also had a habit of giving away the borrowed money to others he considered in greater need. When his great friend Lord Birkenhead died just nine months after Bee, leaving a surprisingly small estate in his will, Oliver and others, including Winston Churchill, formed a special fund at personal cost to secure Lady Birkenhead's future.

Oliver was not the only one feeling the pinch. The Wall Street Crash that occurred in October 1929 saw billions lost from the stock market and investors wiped out. The value of British exports halved, plunging industrial areas into poverty and by the end of 1930, unemployment had doubled to 20 per cent. Firms went bankrupt all over the country and many businessmen and their families were financially ruined. For the many in Cromer working in the hospitality and tourism trade, it was a tough time. Takings plummeted as costs rose and guest numbers dwindled as families sought to save money.

Echoing the mood of the time, Oliver wrote a speculative piece titled 'What I would do, if I were a millionaire', which appeared in the *Peterborough Standard* in August 1930. As well as lamenting his lack of funds, the piece gives a good indicator of the mature Oliver – less materialistic, somewhat wistful and certainly changed as a person by his experiences:

> Values have shifted, and I do not care to be now, what I then wanted to become. I longed for so much money that I could scatter it about and be envied by the crowd. But how much more modest are my desires today! What I like best is a tent on a heath, plain viands, a glass of beer and the sweet communion of my darling books and dearer friends. And I chose my friends not by the hats they wear or the number of studs in their shirt fronts, not because of any property they possess in titles or things. I like my friends for what they are.

One who was within Oliver's trusted circle was his brother-in-law, Augustine Birrell, who, over the years, had become as close as a second father to him. Affectionately known as Uncle Austin to the younger members of the family, they all loved him dearly. After losing Eleanor in 1915, Birrell had never remarried and lived with his unmarried sons, Frankie and Tony, at their home in Chelsea. The trio kept up The Pightle in Sheringham, the holiday home where they had so many memories of the happy days together, but a reduction in income meant Birrell was forced to rent it out for most of the summer months. Always one to look for the humour in a situation, referring to his financial situation, he joked to his stepson Charlie, 'I will have to die soon if I am to appear in recent wills.'

Despite the popular tennis tournaments, Newhaven Court was struggling to make a profit. Accounts for the end of 1928 showed a small loss and
takings remained flat the following year. In January 1931, the bank agreed
a loan to settle outstanding debts but then suddenly demanded repayment,
which the company could not meet. The bank appointed a receiver, Mr
Christmas, to run Newhaven. He proposed to keep running the business
while arranging the sale of the property. He turned a small profit for 1931
but with money owed to various people, including to local Cromer trades-
men, the syndicate received a winding up order in May 1932. Newspapers
reported 'considerable losses due to depression' and the syndicate was liqui-
dated while investors sought to sell the property.[2]

Despite inheriting some of his father's characteristics, namely Frederick's
love of literature as well as his gift for making friends everywhere he
went, as he aged, Oliver was becoming more like his mother, increasingly
militant in his causes. Oliver had always had a particular penchant and
sympathy for the underdog, and it became customary for those in trouble or needing advice in his constituency to 'ask Locker' for help. When
a 24-year-old Birmingham constituent found herself unemployed when
her father's business folded, Oliver suggested she write to the Newhaven
Court manager to enquire whether there would be a vacancy.[3] It is likely
he put in a word for her. He also expended considerable energies on local
projects like pig clubs and allotments for his constituents, as well as standing loyally as a court character witness on several occasions to men who
had served with him in Russia.

Oliver was well known for his intense dislike of communism and throughout the 1920s he had campaigned vigorously in anti-red rallies, going as far
as to form a quasi-fascist organisation, the Sentinels of Empire, which had
its own rousing meeting anthem, 'March On!', with lyrics by Oliver himself.
He even showed early admiration for the nationalist politics of Adolf Hitler.
However, there was one crucial difference between the pro-nationalist senti-
ment of Oliver and the vehemently anti-Semitic ideology of the Nazi Party
– Oliver had always been a supporter of the Jewish cause, and as far back as
1915, Oliver had been reprimanded for wearing his uniform 'in connection
with a scheme for collecting funds to combat antisemitism'.[4] The family had

many Jewish friends and Oliver would also have been aware that Jack, and therefore his nieces and nephews, had Jewish heritage.[5]

Hitler had become Chancellor of Germany in January 1933 and immediately plans for anti-Semitic legislation were drawn up. By April, in the same month that laws were passed excluding Jews from public offices and restricting the number of Jewish students in German universities, Oliver, who had thus far broadly supported the nationalistic element of the Nazi Party, felt increasing concern and sent a telegram to Hitler:

> As a member of parliament and former officer who has always and openly stood for Germany's claims to military equality and territorial revision and who has been for years your sincere admirer, I take the liberty of calling your attention to the fact that the decision to discriminate against the German Jews has had a most damaging effect upon the good feeling for Germany. […] The action against the Jews is making the work of myself and other friends of Germany impossible.[6]

As movements against Jews accelerated, so did Oliver's opposition. In December 1933, he organised a protest meeting against the persecution of the Jews, addressing a large gathering of the Jewish Arts Society. 'Germany had not driven out half-wits, crooks or blackguards; she had turned out the cream of her culture and hunted out the most intellectual people she possessed!' he roared, cheered on by the crowd.[7] The congregation was so grateful for his friendship that they put together a fund to have his name inscribed in the 'golden book' in recognition of his support.

There is good reason to suspect Oliver's increasingly active political career may have been a way of channelling his substantial grief into a cause. Just over two years after the death of Bee, Oliver lost the other most important woman in his life. In March 1933, Maud, his beloved twin sister, died, aged just 52, in her sleep at her home of several years, Pucks Hill in Roughton. Maud had suffered a catastrophic aortic aneurysm, which had ruptured without warning, killing her very suddenly.[8]

The shock to the family was tremendous. Victor, Hermione and Ruth, the latter still just 18 years old, had now lost both their parents and Godfrey, Dolly and Oliver their much-loved sister. Maud had been a favourite aunt to many of the younger generation, particularly Jane, who had loved her dearly and spent many happy holidays with her. In the cool evenings at Newhaven,

Maud used to gather the children around the fireplace and read to them, particularly popular classics such as *Oliver Twist* and *Treasure Island*, but also poems by Tennyson, Byron and Scott.[9] She was active in the community and well known around Cromer as a member of the church, where she made daily visits to unwell parishioners or those down on their luck, cheering them with her friendly, sympathetic nature. Her passing had taken everyone by surprise as, just two days before her death, she had been seen calling on an old cottager who was ill. Locals came in droves to a memorial service in Cromer Church to remember her.

In the same year that Oliver lost Maud, a guest came to stay in Cromer in a series of events so extraordinary it is still remembered by the people of Cromer today. Much has been written about Albert Einstein's visit to Norfolk. However, we will touch on it here as it would prove to be, in the words of author Andrew Robinson, 'Locker-Lampson's version of his friend Churchill's finest hour'.[10]

Oliver had met King Albert of the Belgians on the Western Front during the Great War. He had maintained the friendship, and during the twenties, he and Hermione had holidayed with the royal in Switzerland. Out of the reach of prying eyes, they ate hearty breakfasts of poached eggs on toast to the tune of a gramophone records before spending time teaching the heavy 6ft 4in royal to ski.[11]

Albert's wife, Queen Elisabeth, had become friendly with Professor Einstein following his visit to the Belgian court in 1929, when the two had bonded over their love of music. Fearing for their own safety following public criticisms of the Nazi Party, when Albert Einstein and his wife, Elsa, returned from a visit to California in 1933 they did not return to Germany but to the apparent safety of Belgium. There, they gave up their German passports, rented a villa and were given armed guards on the orders of King Albert and Queen Elisabeth.

Shortly after, Oliver wrote to Einstein via the Belgian royals, offering him a safe haven at his London house for no charge. Oliver was a champion of the underdog, and he was undoubtedly concerned for Einstein's safety, but his offer of sanctuary was not purely altruistic. Oliver knew that having the great German scientist under his protection would be personally very beneficial, deflecting attention from his earlier pro-fascist comments while also publicising his campaign to assist the Jews. At that time, the offer was declined, though the two stayed in contact and a later invitation in July was accepted on the premise of promoting the plight of the Jews in Germany. Einstein stayed with Oliver in London, where he was introduced to Lloyd George, Winston Churchill and Sir Austen Chamberlain.

Einstein spoke little English, 'It just won't stick in my ancient skull,' he wrote in his 1931 diary. However, language barriers were largely overcome due to Oliver's grasp of German, meaning he could converse in depth and translate for others. The following day, and with Einstein watching from the gallery, Oliver tried to introduce a bill in Parliament to promote and extend opportunities of citizenship for Jews resident outside the British Empire. Unfortunately, the second reading of this far-sighted bill was not scheduled before the parliamentary session ended and lapsed.

Einstein returned to Belgium, but rumours were rife of kidnappings and assassination attempts. Following a serious threat to his life in September 1933, Einstein accepted the offer from Oliver to stay with him in Norfolk.

How Einstein travelled to Britain from Belgium is unclear. One credible theory is that journalist Patrick Murphy accompanied Einstein by public ferry from Ostend to Dover and then on by rail to Victoria Station, where he was met by Oliver, who had been at Cromer just the day before.[12]

Did Jack fetch Einstein on Mansura?
(Family collection)

Given the armed guard that was deemed necessary in Belgium and the following secrecy surrounding his whereabouts in England, travelling by public ferry seems a risky endeavour. Oliver had already deliberately fed the press misinformation about Einstein's location, and it is possible that instead of travelling by ferry, Oliver arranged for Einstein to secretly travel across the Channel in *Mansura*, Jack Delmar-Morgan's hybrid propulsion motor cruiser.

The Delmar-Morgans were an adventurous, seafaring family and, under Jack's experienced hand, he, Dolly and the children had cruised extensively on *Mansura* to Germany, Holland, France and the Channel Islands. It was easily within the capabilities of *Mansura* and Jack to have sailed over to Ostend and taken Einstein back to Ramsgate in a twelve-hour run.[13] Under electric propulsion, *Mansura* was silent, which was very useful for an unobtrusive and quiet arrival. It may also explain why, despite the apparent danger of remaining in Belgium, Elsa Einstein did not travel with her husband. At 32ft long, *Mansura* was comfortable for three but would have been a squash for four.

Following a night spent in London, Oliver's two lady secretaries, Barbara Goodall and Margery Howard, took turns driving the group to Norfolk while Oliver sat chatting with Einstein in the back seat. Eventually the group, armed with rifles, arrived at Oliver's Roughton Heath 'camp'.

The camp, in a corner of a field near Roughton in Norfolk, consisted of a collection of wooden huts with thatched roofs. Einstein was housed in one and another hut housed the 'guards', Barbara and Margery. Although it was simple accommodation, in the words of Oliver's son, Stephen, 'They were hardly "roughing it" as Oliver had a butler and a cook with him in the camp.'[14] There was a WC and kitchen and Oliver had water, fresh eggs and milk sent up every day from the nearby Hill Farm.

The land belonged to local farmers, Mr and Mrs Colman, who lived at Hill Farm with their three children, George, Beryl and Phil. The family had long been acquainted with Oliver and Mr Colman was particularly proud to be friends with the dashing commander. Oliver had a habit of popping up to Hill Farm during his visits and on one occasion he arrived with his secretary, local woman Miss Billings. The pair had been busy working on the song 'March On!', the anthem for Oliver's political movement, and knowing the family was musical, Oliver had come to ask for their help in putting the song together. Phil and his mother played the piano and violin while George and Beryl, Phil's siblings, sang the lyrics.[15]

Always one to spot an opportunity to promote himself in a good light, Oliver leaked information to the press and gave the location of the scientist as 'near Cromer', although it was not difficult for anyone to work out exactly where that location was. Several posed pictures were taken of Einstein by the local paper photographer, one of which showed him outside his hut with Oliver sitting on the ground to his side, upright, cross-legged and holding a rifle while Margery looked on. Behind them, keeping guard, is Herbert Eastoe, Oliver's bemused gamekeeper. Oliver sent Herbert to the Colmans to hire their pony for Einstein, which they gave him for 5 shillings a day.

Roughton Heath Camp 1933: (L–R) Margery Howard, Albert Einstein, Newhaven Court caretaker Tom Wilson, Oliver and Barbara Goodall. (Philip Colman, courtesy of Robert Nash)

As well as journalists, sculptor Jacob Epstein was brought into camp to capture a likeness of Einstein, and choice visitors, including Dolly and Jack's daughter Jane (who bought Einstein a replacement violin), were invited to meet the eminent professor. In addition to the lodgings provided at the camp, a room had been reserved at Newhaven Court where on several occasions Einstein was taken. He wandered the wooded grounds with Oliver and the two were spotted watching the tennis and walking, deep in conversation. Back at the camp, Oliver and Einstein sat up late into the night, conversing in German and discussing politics. A plan was forged to hold an ambitious meeting in the Albert Hall at the end of Einstein's stay.

All the newspaper coverage ensured that on the night of the meeting, the Albert Hall was packed to capacity with over 10,000 people. Oliver's exceptional organisational skills, in addition to his many and powerful connections, meant the evening was an enormous success. Austen Chamberlain spoke, followed by eminent scientists, before Einstein took the stand to make a speech to the crowd. Others, such as the prolific writer and orator Hilaire Belloc, had been invited but had to regretfully decline due to the short notice and a heavy workload.[16]

Oliver enjoyed his important temporary position as Einstein's protector, and letters flooded in requesting meetings. One of the letters came from Lord Baden-Powell, later famous for founding the Scout movement, asking if Oliver could arrange for a drawing to be made of the professor.[17] Unfortunately, requests were turned down as, just four days later, Einstein left England and Europe forever.

Barbara, one of the two lady guards, drove Einstein down to Southampton to see him off. With a lost look in his eyes, he said his goodbyes to his auburn-haired young guard, 'I feel just like a parcel. You met me, looked after me, and now you are posting me off.'[18] Rumours of apparent sightings of Einstein cycling around the Norfolk coast perpetuated for many years afterwards. In fact, the grey-haired, German-speaking gentleman the locals saw was Oliver's old friend Karl Ott, who continued to visit Cromer after the war.

The year 1933 had proved a tiring one for Oliver. Just a month after the Albert Hall meeting, he received the sad news that Augustine Birrell had died aged 83. Stubbornly, he had clung onto The Pightle until just a few months before his death, when a serious illness that left him less mobile forced his hand. It was a blow to Oliver to see the Sheringham house sold and his brother-in-law so ill.

The old man kept his humour until the end. The last time his stepson Charlie saw him alive, Birrell was sitting in a wheelchair, having become completely immobile. When Charlie asked how he was, the old man replied, 'The top half is alright,' putting up his arms in a defensive motion, 'but my legs are no good – I could fight but I couldn't run away!'[19]

Perhaps the stress of losing Maud so suddenly, the mental efforts of the summer Einstein visit and the death of Birrell affected Oliver physically, because over Christmas that year, while staying with friends, he was struck down by a violent bout of food poisoning that necessitated several days in hospital.

On Wednesday, 18 January 1933, Newhaven Court, the land, tennis courts and furniture were sold by Hammersley, Kennedy & Co. London auction house for £8,000.[20] The purchaser was 'Newhaven Court Limited'. Records with the precise details of individuals that made up the company are lost and it is difficult to determine whether Oliver kept any small shares in the business. A few years later, three directors are listed as William Foulder Smith, a baronet called Cecil Roll and the managing director, who was to take overall charge of the business and reside in the hotel.

The new resident managing director of Newhaven, ready to turn around the fortunes of the business, was an experienced and energetic Swiss hotelier, 41-year-old Maurice Pierre Berset. Maurice had managed hotels in Norfolk, first at the Royal Hotel in Great Yarmouth and then the Royal Links in Cromer, a 150-room hotel situated on the nearby heathery hills towards Overstrand. He had been married to his first wife, Bertha, in 1918 but the marriage fell apart and she later married a younger man, a barman from the nearby Hotel de Paris in Cromer.

Moving into Newhaven with Maurice was his younger, Surrey-born second wife Irene, then in her late twenties, and their 4-year-old daughter, Judy. Irene, who had lived in Overstrand from an early age, probably met Maurice when he was working at the Royal Links Hotel. Coming from an affluent background herself, the ambitious, enthusiastic hotelier impressed her. The couple had Judy in 1930 and married the year afterwards.

Oliver certainly knew Maurice, the two men having attended the same charity functions in Cromer, and he may have even approached him with the proposition. With many years' experience running large hotels, Maurice was the perfect man to take on Newhaven. 'His good spirits are infectious,' a hotel reviewer later wrote. 'His enthusiasm for good food and wine has no bounds. He can prescribe, produce and pilot us away from depressing thoughts.'[21]

If, indeed, he did suggest the purchase to Maurice, then it was also a pragmatic move for Oliver. The auction sale details that the property and land was bought freehold except for a small portion, about ¾ acre, which remained as leasehold. This was the freehold land on the plot of the tennis courts previously retained by Oliver after the syndicate had bought the rest of the property in 1927. By holding onto a small portion of the land and by having a resident managing director that he knew and trusted, Oliver could still arrange for his guests to stay at Newhaven.

Immediately Maurice tried to modernise the business. In February 1934, he made an application for a licence to sell alcohol on the premises. Oliver had made a similar application in 1927, which had been turned down, but Maurice argued that for a hotel that could accommodate 100 people, asking a porter to walk half a mile down the hill into town for whisky and soda was a great inconvenience. There was opposition by the Methodist Church, who objected on moral grounds, but a month later, Maurice was pleased to be granted a licence, although on the condition that there was to be no public bar.[22]

The Bersets' first large event was the April tennis tournament. Lunch and teas were laid on in the dining room and the ballroom was opened for late-night tournament dances. The next month, chambermaids, porters and waiters were hired, and advertisements appeared once more in the papers, promising first-class accommodation and service, excellent food served in the spacious palm court and charming grounds of woodland, rose and flower gardens to enjoy, all for moderate charges.

Electric fires were placed in every bedroom and damaged or old furniture and linen replaced. Mindful of the exceptional tennis facilities the hotel could offer, outdoor courts in addition to the indoor courts, a resident coach called Allan Lowpe was hired to maximise profit from the guests.

Not forgetting the importance of tasty food, Maurice brought over a chef from Soleure in Switzerland named Werner Otto (Bob) Gasche. Bob, a previous cruise liner chef, cooked the very best in Anglo-Swiss cuisine for hungry diners often using ingredients grown in the large kitchen garden on site. Guests could stay for one night, for bed and breakfast, or longer all-inclusive stays. Special terms were offered for parties or those looking for a semi-permanent home.

The family brought life and energy back to Newhaven, which had been lacking since the death of Bee. Maurice and Irene were determined to make a success of their business and the energetic pair laid on event after event to bring in the crowds. During their first summer, the couple managed to hire composer Jimmy Campbell to entertain at a special late-night dance. Extravagant Campbell was one half of a famous songwriting duo who used the pseudonym Irving King for their compositions, which included the familiar hits 'Show Me the Way to Go Home', 'Goodnight, Sweetheart' and 'Try a Little Tenderness'. It is likely these hits were played as the couples swept around the dancefloor.

A dance held on New Year's Eve 1936 was typical of the events Maurice and Irene held at Newhaven. The ballroom, filled with over 100 couples in fancy dress, was bedecked with special decorations and strung with glittering lights that twinkled as a band played for the dancers who spun around the

floor beneath. Mona Lewis & the Six Dancing Girls were brought on to entertain and there were competitions and prizes. Just before midnight, long-term
Newhaven caretaker Tom Wilson came in dressed as 'Father Time', complete
with a scythe. At the stroke of midnight and to the delight of the guests, little
7-year-old Judy Berset danced in to join Tom, dressed as 'Miss 1937'.[23]

Saturday night dances soon became a fixture at Newhaven. The couple
were sociable and could be found in the ballroom mingling with the guests,
where Irene showed off her prize-winning dancing skills. In the little time
she had for herself, Irene worked on a large tapestry of the house to hang
in the entrance hallway, a mark of pride the couple had in their new home
and business.

With the Bersets now running Newhaven, Oliver spent much of his
time close by in the camp at Roughton, enjoying the solitude and quiet. It
allowed him time to indulge his love of writing and he was often found in
one of the huts or his bell tent surrounded by his books or dictating to one
of his secretaries, who sat bent over a typewriter.

Tapestry of Newhaven Court, completed by Irene Berset, 1936. (Author's own)

Often harried and running late, Oliver hired Phil Colman from Hill Farm as a driver to ferry him to Cromer or Norwich. It often resulted in a memorable day. Phil later recalled an occasion when he was approached by gamekeeper Herbert Eastoe, who told him Oliver wanted to catch the ten o'clock train from Cromer to Norwich:

> About three minutes to ten, Locker would fly out his tent, leap in the back and Herbert would jump in front with me. Locker would yell 'drive on, drive on, faster, faster!' all the way to Cromer station. We went like hell in the 1927 Morris Cowley, only one wheel had a brake.

After reaching the station in record time, Oliver would jump out shouting, 'Bravo! Well done!' before leaping into a first-class carriage.[24]

Oliver was still keen to invite his special visitors to stay at Cromer and in the same year, along with Barbara Goodall, the secretary who had seen Einstein off at Southampton, he was at Newhaven to greet the golden-haired royal, 13-year-old Prince Philip of Greece. Following the overthrow of the Greek monarchy in 1922, Philip had spent much of his childhood being moved from one house to another, relying on the generosity of family and friends. Oliver, who had put up such a show in 1926 for Philip's cousin, King George of Greece, was happy to offer a home to the young prince for the holidays and consulted with Berset to house Philip in one of the chalets in the grounds.

In a foreword to *The Czar's British Squadron*,[25] the Duke of Edinburgh recalled his stay at Newhaven Court in the summer of 1934. He remembered Oliver vividly and suggested that the visit had made a great impression on him. During his stay, Oliver pulled in a favour and asked King George of Greece to persuade Philip to give out prizes at a charity event he had organised in benefit of a relief fund for the families of the 1934 Cromer crab boat disaster.

On 27 July 1934, a little crabbing boat called *White Heather* had set off from Cromer. In the boat were brothers-in-law Charles Cox, who was 57, and Gilbert Mayes, aged 62. Both men were members of the Cromer lifeboat crew with over thirty years' experience and both had received medals for gallantry. When the boat was a mile or two from shore, the weather changed and, in what was later described as a sudden gale, the sea hit the boat hard on the starboard. Before the vessel could right herself, another wave hit and the boat capsized, hurling the two men into the water. The sudden shock of being immersed, combined with the heavy crashing waves meant the two men immediately began to struggle.

The whole event had been witnessed by a member of the lifeboat crew who had been keeping watch and the lifeboat was launched immediately. As members of the public crowded the pier to watch the spectacle, the boat raced out and found Cox floating face down near the boat. There was no sign of his brother-in-law.

Cox was hurried back to the pier, where resuscitation was attempted. He made it to hospital but died later that day. Mayes was lost at sea.

The disaster sent shockwaves through the town. Accidents and drownings at sea were unfortunately not uncommon, but for the sea to take two such experienced and revered men was unthinkable and troubling. Concerts and subscriptions followed, raising money for the bereaved families. For his part, Oliver organised a gymkhana, a day of horse-riding events and competition. Alongside Prince Philip giving out the prizes, he also used his extensive contacts to persuade ex-Foreign Secretary and Nobel Prize winner Sir Austen Chamberlain to officiate.

Prince Philip of Greece, later HRH The Duke of Edinburgh, at the gymkhana fundraising event arranged by Oliver, for the families of the White Heather disaster victims, 30 August 1934. (Mary Olive Edis, Cromer Museum/Norfolk Museums Service, CRRMU: 2008.14.209)

It is easy to imagine the teenage blond prince exploring the wooded grounds at Newhaven. The house stood as grand and solid as the day it was built fifty years before, but by the 1930s Newhaven was surrounded by numerous outbuildings, huts, garages and the covered tennis courts. Ivy had crept up the walls, softening its once harsh new brick, and the trees planted by Frederick were now thick and lush to give welcome areas of shade. Perhaps Philip walked down the drive, past the gatehouse lodge and left onto the Norwich Road that led into town to visit the lifeboat station on the pier or to look for fossils on the beach. He was an athletic young man and undoubtedly took advantage of the tennis facilities and the opportunities to bathe in the Cromer waters.

Barbara had taken part in one of the charity equestrian events and, by this time, she and Oliver were in a relationship. After the death of Bee, Irish playwright George Bernard Shaw had written to Oliver, 'So you are a widower. That is the worst (or the best) of marrying angels: they soon fly away. Be content with a comfortable plain woman next time.'[26]

Oliver did not heed his advice for, in December 1935, he married the attractive, red-headed Barbara in Blarney Church in Ireland.[27] As when he married Bee, the wedding was a quiet affair and Barbara was simply attired in a brown travelling suit with matching hat, accompanied by nothing except a bouquet of chrysanthemums. The official reason given for the quiet ceremony was due to family bereavement. Frankie Birrell, the small, energetic, radical and witty son of Birrell and Eleanor, died in January 1935, having shared the fate of his mother, suffering for over a year with an inoperable brain tumour. Soon after, Lalla, Godfrey's beloved wife of nearly three decades, died in March 1935 after a long illness.

The following August, Oliver and Barbara were waiting at Cromer Station to greet the arrival of an old friend, Princess Louie, who had come to stay for a week. It was arranged that she would stay at Newhaven but take some meals with Oliver and Barbara at the Roughton Camp. The princess was given the finest accommodation in the house, the corner turret room named aptly the Royal Suite, which afforded a grand sea view. Godfrey was at the camp, along with Jack and Dolly's youngest daughter, Jane. Eight days later Louie left, holding a bunch of orange carnations given to her by little Judy Berset, who waved her off at the station along with Maurice, Irene and the Locker-Lampsons.

✻　✻　✻

Oliver remained one of the most outspoken and independent MPs and as the Nazi policies of anti-Semitism became more radical, so did so Oliver's campaigning. In 1936, he arranged a town meeting at Ealing, where he started a relief fund. 'I think it is the most caddish thing to persecute people because of the blood in their veins,' he told the crowd. Over £400 in donations flooded in.[28] Articles were written for papers to stir up public interest in the issue. In 1938, after allegedly having been called a 'Jew and a communist' by Adolf Hitler himself, he again sent a series of telegrams directly to the Führer, telling Hitler if he must bully people then 'chose someone bigger than himself'.[29]

By 1938, Oliver ramped up his efforts to remove as many Jews out of the Nazi-occupied areas as possible. Despite lukewarm public opinion, he pressed ahead with forming the Polish Jewish Refugee Fund (PJRF) with Left-leaning MP George Lansbury. The fund soon turned to fundraising in aid of the Kindertransport movement, which was government facilitated but privately funded and by 1940 had helped over 10,000 unaccompanied children to escape Nazi-occupied areas and come to the UK. He spent hundreds personally sponsoring others to get to the UK and accounts exist that show he was assisting families who were in desperate need of help and had been turned away elsewhere. Jack and Dolly also took in Liesl and Elizabeth, two girls who came over as domestic servants, an occupation that allowed Jewish adults to legally enter the country.[30]

Oliver was back in Cromer in August 1939 again to greet Princess Louie, who had come for a stay at Newhaven. He accompanied her up the hill to the hotel, where they met Maurice and Oliver's niece, Jane Delmar-Morgan, who had become a frequent companion to Oliver and Barbara's little sons.[31] As soft clouds glided overhead, the group enjoyed tea on the patio in warm sunshine and conversation turned to the recent burglary at Newhaven, where a thief had stolen over £7 worth of takings from behind the bar.[32] Later in the day, Oliver and Jane went back to the camp where Barbara and the boys were staying.

Oliver was gaining a reputation around this time for his increasingly eccentric antics. Phil Colman recollects an occasion when he drove Oliver from Cromer to Norwich Station to catch a train. Having only just made it to his seat in time, Phil watched Oliver take a seat and remove his hat, underneath which was a revolver, which he then placed on the seat next to him! 'No one will come in here!' Oliver laughed, before telling Colman to tip the porters before the train left in a puff of steam.

Another summer when Oliver was with another secretary, Miss Billings, he fancied some pheasant shooting and made a deal with the Colmans to shoot on their land. Off the group went, Oliver with a gun, Miss Billings beside him and Herbert Eastoe with Phil Colman. On seeing a pheasant rise, Oliver fired both barrels at it. Herbert would say, 'You've hit it Sir, it's gone down over the hedge.' Away Herbert would go and then return with the pheasant in his hand. 'Well done, Sir, I knew you'd hit it,' he said, showing the pheasant to Oliver, who gave him a shilling tip. However, what Oliver did not realise was that Eastoe had a large inside pocket in his jacket where he had hidden a dead pheasant and rabbit in advance of the shoot. Herbert later told Phil, 'I have to do this, as he can't hit a haystack.'

Sometimes at harvest time, Oliver would go down to the farm where ten or so men were hard at work. 'Throw up your hats!' he would yell. As they did so, he fired at the hats, shot after shot. He told Phil to give the men whose hats he had shot money in compensation. All the men cried, 'mine's got a hole in!', at which Oliver would be tremendously proud and pay out, never realising he had never hit a single hat.[33]

Little did the happy family group who gathered at Newhaven and in the huts on the restful landscape of Roughton Heath that warm summer of 1939 realise that it would be the last happy time they would spend in Cromer together. As Oliver played high jinks with little son Jonathan, his niece, Jane, who was close to them all, laughed and took some pictures, capturing the family in time.

However, storm clouds were gathering overhead and the second horrific world conflict in twenty-five years was on the horizon. It would ultimately end the Locker-Lampson association with Cromer and Newhaven Court.

Jane Delmar-Morgan on a visit to Newhaven Court, 1939. Next to her is probably Maurice Pierre Berset. (Family collection)

Oliver with his son Jonathan (Jack), Roughton Heath Camp, 1939. (Family collection)

NOTES

1 Dorothy Delmar-Morgan to Oliver Locker-Lampson, Norfolk Record Office, OLL2723/1-79/323X5.
2 *Eastern Daily Press*, Tuesday, 1 November 1932.
3 Letter to the manager of Newhaven Court (family collection).
4 Oliver Locker-Lampson, military record, National Archives, ADM337/118/109.
5 The grandmother of Jack Delmar-Morgan was Louisa Thomas, granddaughter of wealthy Jewish banker Benjamin Goldsmid.
6 *Leeds Mercury*, 1 April 1933.
7 *Birmingham Daily Gazette*, 11 December 1933.
8 Death certificate of Maud Fisher-Rowe.
9 Source: Jane Madden, née Delmar-Morgan.
10 Andrew Robinson, *Einstein on the Run: How Britain Saved the World's Greatest Scientist* (2019) p.249.
11 Stephen Locker-Lampson, *Nothing to Offer but Blood*, p.240.
12 Stuart McLaren, *Saving Einstein: When Norfolk Hid a Genius. The Double Life of Oliver Locker-Lampson* (2021). p106.
13 *Mansura* could average 5 knots and was known to achieve 7–8 knots when required. She could run for fifty hours at a stretch. Ostend is approximately 50 n.m. from Ramsgate, which is a twelve-hour run. Information courtesy of Miranda Delmar-Morgan.
14 Stephen Locker-Lampson, *Nothing to Offer but Blood*, p.243.
15 Philip Colman recollections, courtesy of Robert Nash.
16 Letter from Hilaire Belloc to Oliver Locker-Lampson (family collection).
17 Letter from Baden-Powell to Oliver Locker-Lampson (family collection).
18 Stephen Locker-Lampson, *Nothing to Offer but Blood*, p.244.
19 Charles Tennyson, *Stars and Markets*, p.136.
20 Approximately £600,000. Source: Bank of England Inflation Calculator.
21 *Illustrated Sporting and Dramatic News*, 6 March 1942.
22 *Eastern Daily Press*, Tuesday, 6 February 1934.
23 *Eastern Daily Press*, Saturday, 2 January 1937.
24 Philip Colman recollections, courtesy of Robert Nash.
25 Bryan Perret and Anthony Lord (1981).
26 Stephen Locker-Lampson, *Nothing to Offer but Blood*, p.242.
27 Barbara Goodall was aunt to English primatologist Jane Goodall.
28 *Middlesex County Times*, Saturday, 30 May 1936.
29 *Coventry Evening Telegraph*, Saturday, 25 June 1938.
30 Jane Madden anecdotes.
31 Oliver and Barbara had two sons, Jonathan Hawke and Stephen Reginald Vermont Locker-Lampson.
32 *Eastern Daily Press*, Friday, 7 July 1939.
33 Philip Colman recollections, courtesy of Robert Nash.

12

Conflict

At a quarter past eleven on the warm Sunday morning of 3 September 1939, families in Cromer and all over the country gathered around their wireless sets to listen to the address by Prime Minister Neville Chamberlain. In sombre tones, Chamberlain informed the people of Britain that Hitler had failed to respond to demands to leave Poland and therefore the country was at war with Germany. It was a desperately bitter blow to Chamberlain, who remembered the horrors of the Great War first-hand and had done everything in his power to avert another conflict.

Following the five-minute broadcast came a series of announcements that were frightening enough to send a shiver through those listening. Civilians were warned not to crowd in public places except for church and all places of entertainment were to close with immediate effect. Details were given as to what should be done in the event of an air raid siren.

Dreadful as it was, the news was not unexpected, and the government already had detailed war plans in place. Following Hitler's invasion of Poland two days previously, a scheme to evacuate schoolchildren was initiated with immediate effect. By the time Chamberlain addressed the nation, children from towns and cities considered danger zones were already on their way to safer areas, including Norfolk.

It is plausible that Maurice Berset and his family were listening to the broadcast at Newhaven Court, but however he heard the news, he certainly would have immediately understood the implications not only for his family but his business. Within a stroke, the tourist trade dried up and visitors already at the hotel started to check out. One must also presume the telephone would have been busy with others cancelling their bookings.

Though fearful for their jobs, staff were kept busy in assisting with the imposed safety measures, taping glass to prevent shattering and creating blackout materials for all the windows. It was a mammoth job for a house that had been designed with so much glass to maximise its scenic views. All exterior lights were turned off and outside pleasure buildings, the courts and the ballroom were plunged into darkness and locked up. Although those housed in the hotel could have used the cellar in the event of a bombing, it is likely the fitter, younger members of the hotel staff were tasked with digging out an area to house an air raid shelter in the grounds for those living in the chalets or caught outside.

Petrol was immediately put on ration and staff were ordered to always carry their gas masks. Soon after, handbills, flyers and the news warned the town's population of a census to be taken on the night of 29 September 1939. The register, which recorded every living person in the UK, was to be used to monitor the population and to issue identity cards. With streetlights turned off, civilians were warned to be extra cautious in the blackout, staying near to buildings or the kerbside to avoid disorientation. There was a degree of panic buying of essential items. Nightlights, candles and black paper all sold out and people quickly began to hoard food items such as tinned foods, sugar and jam.

When war was declared, Oliver, who had been with Princess Louie in Cromer just a fortnight before, rushed back to London, where he was needed in Parliament. The 1939 register captures him staying at the Charing Cross Hotel in London. Never a man to shy away from danger, Oliver may have stayed in one of the upper floor rooms, which because of the risk of air raids, perhaps afforded him luxury at a cut price.

Alongside Oliver, but in one of the safer basement rooms, was his wealthy but notorious rogue criminal cousin, Sir Curtis George Lampson, grandson of the first Sir Curtis and nephew of Janie. Described by author Matthew Sweet as 'the most aristocratic con artist of his generation', Curtis got himself into hot water by telling the other young men in the hotel that 'a commission in one of the less bullet-pocked parts of the armed forced could be theirs – for a few fat envelopes of used oncers'. Swindler Curtis was caught out by the police and MI5, who had been secretly monitoring his transactions.[1]

Although not swarming with aristocrats and Cabinet ministers, Newhaven was soon to host a visitor who was remarkable as one of a team of eight brave and talented women who broke into a field of war work previously only undertaken by men. Winifred Crossley was born Winifred Harrisson in the year 1906, one of twin daughters, the second and third of five children born to Doctor Ernest Harrisson and his wife at St Neots. Ernest had achieved minor celebrity status in 1935 as the doctor who delivered the world's first surviving quadruplets.

Winifred, known to her family as Winnie, was ambitious and sporty, growing into a talented tennis player, at one time representing Bedfordshire at the sport. At the age of 20, the tall, dark and athletic Winnie married James Francis 'Frank' Crossley, and three years later gave birth to their only child, John James.

When John was still very small, Winnie and her twin sister, Daphne, trained as pilots at the Norfolk and Norwich Aero Club, then based just outside Norwich at Mousehold Heath. By 1935, she was the owner of a De Havilland Gipsy Moth I.

Winnie was fortunate to have a bank balance sufficient to support an interest that was barred to so many others, but she quickly showed real talent. In September 1936, she was performing stunt aerobatics in an aerial circus capturing the attention of local press. 'Mrs. Winifred Crossley provides one of the most amazing features of the display,' said one reviewer of the circus. 'She is the first acrobatic pilot, and although she has only been flying for two years, she has reached a surprisingly high standard.'[2] In the years leading up to the war, she worked in air publicity, towing advertising banners. Just a month before the war, she wowed audiences with a display of aerobatics in her Tiger Moth, looping, spinning and rolling through the air with ease to raise money for charity.

By September 1939, she was living separately from her husband and the 1939 register records her staying in Bedfordshire with Daphne and her housekeeper, Margery Gregory. However, within a couple of months, Winnie and Margery had moved temporarily to Cromer and into suites at Newhaven Court, organised as a favour by Oliver.[3] It is likely that the Harrisson family had met Oliver during his time spent as an MP for Huntingdon. Winnie's twin Daphne had been interested in Oliver's political movement and was friendly enough with him by 1930 to borrow his two-seater Buick, which she used to drive herself to his meetings.[4]

Winnie was soon headhunted by the War Office for her flying skills and may have moved to Newhaven Court while awaiting communications from the War Office. She was sent official paperwork, which was promptly filled in, with Margery Gregory acting as a witness to the signature. Both put Newhaven Court as their home address. Winnie had probably stayed at Newhaven before, while playing tennis for Bedfordshire or perhaps as a guest of Oliver. It is tempting to imagine her in one of the little second-floor rooms, keeping warm by the little electric fire, wistfully looking down at the courts and wondering what the next few months and years would have in store for her.

The organisation that had head hunted Winnie was the Air Transport Auxiliary (ATA). The ATA was set up on the outbreak of the Second World War, designed to assist the war effort by ferrying aircraft, personnel and medical supplies. Initially, the ATA recruited qualified pilots who were unfit for regular service in the RAF or Fleet Air Arm due to reasons such as age or physical disability. However, very quickly, the ATA found it necessary to recruit anyone with flying experience and soon began to look to women to fill the vacancies.

Pauline Gower, daughter of an MP, had been fascinated by flying from an early age and by the tender age of 21 was an accomplished pilot. With Dorothy Spicer, the first woman to gain an advanced qualification in aeronautical engineering, she founded an air taxi and joyriding service in Kent. On the outbreak of war, 29-year-old Gower was tasked to set up a women's section of the ATA and by December 1939 she had formed a ferry pool of eight female pilots, including Winnie. The talented 'first eight', as they became known, were appointed on New Year's Day, 1940.

Cromer soon rallied from the initial news of war and, in support, events were held to raise money for the well-being of the troops. In March 1940, a licence was granted to Mr Harrison, proprietor of the Regal Cinema, to hold a special showing on Good Friday evening in aid of a fund for the comfort of local soldiers. Maurice Berset decided to follow suit and applied successfully for a licence extension to host a dance in the Newhaven Court ballroom.

The licences were granted as, despite the lengthy preparations, there was initially no aerial bombing and so little fighting that the period started to be dubbed 'the Phoney War'. Civilians began to leave their gas masks at home and many evacuees returned home. Cinemas were reopened and there were a decent number of Easter visitors to the town, which cheered local shopkeepers.

However, fighting soon intensified and in April 1940, Germany invaded Denmark and Norway, followed by Belgium, Luxembourg and the Netherlands in May. By June, Hitler's tanks were in France. With the Nazis just across the Channel, the war became suddenly frighteningly close and real. Having initially been an area of refuge for evacuees, worried officials now saw Norfolk as a danger zone and on 2 June 1940, evacuation started from Cromer.

Servicemen and women flooded the area. Local hotels were quickly requisitioned by the government, including Newhaven Court. The Bersets would have been given notice of requisition in early 1940. Valuable furniture and equipment were swiftly moved out of the property to be safely stored elsewhere in Cromer for the duration of the war and military equipment, camp beds and personnel moved in. The Bersets moved into one of the small cottages on site, next to Newhaven's gardener Ernie Griffin and his wife. The kitchen garden would have been put to beneficial use and enlarged to help in the 'Dig for Victory' campaign to help feed the troops billeted at Newhaven.

Ernie, David and Lenny, the three sons of gardener Ernie Griffin, in wartime uniform outside the Griffin cottage at Newhaven Court. (Courtesy of Philip Griffin)

The number of serving personnel quickly altered the fabric of the town. Traders reported worrying cuts in takings, made significantly worse when the order came in June 1940 that it would now be an offence for anyone to arrive in Cromer for the purpose of a 'holiday, recreation or pleasure'. The pretty and elegant seaside resort was now stripped of visitors and reduced to a military base for troops.

Due to its proximity to Europe, Cromer was considered a likely target for bombers. Pillboxes, guns and air raid shelters sprung up along the cliffs, replacing the grassy scenic views with concrete and ugly rolls of barbed wire that stretched along the beach. Worried that it could be used as a potential landing area for invading German troops, the Royal Engineers sectioned the pier without considering the lifeboat station located at the furthest end. Hastily, the gap was bridged with planks that could be easily removed in the event of an invasion threat.

The Battle of Britain of July 1940, a fight for the supremacy of the skies, brought the war to civilians' doorsteps. Those staying at Newhaven would have heard the deep rumble of heavy bombers and fighter aircraft, both enemy and friendly, that flew through the skies above on their way to and from the Continent. Unwilling to fly back to Germany with bombs still on board, one German Dornier 217, returning to base in the early hours of 11 July, dropped a stick of bombs on Cromer, which landed on a newsagents, killing Edward Munday and his sister, Elizabeth. The plane then flew across the town, machine gunning indiscriminately.

London was bombarded that summer, and in November the same year a German bomber hit Central Road in Cromer. One explosive dropped on to a bedroom at No. 18, killing young Doris King instantly. Another raid, with several fatalities, on 11 April 1941, saw the Lyndhurst Hotel at the bottom of Alfred Road destroyed. Servicemen were killed in the hotel as well as Mr Jillings at No. 7, who was rescued but died later in hospital.

It was sobering news for the Bersets, who for the duration of the war made their home in the thatched cottage in the grounds of Newhaven. The position of the hotel on an incline must have made them feel particularly vulnerable, although living on a large plot of land had its benefits. It is likely they were well fed with fresh vegetables from the large kitchen garden and they also had beehives for honey. The wooded areas housed rabbits, pheasants and pigeons, which would have been easy to catch and would have been a welcome supplement to the family's weekly rations.

Clearing up the damage in Church Street, Cromer, Norfolk, after an air raid in July 1942. (H.H. Tansley, Cromer Museum/Norfolk Museums Service, CRRMU: 2003.18.162, courtesy of Tansley family)

Although not directly bombed, the Bersets did suffer a fire themselves on the morning of Wednesday, 5 March 1941. It is not known what started the blaze, which took hold in the thatched roof of the cottage, but the fire crew was quickly in attendance and managed to subdue the fire before nightfall.[5] For Irene Berset, who had been alone in the cottage when the fire started, the damage was another hurdle to overcome.

They were not alone in coping with fire. Cromer suffered several more bomb attacks and small raids as well as sporadic machine gunning. One of the most devastating raids started around midnight on the night of 22 July 1942, when a string of bombs hit the town centre, just missing the church. The Rounce & Wortley shop was destroyed on the corner of High Street and Church Street as well as Thurgarton Dairy. Several people were killed, the church was damaged, and areas of the town were reduced to rubble.

Another serious raid occurred on 19 October in the same year, which came within touching distance of Newhaven Court. A bomb was dropped on Norwich Road, hitting a house belonging to Dr Vaughan. Thankfully, he and his children escaped injury as they were out at the time of the blast, however, Mrs Vaughan and her housekeeper were inside the property, which was destroyed. Both survived, although the two decorators working on the site were not so fortunate.

The constant threat of aerial bombardment, food and fuel rationing and the curtailing of rights took their toll on the frayed nerves of the people of Cromer. Some townsfolk were constantly on edge and terrified of a German invasion, while others took the fatalistic attitude of staying in their beds during a raid, believing that they were just as safe there as anywhere else.

The war had also taken its toll on Cromer itself. The town was ravaged and completely altered from the happy holiday resort of a decade earlier. Previously bustling streets were largely deserted, and the buildings were battle scarred and neglected. Instead of a beach of golden sands, huge rolls of barbed wire stretched along the shore.

The D-Day landings of 6 June 1944 came at an enormous human cost, but they were successful in pushing back the German armies. By September 1944, the desperate Germans deployed a new weapon – missiles known as V2 rockets – but by the end of the month, with the Allies advancing through southern Holland, the only area the rockets could now reach was Norwich. On clear days, it was possible to stand on the Cromer cliffs and see the rockets being launched.[6] During the next month, those in Cromer read frightening reports about the indiscriminate bombings around the city, praying that their town would not be next.

The raids could not last. As the retreating German armies were surrounded in May 1945, Victory in Europe was declared. Wild street parties and celebrations followed, and troops billeted in the town's hotels, including Newhaven Court, ripped down the blackouts in ecstatic delight, piling the wood and paper onto huge bonfires. Further celebrations followed in August when the imperial armies of Japan surrendered, bringing an end to the conflict.

Oliver had spent the war volunteering in the Home Guard while still vigorously campaigning on behalf of the Jews. He was also still working as an MP for Birmingham, Handsworth. Though well into his sixties, he stayed physically fit, even starting a fist fight with a political opponent after a verbal war in the House of Commons. He was, however, scared of bombs and moved around the country in an attempt to outrun the danger. Though Oliver, Barbara and the two boys escaped injury, bombs found them, one dropping near Barbara as she lay taking a bath.[7]

The Bersets had also survived the war, as had Newhaven Court. As troops began to leave the town and life gradually began to return to normal, those left behind started to look to the future. Although the conflict was at an end, rationing continued, parts of the town were reduced to rubble and the economy was shattered.

In September 1945, Prime Minister Clement Atlee announced a special 'Thanksgiving Savings Week', an appeal to raise funds to a target of £125 million to assist in rebuilding Britain and bolstering the shattered post-war economy. Atlee made a speech to drum up support for the cause. 'The achievement of victory was not the end but the beginning,' he told the beleaguered nation. 'Until better times come to us, it is our duty to save all we can and devote our savings to the task of peace.'[8]

For the first time in over five years, Newhaven Court was opened to the public for events in support of Thanksgiving Savings Week. The ballroom doors were flung open and the cobwebs dusted away, ready for a carnival dance on 24 September 1945. It was a bright, colourful celebration in contrast to the drab grey of post-war Cromer.

Another dance was organised by the Women's Institute, followed by a Suffield Park Girl Guides whist drive. Local advertising stated that all events were to raise money for the Thanksgiving Savings Week, to save enough money to 'bring our lads home and rebuild the nation'.[9]

The Thanksgiving Savings Week events were to be the last the Berset family would hold at Newhaven. Early on during the war, Maurice and Irene may have experienced trouble in their marriage and much of Maurice's war was spent at a hotel in East Grinstead, Sussex, leaving Irene and Judy in Cromer. Perhaps this is where Maurice met Marjorie Hill, who he later married in late 1946.

As Newhaven was de-requisitioned and troops left Cromer, the estranged couple had nothing left to hold on for, and by Christmas 1945 they had decided to move on. As a new year dawned, lawyers were consulted, and preliminary auction advertisements appeared in newspapers.

Newhaven Court was to be sold furnished, and considerable time was spent by agents going from room to room listing the furnishings and contents. A large, detailed brochure, along with an inventory of furnishings, were drawn up for interested parties and by February 1946, in exceptionally mild weather, the family were busy packing their belongings to move out of Newhaven Court forever.

From such a promising start more than a decade before, Maurice and Irene divorced and went their separate ways. Maurice continued as a hotelier until his death in London in 1952, at the age of 58. Recorded as 'death by misadventure' by the coroner, Maurice had been resting after having consumed a fine meal with his latest fiancée, Gloria de Maria, when he was seized with convulsions. For such an optimistic, charismatic and sociable man, Maurice died a lonely death on the way to hospital, choking on his own vomit following heart failure.[10]

After her divorce from Maurice, Irene also moved swiftly on and left Cromer for London with Judy. Like Maurice, she stayed within the hotel trade and by 1946 she had settled down with her second husband, another Swiss hotelier and manager of the Ritz, Eduard Schwenter.

NOTES

1   Matthew Sweet, *The West End Front: The Wartime Secrets of London's Grand Hotels* (2011) p.133.
2   *Northern Wing*, 3 September 1936.
3   Information courtesy of Terry Mace.
4   *Peterborough Standard*, 23 May 1930.
5   *Eastern Daily Press*, Wednesday, 5 March 1941.
6   George Baker recollections.
7   Jonathan Locker-Lampson recollections.
8   September 1945, Prime Minister Clement Atlee.
9   *Eastern Daily Press*, 24 September 1945.
10 *Marylebone Mercury*, 11 January 1952.

13

The Last Dance

O n 15 March 1946, the same day long queues formed in a Norfolk village to buy the first bananas for sale there since the war, crowds were gathering at the premises of London auctioneer William Ridgway.[1] Those in attendance that day witnessed the sale of Newhaven Court for £27,650.[2] The purchase included the fully licensed hotel, with its magnificent public rooms, including drawing room, dining room, restaurant, atmospheric walnut-panelled, vita-glass palm court with bar, sun lounge, kitchen, staff room, offices and twenty bathrooms with hot and cold running water. Outside, in 10 acres of timbered, mature grounds, were a hotel annexe, guests' flats and chalets, the detached, thatched bungalow, maple-floor ballroom, twelve lock-up garages and the world-famous tennis courts with space for 2,000 spectators. All contents, including the furniture and linen, which had been carefully stored elsewhere in Cromer during the war, were included in the sale.

The successful bidder at the auction that spring morning was ambitious businessman Roy Walter Marsh, proprietor of many London houses, including The Mitre at St Martins Lane, a busy pub in London that he had owned since 1944. Newhaven was one of several hotels bought up after the war by the entrepreneur, who was looking to take advantage of the depressed post-war prices.

Though the auction catalogue clearly outlined the leasehold plot of land held by Oliver, a later record shows that the land was reverted to freehold, suggesting this piece of land was sold to Marsh, either at time of sale or shortly after by Oliver.[3] How Oliver felt about the sale is unknown, although we must assume his feelings would have been mixed. Presumably, he would have been sorry to see the Bersets moving on as the couple had run the hotel so successfully prior to the war. Though he had not lived at Newhaven

Court or his Roughton Heath camp in several years,[4] he must have felt sad to let his link to his old family house go entirely, his last attachment to so many happy memories of his family and his early life. Cromer had always held a special place in his heart, and for many years he had considered the town his home. But war had come and swept away the old, leaving a new and very different world. His nieces and nephews were now grown up, most with families of their own, his sons were away for much of the time at boarding school and his marriage to Barbara was strained. Perhaps he felt there was little in Cromer to hang on to.

He was also now retired and living on a reduced income, which caused him considerable financial strain.[5] Always on the fringes of his political party, his behaviour during the war had become increasingly disruptive and markedly more eccentric and outspoken, leaving him an isolated and sometimes disliked figure in the Commons. His fixation on Hitler and his campaigning for the Jews, though admirable, came at the cost of speaking on local issues. Gradually, the electorate support, which had always come so easily to him, began to wane and in May 1945 he was deselected by the Conservative Party. Though declaring he would stand as an independent MP, he withdrew before the election, fearing defeat. In the same year, his great friend Winston Churchill was ousted from office in the first election since the war.

As the new owner and director of Newhaven Court, Marsh employed Mr Howard Smith to manage the day-to-day running of the hotel. Marsh had taken a gamble that the summer would see a boom in visitors wanting a holiday after years of war. He also planned to reinstate the autumn tennis championships, which were always a draw. Advertisements were placed in the newspapers and Newhaven was set to open again in July 1946.

Hired staff busied themselves getting the hotel ready for the new summer visitors. Like many other hotels requisitioned during the war, the billeted troops had caused some damage and there was minor maintenance work to be completed before guests arrived. In addition to getting the hotel in good order, Smith found running such a large hotel in an era of post-war rationing posed certain problems. Essential items that were needed to run the hotel, chiefly soap and linens, were hard to come by. A government order of March 1946 made it an offence to serve bread with a main meal, except if specifically asked for by a guest, and the situation worsened in July 1946 when bread was rationed for the first time. There were rigidly enforced allocations of fuel and power and though petrol for private use had become available, it would still be rationed until 1950.

Newhaven Court after the war showing the 'vita glass' dining court and the detached ballroom. The roof of the indoor tennis courts can be seen behind the trees. (Courtesy of Anna Jansz)

It was not just Mr Smith who was struggling to reopen a business. Having no industry and heavily reliant on its summer tourist trade, in June 1946, the Cromer Urban District Council held an urgent meeting to discuss post-war recovery plans for the town. All felt it was imperative that Cromer should be ready for the 1946 season, hotels repaired and made ready, as well as clearing the clifftop walk of barbed wire, minefields and gun encampments. Many also suggested it was important, moving forward, that the town had indoor recreation space to 'hold on' to its summer visitors.

Ideas put forward included plans for winter gardens, a conference hall, boating lake, swimming pool and sports hall. Despite wishing to modernise, the plans were not actually for turning Cromer into a regular seaside holiday destination. The local press reported on the meeting the following day, remarking there was to be 'no fun fair, no cockle stalls and none of the rude delights of plebian popular Yarmouth' and 'Cromer intends to retain, as far as possible, in this noisy age that distinction which earned it modest fame as a resort of the well to do'.[6]

Somehow, Smith muddled through. July arrived and with it came the British summer weather, with thunderstorms and rain over much of East Anglia. But there were fine spells, and the first summer trade at Newhaven was considered successful. By late summer, the courts were being prepared for the first hard-court indoor tennis championship since 1939 and Mr Smith reported to the papers that there had been much interest and a good entry for the competition.

As the year wore on, Newhaven continued to attract guests and bolstered its income with functions such as the one in December when the dining room was filled with eighty ex-servicemen and women, who were entertained at the expense of the Appreciation Fund. T. W. Abbs, the committee chair, gave a speech and toast to the 'returned'.

Soon after Christmas, the weather turned bitterly cold, and the winter of 1946–47 would go down in history as one of the coldest on record. The notorious winter freeze saw two months of blizzards and snowfall, hitting a nation already struggling in post-war austerity. Cromer, like the rest of the country, suffered from frequent power cuts, which would plunge Newhaven into darkness. Always prone to chilliness, even in fine weather, a huge fire was lit in the dining room to try and warm the house from within, although a nationwide coal shortage crisis made this difficult.

In contrast to the perishing winter, the following summer saw a severe drought, following a long August heatwave. As with other long spells of hot weather, folks rushed to the beach and Cromer was full of visitors looking to eat ice creams and cool down in the clear waters. Bookings must have come in for late summer stays as the hotel was still busy enough in September to warrant advertising for extra staff.

It was the start of the heyday for the great British seaside holiday. Most people holidayed at home, and week-long breaks had become more affordable and possible through paid annual leave, thanks to the Holiday with Pay Act of 1938. Visitors from across the country flocked to Cromer by car and train to stay in the numerous guesthouses, hotels or B&Bs. In all weather, deckchairs and windbreaks were carried down to the beach or hired, allowing the adults to relax while the children dug in the sand, explored the rockpools and paddled in the sea. Pier shows, long walks on the cliffs or a film at the cinema filled the evening hours.

Despite the wartime bombing, Cromer Council had achieved its aim of retaining its pre-war image of attracting more upmarket visitors. Newhaven, which still sat resplendent in its large grounds, could offer a guest more than just a bed for the night. It offered a real haven, tucked away from harsh post-war austerity and the bomb-damaged streets below, and guests did not necessarily have to leave the beautiful estate during their stay. Those who wanted to stay closer to their accommodation enjoyed walks through the cool, wooded areas of the estate, carefully looked after by the gardener Ernie Griffin, where they could stop to picnic in dappled sunshine or hire a court for the afternoon for a spot of tennis.

Gardener Ernie and his wife Violet, both now around retirement age, were long-established residents of Newhaven, still living simply in the three-bedroom gardener's cottage on site. Ernie was a keen sportsman and life member of Cromer Football Club, winning many honours for his team. Violet was a wonderful cook, and their three sons always enjoyed the dinners in the pleasant little cottage.[7] As Violet pottered around the kitchen, Ernie kept up the courts and tended to the lawns and kitchen garden. In fact, Ernie's work in keeping the kitchen garden meant that vegetables and fruit from the garden and honey from the ground's beehives supplemented what meagre supper fare most hotels at that time could offer and any excess was canned for winter use.

By 1948, Mr Smith was replaced as manager by Mr White, who continued to provide the best food possible for his guests, once landing himself in court for his endeavours, having been charged with failing to keep stock of rationed food and obtaining eggs without a permit. The horrified manager pleaded that he had honestly believed he could buy the eggs and that the stress of the situation had made him ill. Director Roy Marsh was not happy when the company was blamed for not supervising their manager and were ordered to pay a large fine of £455.[8]

In its large, leafy grounds, with its interesting history, imposing architecture, world-famous tennis courts and magnificent interiors, Newhaven was still looked to by the people of Cromer as an unrivalled space in which to hold functions. When a new Cromer and North Norfolk Festival of Music and Dance was announced, the organisers looked to impress the audience on its opening night by holding the first events in the dining room at Newhaven. Four years later, the festival, which had started small at Newhaven, had grown into a much-anticipated and enjoyed annual event.

As the forties made way for the fifties, Sidney and Blanche Welham replaced Mr White as resident managers. Sidney had married Norfolk-born Blanche May Rudrum in 1922, before having daughter Joan in 1923, followed by Brian on New Year's Eve, 1938.

One of the upstairs guest bedrooms at Newhaven Court. (Taken from Newhaven Court brochure, courtesy of Roy Boyd-Stevenson)

The experienced hoteliers, both in their early fifties, were under instruction to only open Newhaven during the warmer months, so for a portion of the year the house was unoccupied. During the dark winter months, young Brian found the big house 'lonely and scary'. He frequently ran the poorly lit path that led through the gardens to the hotel as fast as his slim frame would allow, his imagination running riot about what might be lurking in the shadows.

The summer months, in contrast, were full of happy memories, playing on the outdoor croquet pitch, watching the rabbits and pheasants or playing tennis on the indoor courts, although they tended to get uncomfortably hot in the warmer season. Bright and intelligent, Paston Grammar schoolboy Brian showed talent as an angler. He frequently walked the ten minutes to the pier, where he would set up to fish off the end, once catching a tope that was so large it made the local papers.[9]

✳ ✳ ✳

Nearly a decade after the end of the war, the demolition of urban slums and the many left homeless after the bombings meant the country was facing a housing crisis. More houses were needed than ever before, and quickly. Sensing an opportunity, in December 1954, Director Roy Marsh put forward a proposal to the County Planning Authority and Cromer Urban District Council to develop the 10 acres of the hotel estate. The proposal was for fifty-four houses with estate roads. Faced with some disquiet from the local community, Marsh tried to scale down his plans to a local reporter, saying there was no question at this stage of pulling down Newhaven and, if permission was granted, Marsh thought he may 'build perhaps twenty-five small, good class houses', but added ominously that if there was demand, he might consider 'full scale development'.[10]

The plans were turned down. Frustrated and demoralised, Marsh closed Newhaven and the Welhams were given notice that the hotel was to be offered for sale. Marsh informed property dealer Goddard & Smith of St James Square, London, that he intended to put Newhaven along with another eight of his hotels up for auction. Though an attractive brochure was produced, listing the particulars, interest proved lukewarm. On a bright spring day at the end of March 1954, the auction began, but disappointingly the reserve was not met and Newhaven Court remained unsold.[11]

With no sale and the building plans stalled, Marsh actively looked around for offers. In March, it was reported that the Royal Hospital Board was interested in using Newhaven as a hospital for chronically sick patients, but again, the idea never came to fruition. Later that month, businessman Frank Thrower of London approached Marsh with an offer that was accepted, and the ownership of Newhaven changed hands once more.

Although Thrower quickly reopened the hotel to recoup some money, throwing open the doors for Saturday night dances, he had bought the estate with the idea to turn the grounds into a site for 100 caravans. When those plans were turned down in December 1955, Thrower closed the doors again in frustration. 'My protracted unsuccessful negotiations have been both costly and frustrating, so much so that I have decided to cut my losses,' he told a local paper.[12] He tried once more, the following month, with some support from respected coxswain Henry T. Davies, the nephew of Cromer lifeboat hero Henry Blogg. Davies, who had initially been appalled by the idea of a caravan site, had changed his opinion and spoke in support of the plans. 'Cromer is going downhill,' he said. 'I do not want to see another derelict hotel.'[13]

Davies' words were in vain. Newhaven was closed, awaiting a new owner.

❊　❊　❊

Having expected for some time that Newhaven would close, Sydney Welham had been looking for other work. In the early summer 1955, he was offered the post of manager at the substantial mid-Victorian East Anglian Hotel in King's Lynn and the family packed their bags. Their teenage son, Brian, was disappointed that his days angling from Cromer Pier were over and he missed the blue sea and green lighthouse hills.

On Boxing Day, 1956, aged just 17, lured by sunshine and green pastures, he sailed for New Zealand as a 'ten-pound pom' on an immigrant passage. Landing in Wellington in February 1957 with just £15 in his pocket, Brian quickly made a new life on the other side of the world. Sydney and Blanche Welham retired in 1967 and Brian remained in New Zealand.[14]

As the Welhams started their new life in King's Lynn, a family 5,000 miles away in New Mexico, USA, were considering their next moves.

In early 1955, Elton Joseph Lowell, a member of the United States Air Force, was transferred from his base in the sunny climes of Sandia, New Mexico, to the US base at Sculthorpe in north Norfolk, England. He had left behind Anna, his wife of two years, three young stepsons, Arnie, Phillip and Lee, and his baby daughter, Nesha. He missed them dreadfully.

Once settled, Elton began to make immediate enquiries to find his wife and children a home nearby so they could join him in England. Johnny Bullock, a civilian friend working on the base, told Elton of a house he knew was available on the old Newhaven Court estate in Cromer, just over 20 miles from the base. The house available was the Boulton & Paul gate-house lodge, on the driveway by the Norwich Road. With four bedrooms, a bathroom, cosy sitting room and open kitchen-diner, Elton felt the thatched cottage, though a little chilly, was perfect for his family.

Anna was told to pack, and in the winter of 1955, she and the children boarded the US Naval ship *Geiger* and made the choppy journey across the Atlantic Ocean. Elton met his family at Southampton and after a welcome meal and night in a hotel, the family made their way to Cromer.

As Anna familiarised herself with the cottage, the children explored the grounds of Newhaven Court. The three young brothers ran in and out of the dense, wooded areas opposite their cottage, crunching over a thick bed of pine needles, before stopping to stare at the grand house above them. They were told by their mother not to venture near the property but were happy, nonetheless, to stay in among the trees. Phillip, just 7 when the family moved in, remembers the grounds, describing them as 'a gigantic yard idyllic for us four children to play'.

Over the next eighteen months, the children made friends and settled down to life in Cromer. Phillip, his brothers and friends spent the happy months of 1956 roaming the grounds picking buttercups, climbing on the horse chestnut tree and picking blackberries to satisfy their sweet cravings. Occasionally, they ventured through the woodlands at the back of the house until they found an open field with another grand house, Cromer Hall, where the children agreed, 'the Queen lived'.

The winter of 1956 turned cold, and as snow fell, the children enjoyed snowball fights in the grounds and kept warm by running races with their dad up the gravelled drive. It was the last winter the family stayed in the property, and although the time they spent in Cromer was short, the happy memories remain.[15]

Arnold, Phillip and Lee Shaw playing in the snow in the grounds of Newhaven Court, 1956. (Courtesy of Phillip Shaw)

During their stay at the gatehouse lodge, the Lowells never saw anyone else living on the site except for Ernie the gardener, but as the family moved out in spring 1957, a deal had been made with a new buyer to open Newhaven Court once more. Charismatic London entrepreneur Harold 'Bill' Alfred Towle, described by his daughter as a man who was 'good at making money, but better at spending it',[16] was next to take a gamble in turning around the fortunes of the hotel.

Ex-paratrooper Bill, dark haired, broad and standing at 6ft 4in, towered over his petite and gentle red-haired wife, Josie, and had a larger-than-life personality to match his height. Intimidating on first impression, those who became more familiar with the entrepreneur found him lively, adventurous, fun and engaging. Bill was a risk taker and his numerous ventures had seen his family experience a roller coaster of the high life alternating with periods of relative hardship.[17]

While working for the Hille Furniture Company, Bill had met an American serviceman, who planted the idea of a transit hotel for serving men and their families coming to England. Presumably, he saw Newhaven Court for sale and made an offer.

In late November 1957, Bill, Josie, their children, 13-year-old Anna, 10-year-old Philip and their loving little dog left their three-bedroomed council house and drove to Cromer. Heading down the Norwich Road, past the railway station and towards the town, the family saw the sea stretching out before them on the horizon. All were longing to reach their new home and the atmosphere in the car was one of excitement mixed with trepidation.

As they approached the tennis club on the right, the car slowed and swung a left through two brick posts and past the gatehouse lodge, before travelling up the long, tree-lined, sweeping gravel drive to Newhaven Court. Parking directly outside the front porch, the family entered the grand entrance hall. Anna was immediately taken by the 'amazing, huge house', and she and little Phillip, with his red, curly hair, bounded with excitement through the hotel, exploring the ground-floor dining room with its large fireplace, original oak-panelled rooms and modern commercial kitchens before running up the staircase, where they found a further two floors containing twenty-three bedrooms stuffed full of furniture. Running in and out of numerous doors, they soon found a rundown annexe extension of another twelve bedrooms and four apartments that had been used for billeted troops during the war.

Above left: *Harold Alfred 'Bill' Towle and his wife, Josie. (Courtesy of Anna Jansz)*

Above right: *Philip Towle outside Newhaven Court. Philip and his sister ran wild around the house, sleeping in a different bedroom every night. (Courtesy of Anna Jansz)*

Outside they found that the front brick steps leading down to the gardens were broken in places and in need of repointing, but they opened onto an attractive, grassed area and a path that led down a slope through the wooded area towards the Norwich Road. The mature grounds were full of trees and shrubs and as the children ran around the outside of the house, they came across the overgrown outside croquet and tennis courts. A pretty rose garden, left bare in the autumn sunshine, was next to a paved sitting-out area that led on to the locked-up ballroom. There, they found the stage and maple-sprung floor in need of cleaning and repainting. Chalets standing in an L-shape nearer the Norwich Road on the bottom of the estate were also in a poor state and considered uninhabitable, the cost required to fix them up being inhibitive.

Around the back of the hotel they found the kitchen garden, and then before them stood the marvellous indoor tennis courts, arguably the star of Newhaven. Through the entrance they found the changing rooms, lounge and the spectators' galleries that, in comparison to the outside courts, had been well looked after.

Initially, just Josie, the children and 'Bosoms' the dog occupied the house. Anna and Philip enjoyed exploring every corner, often sleeping in a different bedroom every night. Anna's favourite was the pretty corner turret room. Though initially closed to paying guests, the tennis courts were opened for business and Josie made some extra money by serving teas out of the ground-floor commercial kitchens.

Instead of running Newhaven as a hotel, which had not proved successful in recent years, Bill had been in negotiations with the USAF to develop his idea to let Newhaven to US servicemen who were in transit between America and the US base at Sculthorpe. The suggested plan was for Newhaven to accommodate the families of men who had finished their tours of duty in the UK and had given up their accommodation pending transport for their return home. Similarly, the hotel would accommodate new arrivals until suitable flats were found, serving as 'a welcome mat to Europe'.[18]

The initial five-year lease contract was signed on 3 January 1958. A clause in the paperwork, designed 'as a gesture of Anglo-American friendship', ensured members of the local British Tennis Club would be permitted to use the tennis courts.

Keen to make money from his purchase, before he brought his family to Newhaven, Bill had approached local Cromer building firm H. Bullen & Son in the late summer of 1957 to discuss plans to put forward to the Cromer Urban District Council to develop 4 acres of the estate on the southern boundary abutting the Fletcher Convalescent Home.

Founded in 1895 by carpenter Herbert Bullen, the business had a reputation for thoroughness and hard work and was well respected in the town. This may have helped the preliminary plans to be initially approved in October 1957 and with funds secured from the future building plans, Bill set about giving the 75-year-old house a much-needed makeover. Electrics and plumbing were overhauled, and the house redecorated.

By the end of January, Newhaven was opened once more and, shortly after, the Americans, in their large, shiny cars, came rolling up the hill to take possession. USAF Sgt Ferdinand Peche was the resident manager, the only military man assigned to the hotel, which employed fifteen Cromer locals.

Peche thought of everything to make the lives of transient USAF families more comfortable, including a supervised playground, tree-shaded grounds where children could play away from traffic, a putting green, croquet court, an all-night formula service for babies, a laundry room with washing machines and a full entertainment programme. Swimming was encouraged in the warmer months and all year round, Peche had two 35ft pleasure boats for inshore fishing and cruising for the sole use of the hotel's occupants. The services that Peche provided, as well as the low-cost rooms and calm and restful atmosphere of the hotel, made 'travel weary airmen and their families perk up after their long trips'.[19]

With development plans in place and the Americans occupying the hotel, Bill and his family moved into the two-storey cottage on the grounds near to the tennis courts. It was far from luxurious accommodation, compared to the hotel, for the cottage had originally been the stables, but it was quaint and comfortable. Spacious living rooms were on the ground floor and a set of stairs with a rope banister took the family to their sleeping quarters. Bill and Josie were in the largest bedroom and the two children had a smaller bedroom each. Anna's bedroom window in the old stables faced the church and when she woke in the mornings, she could see the time on the clock tower.

It was the start of an incredibly happy period for the family. Both children enrolled at local schools and began to make friends in town, especially pretty, dark-haired Anna, who found she soon made friends among the local teenagers from all diverse backgrounds, who socialised together 'happily and easily'.

Jenny Scally, daughter of a Cromer hotelier and niece of Cromer fisherman Shrimp Davies, became a best friend, and the two girls spent many happy hours together. Occasionally, they would help Jenny's mother with her grocery deliveries, or on a warm day, the two girls would head down to a mutual friend's beach hut, where they would congregate with other teenagers to laugh, chat and swim. Another favourite hangout was the coffee bar in town.

Friday nights were reserved for an evening at the roller drome and Saturday afternoons for a cinema matinee. Most afternoons after school were spent knocking a ball back and forth on the tennis courts, and sometimes they would sneak into the spectators' gallery to watch a well-known player at practice, particularly when the handsome junior Wimbledon ace John Baker was there.

Bill was a sociable man and Anna found her friends were always welcome back to Newhaven, where they would be cooked for by her father. In Anna's words, 'it was a wonderful, innocent teenage life'.[20]

Anna Towle (right) with her best friend, Jenny Scally. (Courtesy of Anna Jansz and Jenny Scally)

The family were also involved in running the hotel. As well as preparing meals for his daughter's friends, Bill cooked for the Americans. Josie worked tirelessly to look after the hotel and, in addition to this and the demands of looking after two children, continued to make some extra money by selling teas. Anna and her best friend Jenny were at times called upon to babysit the children of the Americans, something they did not enjoy, although occasionally they were given chewing gum and comics, which made it bearable. Anna also worked briefly as a waitress but found the work monotonous and dreary.

The staff in the hotel became good friends with the Towles – Bob and Poppy Murray, who helped to run the hotel; Frances, a waitress; the local kitchen porter; and another waitress, Shirley Flower, known as 'Blossom'. Blossom, who cheered everyone with her pretty smile and 'optimistic spin on life', was simply delightful company, becoming a good friend to Josie and a regular fixture at the Towles' cottage.[21]

Ernie Griffin, the gardener, was still living with Violet in their cottage, but now in their late seventies, they enjoyed a simple life. There were frequent visits from grandchildren, dinners by candlelight – for the cottage had no electricity – and time was spent feeding the tame little blackbird affectionately named 'Peter', who hopped around outside.[22]

His predecessors having failed, Bill Towle was making a success of his business at Newhaven and by September 1960 he was putting forward plans to develop a further part of the estate into housing fourteen new bungalows. But a disaster was looming for the Towle family.

Around 3 a.m. on Saturday, 21 January 1961, Charles O'Regan, the night porter, heard a crackling noise. On investigation, he saw one end of the indoor tennis courts on fire. O'Regan ran back inside to call the Fire Brigade, but by the time they arrived the entire 150ft roof was fierce mass of flames. Thirty firemen worked tirelessly, using five different water jets to stop the fire spreading to the outbuildings and ballroom but were hampered at times by low water pressure.

The Towles had also awoken to crackling and had immediately evacuated their accommodation. By this time, red embers were floating over the town and the blaze could be seen from Sheringham. Locals woken by the commotion and noise wandered up the hill towards Newhaven. Anna stood in her pyjamas with her friend, watching the blaze with her devastated parents.

The tennis courts had a metal frame but wooden walls and a glass and asbestos roof. Once alight, they were almost impossible to save. The courts had been in use just the evening before the fire and the resulting loss to county and national tennis was considered severe.

Over the following week, Towle weighed up his options while waiting to hear back from the insurance company. 'Naturally, I would like to see the courts back again. Their loss was a great blow,' he told reporters, although, he added 'everything hinges on finance'.[23] Contractors were called in to assess the work needed to rebuild the courts, various quotes coming in between £27,000 and £48,000 – huge sums. 'I have our own architect designing something of a less ambitious nature,' he added a few weeks later, 'but no decision has been made.'[24]

The cause of the fire remained unclear, but upon learning that couples sometimes used the courts as a late-night rendezvous, the Fire Brigade proposed a theory that a carelessly discarded cigarette may have accidentally started the devastating blaze. In fact, soon the family were to learn the devastating news that they would not be receiving any compensation for the loss of the courts, which now sat as a ruined mass of twisted and burned metal.

By March, Bill Towle made the decision to sell. The purchaser was established, family-run local building company A.G. Brown. The firm had already been involved with building the small bungalow estate of Newhaven Close, which ran along the southern boundary and future plots of land were rumoured for imminent development.

The Towle family packed up and reluctantly left Cromer, the town where they had made lifelong friends and so many happy memories. Soon after, they moved to Ipswich, where Bill opened the first tenpin bowling alley in town.

It may have been the tennis court fire that earmarked Newhaven Court to be one of the six US military hotels in Europe to be shut down by the Pentagon, who were looking to trim defence spending abroad. In May 1961 came the decision from Senator Al Gore that Newhaven Court, along with several military hotels in Germany and France, were to be closed with more on the list to be closed later. Gore had criticised the 'ridiculously low rates' charged by the hotels.[25]

The twisted ruins of the covered tennis courts. (Courtesy of Anna Jansz)

Given notice that Newhaven would be closed, the twenty-four English staff, cooks, waitresses, cleaners and barmen were facing unemployment. 'I suppose we shall have to look around for other jobs,' one told the local paper at the end of May 1961.[26]

The next month, Newhaven was busy with cars and trucks as the Americans packed up and moved out. As the last people left the building, the American connection with Newhaven, which had started with Sir Curtis Lampson eighty years before, was severed forever.

NOTES

1   *Eastern Daily Press*, Friday, 15 March 1946.
2   Approximately £1.2 million. Source: Bank of England Inflation Calculator.
3   1954 auction catalogue, 'Terms of Sale', Cambridge University Archives.
4   The Roughton Camp had been requisitioned for military use during the war.
5   Stuart McLaren, *Saving Einstein: When Norfolk Hid a Genius. The Double Life of Oliver Locker-Lampson* (2021) p.204.
6   *Eastern Daily Press*, 13 June 1946.
7   Philip Griffin recollections.
8   *Eastern Daily Press*, 19 July 1949. Approximately £17,000 Source: Bank of England Inflation Calculator.
9   Brian Welham recollections, 2022.
10 *Eastern Daily Press*, Friday, 7 December 1954.
11 1954 auction catalogue letter, Cambridge University Archives.
12 *Eastern Daily Press*, Wednesday, 11 January 1955.
13 *Eastern Daily Press*, Tuesday, 13 March 1956.
14 Brian Welham recollections.
15 Philip Shaw recollections.
16 Anna Jansz recollections.
17 Anna Jansz recollections.
18 *USAF Stars and Stripes*, Wednesday, 22 January 1958.
19 *Ibid.*
20 Recollections of Anna Jansz and Jenny Scally.
21 Anna Jansz recollections.
22 Philip Griffin/Jacqueline Regis recollections.
23 *Eastern Daily Press*, Saturday, 21 January 1961.
24 *Eastern Daily Press*, 15 February 1961.
25 *USAF Stars and Stripes*, Thursday, 25 May 1961.
26 *Eastern Daily Press*, Thursday, 25 May 1961.

14

Fire and Ice

The beginnings and endings of all human undertakings
are untidy, the building of a house, the writing of a novel, the
demolition of a bridge, and, eminently, the finish of a voyage.

John Galsworthy

When the news was announced that Newhaven was to be closed once more, new owner Albert Woodrow, of A.G. Brown Builders, was approached for comment. 'Will you demolish Newhaven?' asked the journalists. 'I haven't thought that far ahead,' replied Woodrow.[1]

As the builder deliberated, Newhaven Court stood empty. For nine months the estate was quiet, until in spring, as golden daffodil buds emerged from the cold sandy soil, Newhaven unexpectedly found a new owner.

Ambitious Violet Boyd-Stevenson, previously proprietor of The Swan in Harleston, saw an opportunity and signed a contract with A.G. Brown. Violet hoped to use her experience to turn a good profit as manager and Newhaven Court was handed a lifeline and reprieve from likely demolition.

Cromer folk were pleased to hear the hotel would be occupied once more, albeit surprised, as many assumed the hotel would be knocked down to develop the prime building land. Newhaven, still resplendent in its Victorian elegance, increasingly looked like an anachronistic misfit on the landscape. Encroaching on the southern side of the hotel boundary was a development of newly built houses, alongside a block of chalets facing the road to the east.

In late May 1962, Violet and her family, husband of eighteen years, Donald, and her sons, Ian, 15, Christopher, 11, and Roy, 9, packed their possessions and travelled 45 miles north from Harleston, south of Norwich, to Cromer. Initially, they settled into the cosy accommodation in the grounds that had recently housed Bill, Josie, Anna and Philip Towle.

Violet had met Donald during the Second World War while both were serving in the Royal Air Force. Violet was a warrant officer and Donald a bombardier and senior squadron leader. Donald was much taken by Violet, with her pretty dark hair and interesting background, for although she was raised in Britain, her father, Antonio Guitard, had been an Argentinian Consul, who had moved his family from Buenos Aires to Newcastle in 1919 after being posted to the UK. Donald and Violet had married toward the end of the war in 1944, settling initially in Hertfordshire where their eldest son, Ian, was born, three years later.

The couple immediately set to work getting the hotel ready to receive guests. Staff were hired, linens washed, the exterior was stripped of ivy and the window surrounds were given a fresh coat of white paint. The hotel reopened just in time for summer. Though the star indoor tennis courts were no longer part of the property, Newhaven proved it still had the power to draw in a crowd and the holiday season that followed was hectic. Rooms were full of visitors determined to enjoy all the attractions Cromer had to offer – golden sands and refreshing sea bathing, scenic walks along the cliffs, skating at the roller drome, model railway, entertaining shows on the pier and the floats and fun of the summer carnival. The American-style, sprung maple-floored ballroom remained an added attraction and was considered by many locals to be the best dance floor in town.

The family had settled down to life in Cromer and made friends in the town. Donald had an interest in the RNLI and the lifeboats, helping him to make connections with the locals. The children were mixing well at school, and for the carefree younger boys, Christopher and Roy, living at Newhaven was simply 'paradise'. The old-fashioned house with its spacious bedrooms seemed an endless maze filled with grand staircases, endless nooks and crannies and large outbuildings, affording plenty of space to run and play games such as hide and seek and tag. Outside, the wooded area sloping down to the road was ideal for climbing the large horse chestnut and pine trees, sledging, playing bows and arrows and other fun adventures.

Cromer in the late 1950s. The Regal Cinema is on the left. (Courtesy of Phillip Shaw)

Occasionally, the boys helped their father prepare for a dinner party by plucking chickens in the large industrial kitchens at the back of the house. At other times, they joined their father wandering through the town streets to the beach, where they watched transfixed when a lifeboat was launched. An aunt who lived nearby kept a boat on the Norfolk Broads and happy days were spent playing in the boat or trying to spot monstrous coypu among the reeds – the large rodents were once a common sight in the waters around East Anglia.[2] For Roy, especially, it was a fun time, making many happy memories with his parents and brothers.[3]

At 15, Ian experienced a somewhat different life at Newhaven to his little brothers. Donald had insisted his son leave school to help in the hotel, despite Ian showing promise as a talented young architect. This was not unusual at a time when older children were not consulted by adults but deemed quite capable of bringing in additional income or assisting in the family business. Much of Ian's time was spent in monotonous hotel work, pot washing, waiting on tables, lighting the huge hall fire and scrubbing and polishing the guests' shoes, which were left outside the bedroom doors for him to clean. This last job, the most hated of all, must either be done late at night or, conversely, very early in the morning, leaving Ian with little free time for the normal teenage pursuits.

Violet was upset when her eldest son missed his exams and successfully persuaded her husband to allow Ian to join a day-release catering course at the City College in Norwich. Once a week, Ian walked the ten minutes to the station to catch the early train.[4]

Despite it being hard work, the family's efforts paid off. As the green leaves of summer turned to burnished shades of orange and then fell in the cool autumnal breeze, the family looked back on a successful summer season, the first, they hoped, of many to come.

As the weather cooled and the summer crowds frittered away, the quieter evenings were filled with wedding receptions, anniversary dinners and parties. Every Monday evening, young people flocked to Newhaven for 'teenage night' to dance away to the latest rock 'n' roll tunes played by the band Tony and the Starbeats. A popular part of the evening was the Twist Championship, which involved couples competing against each other in a dance-off. The victor was reigning champion until the following week, when they would be challenged by others.

The cosy wood-panelled hotel bar also continued to attract a steady flow of the older locals, some of whom were residents of the neighbouring houses. Relations with the neighbours were cordial, so much so in December 1962 that the residents of the eleven properties at Newhaven Close, mostly retired older couples, were invited to dine together up in the 'big house' in the spirit of neighbourly friendliness.[5] The hardworking and respectable Boyd-Stevensons were proving a valuable addition to the town and locals were grateful to see the hotel occupied and thriving.

The winter that followed proved unusually severe and the coldest since 1947. Snow started to fall in Scotland on Boxing Day 1962 and by January, every part of the country was either dowsed in thick coatings of snow or frozen in ice and remained so until March. Newspapers were full of shocking headlines – a milkman freezing to death behind the wheel of his float in Essex, postmen delivering letters on skis and a car driving across the frozen Thames.[6]

Closer to home, locals spoke of the ice in the shallows of the Cromer sea and the story of one little girl who had opened her bedroom window to clear the ice only to find a wood pigeon frozen solid in the tree outside.

Black ice covered the streets of Cromer, making travel perilous. Those who risked walking had to hang on to rails and fences to stop themselves sliding over and others who would normally cycle to work were instead forced to catch an overloaded bus.

At weekends, the more adventurous older children travelled to the Norfolk Broads to enjoy the novelty of walking across the frozen waters, while families wrapped up warm before heading to the nearby hills of Happy Valley to career down on homemade sledges, crashing into the icy bracken below. Those with a little spare cash headed to the popular coffee bar in town or queued around the block to catch a film at the Regal Cinema – the feature playing that January was the epic *Lawrence of Arabia*.

The morning of 22 January started like any other for the Boyd-Stevenson family. There was school for the younger boys and for Donald and Violet the prospect of a busy day ahead. Running a large hotel meant there was always work to be done, and by late afternoon on that chilly, dark Tuesday, Donald, Violet and the children were all home and sat together enjoying their well-earned tea in the hotel lounge. Following the cold spell, the family had moved from the summer cottage in the grounds into the attic rooms of the hotel in an attempt to save money on soaring heating bills. All appreciated the large, crackling fire that warmed the room.

Newhaven c. 1960, after the sale and redevelopment of estate land on the southern boundary for modern housing. (Courtesy of George Baker)

While the family were quietly eating their dinner, they had no idea of the developing disaster unfolding upstairs. An electrical fault, probably caused by old, brittle wiring, had caused a small fire to start in an airing cupboard packed full of blankets and quilts. Within seconds, choking black smoke and heat filled the cupboard, before rapidly moving through a pipe duct to the roof. As the fire grew hotter and more intense, nearby flammable furnishings and objects ignited. Long-forgotten dry papers, boxes and furniture in the roof space curled, crackled and combusted, adding to the growing inferno. Just minutes passed before the glass windows shattered, allowing bellowing flames and thick, hot, noxious smoke to pour from the roof.

The fire was quickly spotted by those nearby and, before long, a man rushed into the hotel lounge to warn the family. Donald and Ian immediately ran upstairs to check what had happened, only to find, in abject shock, their whole living quarters ablaze. They were unable to even get close and were quickly beaten back. Running back downstairs, they found Violet and the younger boys, who were standing outside in the grounds staring up at the smoking roof. Little Roy, just wearing a pair of pyjamas, was extremely upset at having to leave all his new birthday presents inside.

Jamie Edghill, a young fireman from Cromer, just 19 years old, was nearby with his crew in a fire appliance when the call came through to attend to the fire at Newhaven Court. The firemen were returning to base, having spent the afternoon tackling a chimney fire in a house next to the village school in Gresham. They were passing the Lion's Mouth at Aylmerton when the call came through on the radio informing them of the fire. The driver put his foot on the accelerator, and they raced to get back to Cromer.

As the fire engine thundered over the railway bridge, a low cloud of smoke appeared, hanging and drifting over the town. Many Cromer locals, alerted by the acrid-smelling smoke and the sound of sirens, started to gather on the streets outside their houses. Most stood in the cold, exchanging excited commentary with their neighbours, and some began to walk up towards the hotel.

As Jamie's fire engine pulled up at Norwich Road, a crowd stood shivering outside, including the shocked Boyd-Stevenson family. The crew quickly established that the building had been evacuated and the family was safe. In addition to the fire crew, an Eastern Electricity engineer turned up, called out by HQ to cut through the mains electricity supply. This caused a short delay before the fire crews could start tackling the inferno, which was now well out of control, the entire roof now furiously ablaze. 'Flames and sparks' were seen leaping 50ft into the air, illuminating the dark Cromer sky.

Despite his thick uniform, the cold took Jamie's breath away. The crew, already exhausted from tackling the earlier fire, immediately leapt into action. Jamie was told to link up the hose with the water mains. He took the standpipe, key and bar down to the hydrant on the corner of Cliff Avenue and Norwich Road. He tried desperately to get the lid off, but it was frozen absolutely solid.

Jamie ran back to the fire appliance, grabbing a sledgehammer. Despite his strength, it took a long time to smash the frozen hydrant lid and connect the hose, finally securing the water supply for the pump. Soon after, Jamie was pulled off hydrant work and ordered to go inside the hotel to tackle the fire directly, alongside his fellow crew mates, Dennis Green and Geoffrey Newland.

This order was equally terrifying and dangerous. The entire roof was ablaze with scorching, furious flames and there was a real risk of structural collapse. Choking black smoke, sometimes described by firefighters as 'pea soup', due to its density, bellowed from the crackling fire, seriously reducing visibility. Under these challenging conditions, the three men dragged a length of heavily charged hose line, slowly making their way up to the second floor, taking care to keep close to each other and clinging to the walls to avoid disorientation.

As they reached the seat of the blaze, they turned their hose onto the flames, resulting in blasts of burning steam coming back at them. Sweat ran into their eyes and down their backs as they stood with their hose directed at the roaring fire.

The three men were totally unaware that the lower staircase had been set alight by burning debris falling from the roof, potentially risking trapping them on the burning upper floors. Luckily, this developing hazard was spotted by the other firemen on duty, who began shouting at the three to get out and to get out quickly. Jamie later recalled, 'We had to make a quick getaway – that was the fastest we had moved all day. We jumped through the flames and fled outside through the door.'[7]

Joining with the other men, they began using the jets from outside the building, directing it up 50ft to the flames in the roof. Keeping control of the hose was very difficult as the men found themselves sliding on the black ice. This was exacerbated by the returning hose water freezing to the ground beneath them and causing their wet tunics to set solid, making it physically difficult to bend.

By this time, the initial two Cromer tenders had been joined by appliances from nearby Mundesley, Holt, North Walsham, Sheringham and Aylsham. Senior officers arrived, including Chief Fire Officer W.M. Ward. Many of Cromer's citizens stood watching from their windows and doorsteps as hot embers and black smoke blew over the town. As far away as East Runton, parents piled their children into cars and drove to a spot to get a good view of the commotion. The blaze eventually became so fierce it turned the night sky a fiery red.

As the shocked Boyd-Stevensons left the scene, given a bed for the night by the local fishmonger, fire crews battled through the night to prevent the fire from spreading to the lower floors. By daybreak, the exhausted men had gained the upper hand and by 10 a.m., a relief crew from Acle arrived, enabling some of the men to go home and rest. Firemen stayed on site for the rest of the morning dampening down the gutted roof.[8]

If they managed any sleep at all, Donald and Violet must have awoken dazed and confused. The fire had started in the attic quarters – their living space. They had lost not only their residence but also many items of real and sentimental value: toys, clothes, cash, photo albums, important documents and irreplaceable treasures.

Later that morning, wearing borrowed sets of clothes, Donald and Violet walked back up to Newhaven to assess the damage. Although the crews had been praised by senior officials for successfully managing to contain the fire to the top floor, the entire roof of the building was a gutted, smouldering wreck, with blackened, charred rafters and attic quarters open to the elements.

The weather was still bitterly cold. The Acle crew had remained on site, busy undertaking salvage work. At some point, they had been joined by assessors, who were there to gauge whether any repairs were possible, but it was still far too soon to tell. As with every situation of this kind, a fire investigation crew was also called in to inspect the building and try to determine a cause.

Experienced investigators confirmed that the fire had started on the first floor inside the airing cupboard and had originated from an electrical failure.

Unbelievably, the electricity and gas supply were reconnected to the ground floors in time to open the bar that very evening. The external advertising lights were turned back on to show it was business as usual. In an interview with an *Eastern Daily Press* reporter, Donald praised the 'great job' the emergency services had done in getting them back up and running. He further stressed that the twelve or fifteen visitors to the bar that evening were 'regulars and not sightseers'.[9] However, despite this initial show of optimism, the situation was dire. Although the fire had been contained at the top of the building, the damage extended to the entire house. Even in the rooms that were untouched by flames, the intense heat had caused the paint to blister, softened the window glass, charred the wood and caused hidden structural weakness. The ground floors and bedrooms were sodden and the original wood panelling in the downstairs bar was drenched, buckled and ruined. The water damage further compromised the structure and foundations, and the resulting damp would quickly lead to mould. Although much of the elegant furniture on the ground floor was unaffected by the fire, a sizeable quantity was unsalvageable, having been damaged by water or smoke, the odour proving impossible to remove.

The family had no choice but to stay on site until the decision was made that the hotel was beyond any economical repair. Two months after the fire, on 29 March 1963, an auction was held to sell the remaining property and contents of Newhaven Court.[10] Rescued items, including oak desks, dining and writing tables, antique mahogany wardrobes, three-piece suites and sprung mattresses were all listed in the catalogue, as well as 120 blankets and numerous eiderdowns, twenty large Axminster carpets, table cutlery and plate, catering and industrial kitchen equipment and one baby grand pianoforte.

Albert Woodrow and A.G. Brown Builders bought the property back from the Boyd-Stevensons.[11] Picking themselves up from the disaster, the family took the proceeds, a modest sum from the furniture sale and presumably some insurance money, and moved out of area to Hastings on the Suffolk coast to run another pub.

By the winter of 1963, under the direction of builder Albert Woodrow, workmen and machines strode and rumbled up the long, sweeping gravel drive to the empty wreck of the once grand Newhaven Court. Over the following weeks, the rear half of the building and annexe were pulled down to make way for a block of flats.

A crane with a wrecking ball was brought in to topple the red-brick chimney stacks. Trucks came to haul away the rubble, crunching over smashed windowpanes as they drove in and out of the site. Men with chainsaws arrived, come to clear several 60ft trees to make way for an access road, and eventually the last of the rubble from the foundations was removed.

Unlike the previous winter, the weather was generally clear and dry, and Albert Woodrow was making steady progress on site under the interested eye of the town's news reporters. In February 1964, a headline appeared in the local newspaper, 'Old Cromer making way for new'.

NOTES

1   *Eastern Daily Press*, Thursday, 25 May 1961.
2   Native to South America, the coypu could reach 3ft in length and weigh up to 9kg. They were brought to Norfolk in 1929 and bred in captivity for their fur. Following heavy rain in 1937, some coypu escaped and began to breed in the wild. By 1962, with numbers considered out of control, they were subject to an eradication scheme.
3   Roy Boyd-Stevenson recollections.
4   Ian Boyd-Stevenson recollections.
5   *Eastern Daily Press*, Thursday, 13 December 1962.
6   Juliet Nicolson, *Frostquake: The Frozen Winter of 1962 and How Britain Emerged a Different Country* (2021).
7   Jamie Edghill, *Cromer Fire Brigade* 1881–2006 (2006) p.69.
8   *Eastern Daily Press*, Wednesday, 23 January 1963.
9   *Eastern Daily Press*, Thursday, 24 January 1963.
10 *Eastern Daily Press*, Friday, 29 March 1963.
11 *Eastern Daily Press*, Friday, 5 July 1963.

Epilogue

Newhaven Court stood above Cromer for nearly eighty years, the length of an average human lifespan. Through those years, it transformed from a brand new, grand, private family summer home to a military base and training ground during the Great War, then it became a luxury residence for the wealthy, followed by years as an upmarket hotel and a base for American families in transit. It stood solid through the reigns of two queens and four kings and two horrific world wars that changed the very fabric of society forever. During its residency above Cromer town, its occupants witnessed the life-changing inventions of telephone, flight, cinema, the motor car, radio and television. Newhaven was built in the age of the music hall and when it burned down in flames, The Beatles were riding high in the charts.

The last owner of the house was ultimately Albert Woodrow of building firm A.G. Brown, who bought back the property from the Boyd-Stevensons after the fire of 1963. It took time to pull down the old house and flatten the ground, but it was done methodically under Woodrow's experienced direction. Soon after, new houses were erected on the empty land.

Newhaven outlived its most colourful and eccentric owner, Oliver Locker-Lampson, by nine years. The year after his retirement and just after the sale of Newhaven Court, Oliver inherited the Sussex family home, Rowfant, from Godfrey, who had died on 1 May 1946. Godfrey had retired as MP for Wood Green in 1935, the same year he had lost Lalla. He remarried sporty young Barbara Hermione Green, known as Baa, in 1937, and spent his retirement writing and happily enjoying a quiet family life.

A clause in Sir Curtis's will stated that Rowfant would be passed down the male line and Godfrey's three daughters, Felicity, Stella and Betty, and second

Newhaven Court during demolition. (Courtesy of George Baker)

wife Barbara were passed over in favour of Oliver and his sons. Rowfant had been emptied of its treasures over the years as Godfrey had sold many and various irreplaceable family heirlooms. Oliver criticised his brother for the loss of the collection, calling the sale of Frederick's most treasured and valuable books a 'desecration of the grave', but the items were probably sold from necessity. Godfrey also tried to forge a collection of his own, a hobby in which he achieved varying success. By most accounts, he was a kind, gentle person, though perhaps one an unscrupulous seller took advantage of from time to time.

Despite the disagreements over the sale of the family heirlooms, Oliver missed his brother, who he had spent time with during their later years. After Godfrey's death, Oliver remained close to Dolly, Jack and his numerous nieces and nephews. The older among them remember him well, and his eccentric character, which had become more pronounced as he grew older. Hermione's son, Conway, remembers his flamboyant great uncle throwing a noisy fancy-dress party and Janey, Edward's eldest daughter, remembers Oliver as 'great fun', teasing her with stories about him being inventor of a tap that only milk would run out of. Even at a young age, she noticed how he stood out in a crowd by wearing all his war medals at a time when people no longer tended to.

Oliver and Barbara moved into Rowfant in 1946 but the house was neglected and run down, having been significantly damaged by the Canadian Army, who had occupied the house during the war. Already facing financial problems, the couple struggled to keep it up for eighteen months before admitting defeat and moving into a smaller cottage on the estate. The house was let to the Latvian Church in 1953 and then sold to them in 1961. The cottage in the grounds and some adjoining land passed to their eldest son, who still lives there to this day.

Dolly and Jack lived at Tite Street in Chelsea during the war, where they were badly bomb damaged, although all escaped unhurt. Edward married Helena Boyle, a niece of Conway Fisher-Rowe, known to the family as Aunt Dily. The pair worked as ambulance drivers during the war.

After her marriage, Rachel later moved to Hong Kong. She stayed close to Princess Ileana and the royal acted as godparent and sponsor to Rachel's daughter, Rosemary. Curtis, known as Uncle Ben, served in the navy during the war and later married Susan Hargreaves Brown. Dolly and Jack's youngest, Jane, married Commander Humphrey Madden. The marriages produced several grandchildren, who Dolly and Jack were close to.

Julian, the eldest child of Edward and Dily, spent time with his engineer pioneer grandfather on his hybrid propulsion motorboat, *Mansura*. Julian remembers fondly, 'Grandpapa liked to show off by sailing in and out of the harbour silently. People would turn heads and wonder how it was moving so quietly.' Julian's sister, Janey, also remembers Jack taking her on the boat and placing her on the tiller.

Dolly would occasionally take all the grandchildren to the cinema, where she was especially fond of watching a classic. Both Dolly and Jack lived near their youngest daughter Jane until Jack died in 1948. Increasingly frail, Dolly followed in 1950, leaving Oliver as the last remaining member of the Rowfant *quartos*.

Maud and Conway's children, Victor, Hermione and Ruth, all married. Ruth had a daughter and stayed particularly close to her cousin Jane, their children spending holidays together. Hermione, who was so beautiful that she made young men blush when she entered a room, died before her time, leaving a son. Victor married but died without issue.

As Oliver approached the age of 70, he was living quietly with his beloved Great Danes and spent his time reading and writing as well as starting his autobiography, which lay unfinished on his death. His last years were sadly dogged by loneliness and severe depression, made worse by a series of bad investments and financial troubles that caused a rift between himself and Hermione. His physical health began to fail, and he was hospitalised for pneumonia in 1953.

Jack with his grandchildren, Rosemary and Julian aboard Mansura. *(Family collection)*

In 1954, a few months before Oliver died, he was clearly and sadly suffering from poor mental health. Conway Ellison, Hermione's son, who was renting a flat in Pimlico at the time, happened to walk past his uncle, 'wearing an old Etonian tie, standing in a doorway talking to himself'.

Perhaps the last person to see him alive was former RNAS man Petty Officer Rule, who sought out his old commander on a trip to London in 1954. On finding his house and ringing the doorbell, Rule heard shuffling, before the door opened a crack. He was told to wait before the door opened again after a few minutes to the sight of Oliver in 'bedroom slippers, uniform jacket and an old pair of trousers'. Oliver looked visibly unwell and tired, and after a brief conversation, the old man made his apologies and the door was closed. Rule left, shocked and saddened by the sight of his former commander.

On 7 October 1954, likely suffering from severe stomach pains and fever, Oliver entered St Mary Abbotts Hospital in Kensington. Although he may not have realised himself how serious his condition was, he presented as a medical emergency. The following day, he died from peritonitis. He left behind his wife Barbara, who later became Mrs Mulholland, and sons, Jonathan and Stephen.

Oliver was cremated at Golders Green after a short service attended to by family members representing Dolly and Godfrey and his American cousins. A Union Jack flag was fittingly draped over the coffin. Younger son Stephen was moved by the sight of a senior White Russian officer and a further four men who had served under his father in Russia. Wreaths and cards were sent from Winston Churchill as well as Herbert Eastoe, the Norfolk gamekeeper who had several times tricked Oliver into thinking he had shot a pheasant. His ashes were taken to the family plot at Worth, where he joined his grandparents, Sir Curtis and Lady Jane Lampson, his parents, Frederick and Janie, and his beloved first wife, Bee.

Both of Oliver's boys spent time at naval college before joining the Merchant Navy. The streak of adventure, drive and spirit seen in Oliver passed to his sons. Jonathan stayed close to Rowfant, where he married and started a family. Younger son Stephen moved to New Zealand, where he worked freelance in the film industry. Stephen later wrote of his father, 'He was a man of achievement and of vision, a man of vanity and pride. He loved life as he loved nothing else.'

Despite a life of controversy, promise and great adventure, which saw him mix with the most influential and interesting in society, in addition to his links with royalty, Oliver remained on the periphery and never quite achieved the fame he desired or the recognition he arguably deserved. This is especially true when it comes to his unwavering support of the Jewish cause. He was a man of action, as well as words, and his efforts to help the Belgian refugees in the Great War and his campaigning to get Jews out of Nazi-occupied areas is to be commended and undoubtedly saved many lives. His efforts were not forgotten by the community he fought so hard for. Oliver's younger son, Stephen, recalled a memory of walking down a largely Jewish-occupied area in the east end of London, where residents came out of their homes to shake his father's hand.[1]

Though the name Locker-Lampson is no longer familiar to most, Oliver is still remembered fondly in Cromer, though chiefly for his involvement with the extraordinary Russian armoured car expedition and his links to Albert Einstein. A blue plaque of remembrance was placed on the side of the Newhaven Court gatehouse lodge, opened by George Baker, the son of one of Oliver's RNAS comrades.

The datestone on the boundary wall with Frederick and Janie's initials. (Author's own)

The view of Cromer from Newhaven Court by Alice, Lady Lowther, 1873–1939. (Family collection)

The numerous descendants of Frederick and Janie, in addition to many of the later occupants of Newhaven are scattered across the world, as far as America, New Zealand, Australia, South Africa and Canada.

Albert Woodrow built a house on the Norwich Road where, in common with the other bungalow residents, he brought up a family. A.G. Brown remains a successful building firm in Cromer with an excellent reputation.

If one could fly like a bird through the blue skies of Cromer, one would still be able to see the outline of the old Newhaven Court estate, its name retained in the two roads lined with housing, Newhaven Close and Court Drive, which now cover the area. Indeed, although long since destroyed by that catastrophic blaze, the landscape still contains traces of the grand house. The red-brick northern boundary wall remains, running the length of the 10-acre estate. Inlaid at two points are two brick stones commemorating the building of Newhaven and the initials of the long-forgotten Frederick and Hannah Jane Locker-Lampson, along with the dates 1885 and 1890. The Norwich Road-fronted gatehouse still exists, the only remaining structure of the old estate.

Some of those houses retain a little piece of Newhaven, with fireplaces made from the repurposed red bricks, and others have odd garden out-buildings that survived the wrecking ball. If you look carefully, less obvious remnants of the old house still exist – a set of concrete stairs near the site of the tennis courts that lead nowhere, as well as a cobble-top wall that doesn't quite fit within its modern surroundings.

But Newhaven Court is gone, and with it, the Cromer Sir Curtis would have known. Although much changed, the town having come through two world wars and bombing raids, the people of Cromer, kind and welcoming remain unaltered, as does the elegant spirit of the little windswept town by the North Sea.

NOTE

1   Stuart McLaren, *Saving Einstein: When Norfolk Hid a Genius. The Double life of Oliver Locker-Lampson*, p.197.

Bibliography

Allinson, Helen (ed.), *Louisa Thomas of Hollingbourne: The Journal of a Victorian Lady* (Synjon Books, 2011).

Aplin, John, *Memory & Legacy: A Thackeray Family Biography 1876–1919* (James Clarke & Co. Ltd, 2010).

Barratt, David, *The History of Duff Morgan* (Duff, Morgan & Vermont, 2009).

Bates, Madison C., 'Sir Curtis Lampson: Vermont Baronet', *Vermont History*, Vol. XXVII (Vermont Historical Society, January 1960).

Benedict, William Addison and Rev. Hiram Tracy, *History of the Town of Sutton, Massachusetts from 1704–1876* (Standford & Co., 1878).

Birrell, Augustine, *Frederick Locker-Lampson: A Character Sketch* (Constable and Company Ltd, 1920).

Birrell, Augustine, *Things Past Redress* (Faber, 1937).

Bobbitt, Mary Reed, *With Dearest Love to All: The Life and Letters of Caroline Jebb* (Faber & Faber, 1960).

Boyce, A.D., *Harmonious Houses in Exquisite Surroundings* (Cromer Preservation Society, 2008).

Brown, Jane, *Lutyens and the Edwardians: An English Architect and his Clients* (Penguin, 1996).

Cameron, Julia and Anne Thackeray Ritchie, *Alfred, Lord Tennyson and his Friends* (T. Fisher Unwin, 1893).

Clifford, James L., *From Puzzles to Portraits – Problems of a Literary Biographer* (University of North Carolina Press, 1970).

Dent, Major Herbert C., *Reminiscences of a Cromer Doctor* (Holt: Norfolk Press Syndicate, 1922).

Downer, Martyn, *The Sultan of Zanzibar: The Bizarre World and Spectacular Hoaxes of Horace De Vere Cole* (Black Spring Press, 2010).

'Dr Webber's Essay on Cerebro-Spinal Meningitis', *Boston Medical Surgical Journal* (6 September 1866), accessed online: *New England Journal of Medicine*.

Dunlop, Tessa, *Romania's Wartime Queen* (historytoday.com, 6/11/2018). Available online.

Edghill, Jamie, *Cromer Fire Brigade 1881–2006* (Poppyland Publishing, 2006).

Englen, Rodney, *Kate Greenaway* (Schocken Books, 1981).

Eve, Kimberly 'The Poetry of Lionel Tennyson' kimberlyevemusings.blogspot.com

Fowler, Edith Henrietta, *The Life of Lord Wolverhampton* (Hutchison & Co., 1912).

Glendinning, Victoria, *A Supressed Cry: The Short Life of a Victorian Daughter* (Virago, 1969).

Hare, Augustus J.C., *The Story of My Life, Volumes 4–6* (George Allen, London, 1960).

Jebb, Lady Caroline, *The Life & Letters of Richard Claverhouse Jebb* (Cambridge University Press, 1907).

Locker-Lampson, Frederick, *My Confidences* (Smith Elder and Co., 1896).

Locker-Lampson, Godfrey, *Life in the Country* (London: Frederick Muller Ltd, 1948).

Locker-Lampson, Hannah Jane, *What the Blackbird Said: A Story in Four Chirps* (George Routledge & Sons, 1881).

Locker-Lampson, Stephen (ed.), *Nothing to Offer but Blood: The Collected Writings of Oliver Locker-Lampson* (New Zealand, 1998).

Lutyens, Emily, *A Blessed Girl: Memoirs of a Victorian Girlhood* (London: Heinemann, 1953).

McLaren, Stuart, *Saving Einstein: How Norfolk Hid a Genius. The Double Life of Oliver Locker-Lampson* (Poppyland Publishing, 2021).

Nicolson, Juliet, *Frostquake: The Frozen Winter of 1962 and How Britain Emerged a Different Country* (Chatto & Windus, 2021).

Perrett, Bryan and Anthony Lord, *The Czar's British Squadron* (William Kimber & Co., London, 1981).

Pipe, Christopher, *Dictionary of Cromer & Overstrand* (Poppyland Publishing, 2010).

Ridley, Jane, *The Architect and his Wife: A Life of Edwin Lutyens* (Chatto & Windus, 2002).

Robinson, Andrew, *Einstein on the Run: How Britain Saved the World's Greatest Scientist* (Yale University Press, 2019).

Savin, Alfred, *Cromer in the County of Norfolk: A Modern History* (Rounce & Wortley, 1937).

Sayer, Alida, 'The Balcony Hotel' (Felbrigg Hall) www.thebalconyhotel.com

Smith, Michael, *Shackleton: By Endurance We Conquer* (One World Publications, 2014).

Stibbons, Brenda, *The Baker Brothers: Diaries from the Eastern Front 1914–1918. Oliver Locker-Lampson and the Men of the Russian Armoured Car Division* (Poppyland Publishing, 2018).

Sweet, Matthew, *The West End Front: The Wartime Secrets of London's Grand Hotels* (Faber & Faber, 2011).

Tennyson, Charles, *Stars and Markets* (Chatto & Windus, 1957).

Tennyson, Hallam, *Alfred, Lord Tennyson. A Memoir by his Son, Volume 2* (Macmillan, 1897).

Thwaite, Ann, *Emily Tennyson: The Poet's Wife* (Faber & Faber, 1996).

Wiltz, Jenni 'Marie-Louise: The Princess from Nowhere' www.girlinthetiara.com

Woodstock History Center (author unknown), 'Spotted Fever Epidemic' (woodstockhistorycenter.org, accessed 1/2/2019).

Zimmer, Anne, *Jonathan Boucher: Loyalist in Exile* (Wayne State University Press, 1978).

UNPUBLISHED MATERIAL

In footnotes, 'Towle' – The Locker-Lampson family letters were rescued from Newhaven by resident Josephine Towle. Josephine held onto these letters for many years, believing them to have importance. They have proved to be a wonderful resource.

In footnotes, 'family collection' – Documents, letters, diaries, guest book and artwork privately owned by the extended family.

ARCHIVES

ancestry.com
Auckland Central Library
Beinecke Rare Book & Manuscript Library
British Newspaper Archive
Cambridgeshire University Library Archives
Cromer Museum
General Register Office
Hertfordshire Archives and Local Studies

Leeds University Archive
Library of Congress
myheritage.com (courtesy of Patricia Walker)
National Archives
Norfolk Museums and Archaeology Service (NMAS)
Norfolk Record Office
Principal Probate Registry
Sir George Grey Collection

NEWSPAPERS

Birmingham Daily Gazette

Coventry Evening Telegraph

The Daily Telegraph

Derbyshire Times and Chesterfield Herald

Eastern Daily Press

Evening Standard

The Gentlewoman

The Graphic

Horsham, Pentworth, Midhurst and Steyning Express

Illustrated Sporting and Dramatic News

Leeds Mercury

Leeds Times

Londonderry Sentinel

Marylebone Mercury

Middlesex County Times

Newcastle Evening Chronicle

Norfolk Chronicle

Norfolk News

Northern Wing

Peterborough Standard

Portsmouth Evening News

Staffordshire Sentinel

Surrey Mirror

Taranaki Herald

The Tatler

USAF Stars and Stripes

Western Gazette

Further Reading

Anand, Sushila, *Daisy: The Lives and Loves of the Countess of Warwick* (Piatkus, 2008).

Austin, W.H. (Bunny) and Phyllis Konstam, *A Mixed Double* (Chatto & Windus, 1969).

Bates, Madison C., *That Delightful Man: A Study of Frederick Locker* (Harvard Library Bulletin/The Rowfant Club, 1959).

Blackburn, Julia, *Threads: The Delicate Life of John Craske* (Jonathan Cape, 2015).

Boyce, A.D., *Aspects of Design in Cromer* (North Norfolk District Council, 2007).

Brockman, Margaret Drake (ed.), *The Voyage of the May Queen*, diaries and illustrations by Bertha and Mary Dobie (Merlin Books Ltd, 1992).

Brooks, Pamela, *The Norfolk Almanac of Disasters* (Breedon Books Publishing, 2007).

Brooks, Peter, *Coastal Towns at War* (Poppyland Publishing, 1988).

Collins, Jodie, 'Clear Out the Reds! Anti-Communism and the Conservative Right. The Case of Oliver Locker-Lampson 1926–33' (MA dissertation, University of Leeds, 2016. Available online.)

Delmar-Morgan, Edward Locker, *Mansura* (Jimbo Printing Services, 1936).

Desmond, Kevin, *Electric Boats and Ships: A History* (McFarland and Co., 2017).

Fiennes, Ranulph, *Captain Scott* (Hodder & Stoughton, 2003).

Garnett, Henrietta, *Anny – A Life of Annie Thackeray Ritchie* (Random House, 2011).

Hastings, David, *The Many Deaths of Mary Dobie* (Auckland University Press, 2015).

Hitchings, Glenys and Del Styan, *Locker-Lampson: Einstein's Protector* (Norfolk Museums Service, Cromer, 2010).

Hodgson, Godfrey, *People's Century* (BBC Books, 1995).

Hoffman, Peter, *Carl Goerdeler and the Jewish Question 1933–1942* (Cambridge University Press, 2011).

Hutchins, Michael, *Yours Pictorially: Illustrated Letters of Randolph Caldecott* (Frederick Warne, 1976).

Innes Shand, Alexander, *The Life of Edward Bruce Hamley* (William Blackwood & Sons, 1895).

Ketton-Cremer, R.W., *Felbrigg: The Story of a House* (The National Trust, 1962).

Lang, Cecil Y., and Edgard Finley Shannon (eds), *The Letters of Alfred Lord Tennyson, Volume III 1871–1892* (Oxford University Press, 1981).

Locker-Lampson, Oliver, *Frederick Locker-Lampson: A Character Sketch* (Peterborough Press, privately published).

Locker-Lampson, Oliver, 'Kate Greenaway: Friend of Children', *Century Magazine*, Vol. 75 (1907–08).

McDonald, Deborah, *The Prince, his Tutor and the Ripper* (McFarland & Co., 2007).

Massingham, Rochelle Mortimer and Del Styan, *Cromer at War* (Norfolk Museums Service, 2007).

Petersons, Margaret, *The Rowfant Story: A Chronicle of Times Past and Present* (Teodors Puperins, 1980).

Snelling, Steve, 'A Whisker from the Reaper', *Britain at War Magazine, A History of Conflict*, Issue 170 (June 2021).

Spielman M.H., and G.S. Layard, *The Life and Works of Kate Greenaway* (Adam Charles Black, 1905).

Thornton, David, *Echoes of Poppyland 1883–1914* (Poppyland Publishing, 2017).

Ward, Lock & Co., *A Pictorial and Descriptive Guide to Cromer, Sheringham, Mundesley* (Fourth edition, Ward, Lock & Co., 1906).

Ward, Lock & Co., *A Pictorial and Descriptive Guide to Sheringham, The Runtons, Cromer and North-East Norfolk* (Seventh edition, Ward, Lock & Co., 1919/20).

Index